"Through page after page, June shows you how *Keeping Your Cool...When Your Anger Is Hot!* will help you build relationships rather than burn them."

Roger Staubach
Executive Chairman, Americas, Jones Lang LaSalle
Hall of Fame quarterback, Dallas Cowboys

"Our world is a matrix of anger, retaliation, and irreconcilable differences. No one navigates through this maze of explosive emotions like June Hunt. With keen biblical insight and amazing application, June brings God's Word to bear on our generation's desperate need for God's healing and hope."

Dr. Mac Brunson
Senior Pastor, First Baptist Church, Jacksonville, Florida

"For anyone who has ever lost control when angry expressions flared, *Keeping Your Cool... When Your Anger Is Hot!* is a must-read. Cool is desired by all of us who have known the heat of anger and been burned by it. Learn what causes you to say and do the things that hurt so many—and more importantly, allow this powerful author to equip you to live victoriously, wisely handling your most explosive emotion."

Gil Stricklin
Chairman and CEO, Marketplace Ministries, Inc.

"It's impossible to imagine the number of lives damaged by out-of-control anger. By highlighting God's principles, June brings hope and healing to wounded hearts."

Terry Meeuwsen
Cohost, *The 700 Club* and *Living the Life*
Executive Director, Orphan's Promise

"For whatever small brag it may be, in my 40 years of prison mi̶ ̶ ̶ ̶ ̶ken to more inmates than anyone...ever. Many are *angry*. Oft̶ ̶ ̶ ̶ ̶ ̶nger of others. When they deserve forgiveness the lea̶ ̶ ̶ ̶ ̶rist died to show us His forgiveness when we ̶ ̶ ̶ ̶ ̶ ̶h angry people. June shows us how."

Bill Glass
̶ ̶ ̶ Champions for Life
Author̶ ̶ ̶ ̶ ̶ ̶g Power of a Father's Blessing
Fo̶ ̶ ̶er Cleveland Browns defensive end

KEEPING YOUR COOL...
WHEN YOUR
Anger
IS HOT!

JUNE HUNT

HARVEST HOUSE PUBLISHERS

EUGENE, OREGON

Cover by Garborg Design Works, Savage, Minnesota

Cover photo © Chris Garborg

Some of the names and details in this book have been changed to protect the anonymity and privacy of the individuals who shared their stories.

KEEPING YOUR COOL...WHEN YOUR ANGER IS HOT!
Copyright © 2009 by Hope for the Heart, Inc.
Published by Harvest House Publishers
Eugene, Oregon 97402
www.harvesthousepublishers.com

Library of Congress Cataloging-in-Publication Data
    Hunt, June.
    Keeping your cool—when your anger is hot! / June Hunt.
        p. cm.
    Includes bibliographical references.
    ISBN 978-0-7369-2424-5 (pbk.)
    1. Anger—Religious aspects—Christianity. I. Title.
    BV4627.A5H87 2009
    241'.31—dc22

                                                            2009014592

Dedication

With deep respect I dedicate this book to my sister, Swanee Hunt, who has long been channeling her *indignation* over social injustice into *action*. Although we have teased about "cancelling each other's votes," we are always in each other's corner—emphatically—concerning abuse, injustice, and active compassion.

Swanee allowed her *justifiable anger* regarding the worldwide epidemic of sex trafficking to fuel her efforts to combat this horrendous atrocity. Her righteous indignation helped energize the movement, involving world leaders and heads of state, to rescue young women and girls who are victims of inhumane, evil sex traffickers.

Previously as ambassador from the United States to Austria, Swanee saw firsthand the aftermath of brutal savagery from the Bosnian war—the wholesale genocide of almost the entire male population in the town of Srebrenica, all fathers, sons, husbands…murdered. As a result, she assisted the mobilization of women around the globe to take action, to become leaders, to make their world a far more civil place.

With a vision of what could be, Swanee has empowered the weak to be strong, the timid to become bold, the victim to become victorious. Indeed, she has helped the voiceless find a voice.

Swanee has refused to sit behind her mahogany desk at Harvard and merely teach about injustices. Rather, she has rolled up her sleeves, marshaled her assets, garnered her allies, neutralized her opponents, focused her intellect, and thrown her energy into making a significant difference in the lives of those who have been disenfranchised. Swanee's anger propelled her to action…and as a result, she is changing the world.

Acknowledgments

If I were deprived of the opportunity to express in print my deepest appreciation to the dedicated team that helped make this book possible, I might be tempted to become...angry! Therefore, with heartfelt gratitude I joyfully acknowledge...

- *The firefighters of Dallas Fire Station #21, Love Field Airport:* Who provided significant insights into the essential skills of firefighting.

- *Barbara Spruill:* Whose vivid recollections of my early struggles with anger surpassed even my own memories—she lovingly sparked personal recollections of my failures and victories, which are candidly revealed throughout these pages.

- *Lillian Spruill* (whom I affectionately refer to as "the Mother of the World") for keeping the home fires burning.

- *Keith Wall:* Whose invaluable organization of the first draft fueled our creativity.

- *Angie White, Bea Garner, Beth Stapleton, Carolyn White, Connie Steindorf, Elizabeth Gaston, Ginger Swann, Jeanne Sloan, Jill Prohaska, Jody Capehart, June Page, Karen Williams, Laura Lyn Benoit, Steve Miller,* and *Titus O'Bryant* for...

  - keying and re-keying
  - editing and re-editing
  - proofing and reproofing
  - researching and re-researching

  They not only performed with the utmost diligence but also fanned the flame of loving support. (You are my editorial Dream Team.)

- *Kay Deakins:* Who, as my personal assistant, juggled calendars and singlehandedly snuffed out brushfires—enabling the rest of our team to "keep going on all four burners."

I am genuinely blessed by God to have each of you in my life.

— *June*

CONTENTS

INTRODUCTION:
A View Behind the Interview

ARE YOU AWARE that many people who read books do *not* read the introduction? Several people who, even as I write this, are typing and proofing this book have told me they *never* read the introduction!

(But now they have to read it!)

So, since *you* are the exception—and it's "just us"—I'm going to approach this introduction in a way that differs from the norm. In fact, I'm going to "pull back the curtain" and give you a peek inside the book publishing world and share a few tidbits of information you may not know.

First Tidbit: We authors don't just write a book; we are also asked by the publisher to write *interview questions* for the book (for publicity purposes). These questions are for those who don't yet have the book (which isn't you, because right now you are reading it). The obvious aim for these questions is to motivate people to think, *I really need to get that book!*

Second Tidbit: The simplest yet most helpful question to ask any author is this: "Why did you write this book?" For well over 20 years I've hosted hundreds of interviews with authors on our radio program *Hope for the Heart*—especially in the early days. And as an author, I know what it's like to be on both sides of the microphone—as interviewer and interviewee.

Long ago, I realized this question was one of the most helpful. This was my opportunity to share not just my motivation, but also my experience and my heart.

By the way, other key questions will help readers quickly grasp what is really important in the book.

Third Tidbit: Imagine you are an interviewer. One key to a good interview is to ask open-ended questions—that is, questions that cannot be answered with a simple yes or no! By doing this, you can get better and more substantive answers that help your audience.

Now...so that you might get more out of this book right from the beginning, I'd like *you* to take the role of the interviewer. (By the way, if you are a bit hesitant about this, please forgive me. I'm just wanting you to become involved in the contents of this book in a new way. I'm hoping you will allow me just a few moments of creativity. If you'd rather not, it's okay...you can do what some other people have already done. You can go straight to chapter 1...but I *really do hope* you'll stay with me!)

Let's imagine that you're interviewing me. You're asking me questions, and I'm answering them just as if we were sitting right across from each other. If you've never been an interviewer, that's not a problem—I'll be your "coach."

Are you ready? Okay—let's go! Just ask...

Q: *June, why did you decide to write a book on anger?*
  (Good start!)

A: Everyone has struggled with anger...and everyone knows someone who has struggled or is struggling. People want help!

  I became aware of the extraordinary number of people struggling with anger when I was in Arizona in the mid-1990s at Prescott Pines Conference Center. I had been asked to be the general session speaker for a series of four back-to-basics conferences. This was the first time I had ever brought all of our Biblical Counseling Keys from our ministry—100 practical resources that address life's toughest problems. (Each small book contains definitions characteristics, causes, and solutions to a given topic.)

  For more than two weeks, I kept calling back to our office in Dallas, asking staff to send us hundreds more of our Biblical Counseling Keys. By far, the greatest demand was for *Anger*.

(Although not once did I speak on that topic during any of those conferences!)

Today is no different—people are seeking *real answers* for their *real problems*. Fortunately, this book has *real solutions!*

Q: *Over the years, what has been the response to your radio programs on anger?*
(This helps to get a little background.)

A: The response has been overwhelming. For example, after returning from Arizona, I checked to see how our ministry was meeting this need to help people with their anger, and I was surprised at the results. People have been requesting more of our Biblical Counseling Keys on anger than any other topic, just like at those conferences.

Then and today, people order *one-half times* more resources (our Keys and CDs) on anger than all our other most popular topics, including depression, decision-making, addictions, forgiveness, and the list goes on and on.

And of course, the calls, letters, and e-mails we receive about changed lives—*lasting* change—are gratifying beyond words!

Q: *Why is anger such a compelling topic?*
(Great question!)

A: Anger is the most mystifying and powerful emotion we face—and potentially the most volatile. There is much confusion about anger. We often become conflicted over the *shoulds* and *oughts*... like "good people *should not* have any anger" and "you *ought* to get rid of all anger—immediately."

Typically we don't want to acknowledge any anger within us, so... we stuff it, disguise it, medicate it, rename it, anesthetize it—but that only adds fuel to our inner fire.

Q: *You share some very personal examples that have to do with your family. How important is that?*
(The personal touch—very good!)

A: As uncomfortable as it is, I don't know of any other way to write this book on anger—with total integrity—without being candid about my own struggle with it...especially in my younger years.

This means I need to speak about personal events and painful people from my past. Therefore, when I do so, it isn't to be dramatic, but rather to be authentic. My intent is not to hurt, but rather, to help. That is my sincere prayer. And I know from experience that help is possible for *anyone* who struggles with anger.

Q: *Why do you use fire as an analogy for anger?*
(Excellent question—it paints a picture!)

A: Fire seems like a fitting metaphor, because fire can be either helpful or harmful, just like anger. The same embers that toast a marshmallow can also ignite a forest. Just as fire can be a friend or foe, anger can be an ally or an enemy.

The Bible even uses the word *hot* to provide a "word picture" of excessive anger: "A hot-tempered [man] commits many sins," and "Do not make friends with a hot-tempered man."[1] Because anger can fuel us or inflame us, we need to make sure our anger—like fire—is always under control.

Q: *Everyone knows fire can be good, but how can anger be good?*
(Now that's thought-provoking!)

A: Anger is like a red light on the dashboard of your car—a warning light that indicates something is wrong and needs your attention. God's design for anger is to caution us, not control us...and cause us to think about options to bring about change.

Anger should motivate us to try to fix the problem, such as applying justice to an unjust situation. That's precisely why the Bible says, "Be angry, and do not sin."[2] Like all reformers from Jesus to Abraham Lincoln, we need to look for ways to harness our "indignation"—our justifiable anger—for good. Then our lives can make a real difference!

(Good interview—you did well. You may have a new career!)

❋

Now, in all seriousness, anger is not the easiest topic for me to write on—perhaps because it dredges up many memories from the past. Yet I'm writing this book with a heart of sincere compassion and mercy. That's because I'm all too aware of my own faults and frailties, and the need for my total dependence to be on God's guidance and grace.

As we walk together through the pages ahead, please know my intent is to explore this sensitive issue in a spirit of support and encouragement. You'll notice I purposely avoid highbrow and highfalutin language. Anger is a real-world, nitty-gritty issue—and I want to keep my communication with you as practical and down-to-earth as possible.

I'm approaching this book as a conversation between you and me. In our lives—so full of potential traps and trials—we need each other. And as God has promised, He will walk beside us, through this and every other challenge we face. He says, "When you pass through the waters, I will be with you; and when you pass through the rivers, they will not sweep over you. When you walk through the fire, you will not be burned; the flames will not set you ablaze" (Isaiah 43:2).

Right now, I'd like to ask *you* a few questions. Has your heart been singed by scalding anger? Has holding on to bitterness caused you deep regrets? Has rage detonated a close relationship and left it in pieces?

Whatever your unique situation, you want help…and hope. And I want you to know, we're both in this together! My prayer is that this book will help you learn to *address*—not avoid—the anger in your life and help you to learn how you can douse its harmful flames.

Learning about anger has been a journey I've been on most of my adult life…and oh, what I've learned! I've walked through the burning embers of my own suppressed anger, and I've also learned how to take shelter from the explosive, fiery anger of others. Now I want to help you discover the same invaluable lessons I've learned.

I know, with the help of God, you can be successful in *keeping your cool…when your anger is hot!*

Part One

FANNING THE EMBERS:

*The Truth About Anger and
How It Affects Our Lives*

1

THE ANGER BOWL
The Overwhelming Pain of Our Anger

"Get rid of all bitterness, rage and anger"
(EPHESIANS 4:31).

"IT'S TOO MUCH. The pain is just too much!" cried a voice seething with anger. "I'm so upset...so angry...my life has turned into a living hell."

- *The place*: the mountains of Prescott, Arizona
- *The occasion*: a weekend retreat for more than 600 women
- *The setting*: an outdoor pavilion with a large stone fireplace

On a Friday evening, after I had just finished speaking, a distraught woman came forward, baring her soul. Actually, Brenda was supported by—practically *carried* by—three deeply concerned friends. As she reached out, I took her hands and led her to sit down by me. She was overwrought with emotion.

Initially, Brenda didn't want to talk with me. In fact, she didn't want to attend the conference at all. But her friends knew how desperately she needed some kind of intervention—something to pull her out of this emotional "pit," something to get her back on level ground.

"Brenda, please tell me what happened. I can see you're in pain."

Immediately she blurted out, "My daughter died of anorexia*...

Anorexia is a psychological eating disorder characterized by compulsive, chronic self-starvation.[1] It she was just 22!" Heaving sobs poured out between every phrase. "She meant the world to me...she had so much potential...so much future...she was vibrant...and so precious...then she withered...withered away—to nothing."

At the word *nothing*, Brenda's body wilted and she began to wail. I now understood the source of this mother's agony. It was the tragedy of watching her daughter die of self-imposed starvation—shrinking to skin and bones, unaware of her own distorted thoughts...thinking she was much too fat when instead she was much too thin...thinking she was eating too much when instead she was slowly starving.

Within moments, the picture was plain to me. Brenda was definitely in a pit—a pit of anger. It was as though this pit contained hot coals she could pick up and hurl at any time. And indeed, she had been picking up those hot coals for a very long time and pelting those who angered her. Yet she hadn't realized she was the one being burned.

Brenda was consumed with agonizing anger, a bitter wrath...

- *at her husband*—for not taking the problem seriously
   —"She's just going through a phase."
- *at her friends*—for not showing compassion, but stating trite comments
   —"She's cute and trim and doesn't want to be fat!"
- *at her family*—for not understanding the real issues
   —"Just make her eat!"
- *at her doctors*—for not being more proactive
   —"Don't worry. I'm watching her."
- *at her hospital*—for not supplying lifesaving solutions
   —"We're doing all we can."
- *at herself*—for not knowing what to do sooner

is a disorder in which the normal function of the mind and/or body is disturbed. Anorexics weigh less than their ideal body weight, which is different for every person (based on bone structure and the amount of muscle). Body weight that is 15 percent below normal poses a serious threat to a person's physical health.[2]

- *at her God*—for not rescuing her precious child
- *at her daughter*—for not fighting to live, not trying to change, for withering away to nothing, for leaving her, for dying

"I am so very sorry, Brenda. When did your daughter die?" Her answer surprised me. "It's been over three years now…but it still feels like yesterday."

Rarely have I met someone so ravaged by sorrow. My heart hurt for her as I silently cried out to God on her behalf.

For over half an hour, Brenda and I sat together on the first row of that pavilion. Continuing to ask questions, I heard more of her anguishing story—her years of reaching out to her daughter, her countless hours of prayer, her sleepless nights of worry, her failed attempts to find help.

When she finished pouring out her heart, I said, "Brenda, you can find true healing. Though your world feels so painful right now, you can receive real relief from that pain. You may not see it, but there is hope for your heart."

She looked at me as if she wanted to believe, but she had been disappointed so many times it was difficult for her to trust my words.

At that very moment, the Lord put into my mind a symbolic picture of what Brenda could do with her pain. I asked her to cup her hands together in the shape of a bowl. Then I asked her to imagine writing on slips of paper each specific hurt, the names of each person who had caused pain, each angering moment…and imagine placing them one by one into her "anger bowl."

Brenda seemed more than eager to get it all out. Together we verbally "wrote down" every feeling of helplessness, hurt, and heartache related to the death of her daughter. Her sorrow, pain, and anger were so extensive, she agonized to recall each incident as we gathered them into her imaginary bowl.

I believed that Brenda had likely been carrying the burden of anger long before her daughter's eating disorder. My aim was for her to leave the Arizona mountains *totally* free of the charred memories—from childhood on up. I asked Brenda to again imagine writing down the names of the people and events throughout her life that caused her anger and pain not related to her daughter's illness and death, and to place those slips of paper in her anger bowl as well.

"Ask God to bring every person and event to mind so you can find complete healing," I gently prodded. "Include even the 'little' hurts that could still be lingering."

When the last "slip of paper" dropped into the bowl, I asked Brenda if she wanted to keep carrying all that anger or if she wanted to release it. "Oh, I want to release it all. I've carried this anger far too long as it is."

Giving a Sacrificial Offering to God

"Now I want you to take this anger bowl over to the fireplace," I explained, "and empty it all into the fire."

"I really want to empty the bowl," she quickly responded. "I *really need* to empty the bowl."

Putting my hands under her hands, I softly said, "Let me help you." Carefully we both carried the figuratively heavy bowl. "Brenda, although you felt you had the right to be angry, you can now present all your anger to the Lord as a *sacrificial* offering." She nodded. Staring at the fire, she paused, then prayed, "I release my anger bowl to You."

Slowly separating her hands...then slowly turning them over...she poured the contents of the bowl into the fire—her anger consumed by flames. Then with the palms of her hands still over the fire, she spontaneously began moving her fingers up and down—making sure no "slips of paper" clung to her, making sure no sliver of anger remained.

As Brenda presented her burnt offering to the Lord, I believe the God of heaven and earth received it as a sacrifice to Him. He blew away her anger like light ash on a cool breeze. He truly lightened her load.

That Sunday afternoon, after the conference had drawn to a close, Brenda's friends rushed up to me, full of excitement. "Have you see Brenda today?"

"No, I haven't seen her since Friday night." Then they began gushing, their words overlapping one another: "It's amazing…she's joyful…she's glowing…she's radiant!"

Then one exclaimed, "Stay here! We'll bring her to you."

Off they scurried…and within five minutes, the flock of four returned. No doubt about it—their exuberant words were right. Brenda's face was beaming—her eyes bright, her countenance beautiful.

The reason? Brenda's anger bowl was completely empty. She had emptied her heart of all past hurt, all past pain, all past anger. She had yielded her right to hold on to her list of resentments, and had presented her offering to the Lord. He was well pleased.

It's amazing to see how, in a relatively short amount of time, anger that had been smoldering for years could be snuffed out—the coals made cool by the breath of God.

Do You Need to Bring a Burnt Offering?

Has anger seethed in your soul for so long that you sincerely question, "Can it really be contained? Can it be completely extinguished?" Can the strongest of all emotions truly be transformed from adversary to ally?

The answer is unequivocally yes. But, as with Brenda, your starting point will probably be filling your own "anger bowl," then releasing your anguish to the Lord and allowing His purifying fire to burn away the blistering pain that for too long has been harming you and those you love.

If you are tempted to think, *But I have every right to be angry! It's too high a price to let go*, reflect on these words in the Bible: "I will not sacrifice to the LORD my God burnt offerings that cost me nothing."[3]

Realize Jesus promises to be your burden bearer. He gives hope to the hopeless and help to the helpless. Instead of casting hot coals on the people who have angered you, do as the Bible says: "Cast all your anxiety on him because he cares for you."[4]

Every time you pick up burning coals to pelt people who have hurt you, know this: It's like lighting yourself on fire and waiting for the other person to burn.

Golden Bowls: Beauty from Ashes

Tucked within the chapters of this book you will find imagery of bowls overflowing with the fire and heat of anger and our need to present them as a sacrificial burnt offering to God. But in the book of Revelation, the apostle John pulls back the curtain of heaven and grants us a glimpse of an entirely different kind of bowl: a bowl of beauty and blessing...a golden bowl of incense.

And there's more: The incense that is perfuming heaven doesn't originate from ordinary spices and plants. Rather, this incense contained in golden bowls is "the prayers of the saints,"[5] which creates a pleasing aroma enjoyed by our Lord Himself.

Think about it: Over all the years, God has considered and contained every single prayer ever lifted up to Him. Just the thought that He cares that much about your every prayer is absolutely *astonishing*!

What a privilege that, even today, we can release all of our anger into God's purifying fire. We can tell Him about every hurt, every injustice, every fear, every frustration—with the assurance that He cares, and He tenderly treasures every prayer in a golden bowl.

Do you see the beauty from the ashes? When you pour out your anger bowl before the Lord—when you present Him with a sacrificial offering in prayer—it rises up before His throne as a pleasing aroma. When you prayerfully pass up the right to hold on to anger, you stir the heart of God and bring Him pleasure.

Throughout this book, we will view all sorts of imagery relating to anger, but as we do so, meditate on this beautiful vision in heaven. I pray it will encourage you all the more to release your anger to the One who dearly loves you.

TURNING UP THE HEAT
The Four Intensities of Our Anger

*"Do not be quickly provoked in your spirit,
for anger resides in the lap of fools"*
(ECCLESIASTES 7:9).

I HAVE A CONFESSION: For a number of years, I struggled with an anger problem. I had an anger bowl filled with many slips of paper… with only one name alone written on all of them—*Dad.*

But it's probably not what you think. I've never been a dish thrower, wall puncher, or fist shaker. Far from it. And my voice, even when I'm angry, doesn't reach high decibels.

My problem with anger stemmed from total ignorance: first, in having no understanding about it, and second, in not knowing how to handle it. I considered anger as always bad—an emotion to be *avoided* when it flared in others, an emotion to be *extinguished* when it flared in me.

Recently, when I discussed these thoughts with a close friend, she reminded me of how I typically dealt with anger—even as a young adult.

"You used to hide behind doors," she recalled.

"Whenever you would hear your dad walking toward the room you were in, you'd slide behind the door rather than run the risk of facing his rage. Even if he wasn't in a bad mood, you made sure you avoided *it*…and *him*, by staying out of harm's way."

My friend's comment basically captured how I responded to anger, or even the potential for it. I'd try to get out of the way—walk, run, hide, whatever! I'd try to move far away from any bull whose nose was flaring or eyes were flashing. But what I didn't realize, as I grew up in age and height, was that the contents of my bowl of anger were growing as well.

My "disappearing act" concerning my dad goes back to childhood. I was raised in a family that clearly had—to use the vernacular— "anger issues." My father was admired by many—primarily for being a brilliant businessman and a superpatriot, an avid anticommunist. However, he was as *deficient* in his personal skills as he was *efficient* in his professional skills. Sadly, his private life brought pain to most people around him.

When it came to anger, my father was a powder keg always on the verge of explosion. And worse, no one ever knew what might be the match that would light the fuse. For example, one Saturday afternoon, my sister Helen and I were sitting on the floor playing chess in a tiny room off our living room. (At the time, Helen was in the eighth grade, and I was in the twelfth.) I remember hearing my father's heavy footsteps coming closer...and closer. And we became ever so quiet.

When the footsteps stopped, there he stood, towering over the two of us. We looked up at him...and waited...and waited. He kept staring at the chess set.

Finally, he spewed, "PUT THAT CHESS SET UP! DON'T YOU KNOW CHECKERS IS MUCH MORE SCIENTIFIC THAN CHESS!"

Immediately my blood began to boil. Talk about "turning up the heat"! I screamed back (in total silence), "Checkers is NOT more scientific than chess!" We spoke not a word.

In slow, slow motion, we removed each chess piece one by one from the board. The king had bellowed his orders. We two pawns complied. We knew not to counter him. (Instead, I pulled out my imaginary pen and slip of paper, quickly scribble on it, and then dropped the paper into my anger bowl.)

On an emotional level, I believe a modern application of this scripture could explain our fear of his anger: "A king's wrath is like the roar of a lion; he who angers him forfeits his life."[1]

To this day, I remember my father's *exact* words from the sabotaged chess match—both his and mine.

I've often described my upbringing as "walking on eggshells." Yet more accurately, it was like walking through a minefield. I felt I had to tiptoe around, placing one foot cautiously in front of the other, so as not to trigger an explosion.

One specific event had the greatest impact on forming my fearful attitude toward anger, and it occurred when I stepped out from behind the proverbial "door." My dad's involvement with numerous women wasn't exactly a secret. There came a time when I felt he needed to be confronted!

The day came when I stood before my father, determined and fully motivated by my righteous indignation (although I didn't know that term at the time).

My approach was an accusatory, "How could you...?!" He dismissed my words with, "I'm *not* a Christian. I *don't* have to go by Christian ethics!" Then came his allegation that Mother was mentally ill. I followed with a sarcastic remark, and he countered by inflicting multiple blows to my back. End of "discussion"!

The result of my confrontation? The next day, I was promptly sent to boarding school, where I was forced to live for several months. I was exiled from family...expelled from home...punished for *confronting my dad with the truth*. Although the school was only ten minutes from our house, I was prohibited from setting foot inside our home. That crushed my mother. She felt responsible for what happened, yet was powerless to change it.

The only time I had attempted to use anger for a "worthy cause" went woefully wrong. It was an experience that left an indelible impression, to say the least, and translated into one of the deepest wounds in my heart.

And because of my "boarding school banishment," I developed my own personal style of anger management—I became a "peace at any price" person. I did whatever I could to keep the peace to avoid any eruption of anger from others.

> While anger has a legitimate purpose in certain situations, it must always be handled with great caution and care.

In retrospect, by suppressing my true emotions and stifling my sincere convictions, I squelched the person God created me to be. And I unwittingly contributed to an extremely unhealthy family dynamic. Surely, that wasn't what the Lord had in mind when He created human beings with emotions—even the most potentially explosive ones.

To awaken in an unfamiliar bedroom at a boarding school can feel unsettling, especially because you're faced with the fear of the unknown. It's an odd feeling to awaken from a sound sleep and wonder, *Where am I?* And you look around trying to get your bearings, trying to find something familiar.

To be in a stupor of angry emotions and wonder *How did I get here?* can also create fearful frustration that serves as a breeding ground for insecurity and emotional conflict.

What can we do when we find ourselves in such a situation? To arrive at an answer, we must first learn some basics about anger.

Anger 101

What Is Anger?

Anger is a strong emotion of irritation, agitation, or hostility that occurs when a need or expectation is not met.[2] Actually, anger is a *secondary response* to something else—it's an upsetting emotional reaction to an assumed "right" that has been violated or not fulfilled.

Of all our emotions, anger is usually considered the strongest, rawest, and potentially most destructive. We all know people who would fit this description: "An angry man stirs up dissension, and a hot-tempered one commits many sins" (Proverbs 29:22).

Now let's focus on the word *expectation*. When we *expect* something, we feel we have the *right* for that something to happen. And when it doesn't, we can feel irritated...agitated...ANGRY. Who hasn't been there, done that? I know I have. Expectations can be the igniter when it comes to anger.

In the Old Testament, the most frequently used Hebrew word for anger is *aph*, literally meaning "nose" or "nostrils"—figuratively depicting nostrils flaring with anger. Later, *aph* came to represent the entire face as seen in two ancient Hebrew idioms:[3]

- *"Long of face"* (or nose) means "slow to anger." Psalm 145:8 describes God as slow to anger—He is not quickly provoked: "The Lord is gracious and compassionate, slow to anger and rich in love."
- *"Short of face"* (or nose) means "quick to anger." Proverbs 14:17 describes a man with anger that pops off like a firecracker: "A quick-tempered man does foolish things."

You can almost feel the heat radiating from such vividly descriptive words. While anger has a legitimate purpose in certain situations, it must always be handled with great caution and care. As the writer of Proverbs said, "Do not make friends with a hot-tempered man, do not associate with one easily angered."[4] Why? Because someone could, and usually does, get burned by fiery rage. God might as well have said, "Thou shalt not play with fire."

What Are the Different Types of Anger?

Many people assume only one type of anger exists: Hot! However, there are many types of anger.

In my home, the burners on my stovetop come in several sizes. To warm a can of tomato soup in a small pan, I use the smallest burner. To cook bacon strips for ten people, I use the largest burner. Over my four burners is a "hood" with a ventilator, which, when turned on, helps to draw steam and smoke up and out of the kitchen.

The word *anger*—irritating anger—covers four levels of emotional heat, much like a ventilator over a stove covers four burners: indignation, wrath, fury, rage.

> **Burner #1**—*Indignation is "simmering anger"* provoked by something that appears unjust or unkind and thus the emotion seems *justified*. At times the unrighteous religious rulers in the Bible felt indignation over Jesus' miracles and His claim to be the Messiah; therefore, they felt justified in wanting to kill Him.[5] Their perceptions, of course, were unjustified.
>
> Meanwhile, Jesus felt *righteous indignation* toward the religious rulers for their hardened hearts. Likewise, Jesus became "indignant" when the disciples prevented parents from bringing their children to Him so He might touch and bless them: "When Jesus saw this, he was indignant. He said to them, 'Let the little children come to me, and do not hinder them, for the kingdom of God belongs to such as these.'"[6]

Burner #2—*Wrath is "burning anger"* accompanied by a desire to avenge. Wrath often moves from the inner feeling of anger to the outer expression of anger. Vengeful anger can be deadly—both literally and figuratively. An old Chinese proverb says, "The man who opts for revenge should dig two graves."

In the Bible, God expresses His wrath as divine judgment on those who commit willful sin: "The wrath of God is being revealed from heaven against all the godlessness and wickedness of men who suppress the truth by their wickedness."[7]

Burner #3—*Fury is "fiery anger"* so fierce that it destroys common sense. The word *fury* suggests a powerful force compelled to harm or destroy. Respected theologian A.W.

Tozer said, "The fury of man never furthered the glory of God."[8]

Some of the religious rulers were so angry with Peter and the other apostles for proclaiming that Jesus was God, "they were furious and wanted to put them to death."[9] This is an example of why the Bible says, "Anger is cruel and fury overwhelming."[10]

Burner #4—*Rage is "blazing anger"* that results in loss of self-control, often to the extreme of violence and temporary insanity. After an outburst of rage, a cry of remorseful regret or disbelief is often expressed: "I can't believe I did that!"

Yet those who continue to vent their rage toward others, including toward God, find themselves defeated by their own destructive decisions and ruined relationships. "A man's own folly ruins his life, yet his heart rages against the LORD."[11]

Anger's Progression of Intensity

Anger, if not resolved, can move from one stage of intensity to another—from mild irritation to uncontrollable rage.

- Unresolved irritation leads to indignation—justifiably *feeling* and/or acting so that a wrong should be made right.
- Unresolved indignation leads to wrath—*reacting* with revenge.
- Unresolved wrath leads to fury—*reacting* with a furious lack of self-control.
- Unresolved fury leads to rage—*reacting* with violence and temporary loss of sanity.

The School of Life

There is no way you can graduate from the school of life without learning the value of the positives and the negatives of anger.

Forest rangers are trained to fight forest fires, and they know how to "start a fire to stop a fire." Known as *backfires*, these deliberately set fires help deprive the wildfire of fuel so firefighters can better contain the blaze.

God works with your anger in much the same way. For example, He could use your most recent incident of anger to spark *an awareness of the larger blaze* (your unresolved past anger) that may be blocking your growth and hindering your relationships.

How Can Anger Be "Good"?

Anger is a surprisingly improbable instructor, teaching us what we need to be aware of, think about, and reconsider.

The Bible says, "All things work together for good to those who love God, to those who are the called according to His purpose."[12] This means not just all *positive* things, all *right* things, all *wonderful* things work together for our good...but literally *all* things. When we release all of the hurt, injustice, fear, and frustration in our lives to the Lord, He promises to use it *all* in some way for good—even if we don't see how that is possible.

Consider your life from God's perspective. Anger can teach you to...

Address the past
- enabling you to recognize your buried anger
- providing insight into past hurts
- motivating you to seek healing for past hurts

Address the present
- bringing your true feelings to light
- revealing inappropriate efforts to get your needs met
- alerting you to current problems that should be addressed

Address your relationships
- enabling you to protect yourself and others from injustice
- exposing your need to set healthy boundaries
- inviting closeness within your relationships

Address your spiritual life
- helping you realize your need for a relationship with God
- leading you to apply biblical principles for overcoming anger
- encouraging you to display a Christlike response by handling your anger properly

As you can probably tell, I've had a change of heart—a paradigm shift—in my perspective about anger over the years. I've come to realize anger is a God-given emotion and a perfectly normal response mechanism. Yet anger is also an ally that can become an adversary if we don't handle it carefully.

Don't get me wrong: I'm a realist when it comes to anger. I recognize there is a mean and

> Anger is not a sin. What we *do* with our anger determines if it becomes sin.

ugly side to it—a side that tears down rather than builds up. Unfortunately, "mean and ugly" is no doubt the most pervasive kind of anger in our world.

While it's true there are scriptures that tell us anger can be a positive influence, there are even more that warn against a negative, harmful mishandling of our strong emotions. For example, Solomon said, "Do not be quickly provoked in your spirit, for anger resides in the lap of fools."[13]

You may have heard the saying, "The word *anger* is one letter short of *danger*." It's true—our hot-blooded emotions can be dangerous. No one who has had an encounter with out-of-control anger would deny that.

Do You Need an Anger Awakening?

You've heard a bit about my journey down Anger Avenue, so let me ask: Where are you on this journey? Is anger a problem in your life? Or have you been on the receiving end of someone's anger...perhaps once too often? Are you trying to intervene before things get any worse? Is your own anger damaging relationships and causing you regrets? Chances are you have an anger bowl in your life that needs to be emptied.

The most surprising aspect of my "anger awakening" was a straightforward command found in Ephesians 4:26: "Be angry, and do not sin" (NKJV). Since I did not grow up reading the Bible, I can assure you, the concept "be angry" was both perplexing and mystifying.

How could this principle be correct when so many verses in the Bible tell us to, in essence, "turn away anger"?[14] The answer lies in understanding *what kind of anger* we carry in our hearts. For example, Jesus had justifiable anger or righteous indignation, which motivated Him to *right a wrong* when He drove the money changers from the temple because of their fraudulent practices.

Another shocker—for someone who thought anger was always wrong—is the irrefutable truth that anger is a God-given emotion. The Bible never says anger, in and of itself, is bad. Anger is not a sin. What we *do* with our anger determines if it becomes sin.

Now think about this: If God considered anger a sin, then He would have been a flagrant sinner Himself because there are more than 200 references to God's anger and wrath in the Old Testament alone. Because Scripture calls us to be "godly," we can follow God's example and express justifiable anger—the kind that seeks to right a wrong.

Surely it is okay—even honorable—to feel anger in unjust situations. It's *how we handle* our natural feelings of anger that can be constructive or destructive. Anger is like many things in life that can be used for either good or bad. A knife can be used for good or for bad. It can be used for healing in the hands of a surgeon or for harm in the hands of a murderer.

In short, the *existence* of anger isn't wrong. But the *expression* of it can be.

Anger *Is One Letter Short of* Danger

Sam was ordinarily a laid-back and even-tempered kind of guy—a firefighter whose job it was to put out fires, not create them. One morning, Sam finally got the phone call he'd been waiting for—his daughter had gone into labor with her first child. Since the death of his wife eight months earlier, being involved in the lives of his children had become more important to Sam than ever. He had promised his wife that because she couldn't be on hand for the birth of their first grandchild, he would be—no matter what.

Sam lived in a small mountain town, where he had retired after years of service as a forest ranger. The hospital was three hours away in the city. Sam packed a lunch, put his overnight bag in the trunk of the car, and settled in behind the wheel. The tank was full of gas, and the previous week he'd had the oil changed and fluids topped off. There was no reason to expect that when he turned the key in the ignition he would hear the telltale grinding sound of a starter gone bad.

"Dear God, not today," he prayed. "Of all days I need this car to start, this is it!" He tried again. And again. Soon it was painfully clear the car was not going to cooperate. Frustrated, Sam rushed back into the house and dialed the number of his mechanic.

It was Saturday morning, but there was a good chance the mechanic would be in his shop. He was, but a new starter would have to be sent from the city, and it wouldn't arrive until Monday.

Sam's anger escalated, jumping from Burner #1 to Burner #2. Why was God letting this happen? Sam hung up the phone and considered his options. There were no car rental companies in such a little town. He could ask to borrow a car from his two closest friends, but he knew one of them was off fishing and the other was on a business trip. And taxicabs didn't come out to "the sticks."

Sam's only other option was taking the bus, which departed in an hour. Sam grabbed his bag and—15 minutes later—had a ticket in hand. He breathed a sigh of relief and sat down to wait with a dozen or so fellow passengers, his boiling anger cooling back down to a simmer.

But Sam's "bad news day" wasn't over yet. The company had mistakenly sold more tickets for the trip than it had available seats. When the bus arrived, it was already full of passengers.

"I could hardly believe my ears when the driver told us he had no more room," Sam said later. "I was so mad I could hardly see straight."

In an instant his simmering anger on Burner #1 heated up to fury—skipping Burner #2 altogether and landing soundly on Burner #3.

Sam offered to sit in the aisle, but that was against company policy—liability issues. He asked if he could squeeze in with other passengers, assuming he could find someone who would be sympathetic to his plight. Once again, the driver told him that was against the rules. After ten minutes of pleading, it was obvious that no amount of arguing would get him a place on the bus.

Struggling to keep his rising anger at the company's incompetence from exploding into a rage, Sam approached the clerk who sold him his ticket and asked for his money back. The man replied he couldn't do that because Sam had elected to purchase a cheaper nonrefundable ticket.

"I assumed that nonrefundable meant I couldn't get my money back if I missed the bus, not if they didn't have a seat for me," Sam said. "I was so mad my hands were shaking. The clerk saw how affected I was, and, with a sneer on his face, he told me it wasn't his problem and that I should pay more attention next time when purchasing a ticket.

"That did it. My anger just exploded, way out of control. What happened next is just a blur in my mind."

And what happened next is Sam hit the clerk—squarely in the face! Sam punched the clerk and had to be restrained by the other passengers, or he might have kept on punching! By the time the police arrived, Sam had calmed down, but the damage was done. He was charged with assault and had to spend the night in jail.

Later a judge reduced the charge and sentenced Sam to mandatory counseling and community service. He humbly apologized to the clerk. Through it all, he was humiliated and ashamed. Sam's biggest disappointment that day was that his grandson had come into the world without his grandpa there to greet him.

You Can Clear Out the Deadwood

When Sam and I talked, I gently told him that he, of all people, should know that it usually takes more than a single spark to start a destructive forest fire. Before a blaze can take off and rage out of control, it needs something besides a source of combustion. It needs *fuel*—the right kind and in the right amounts.

Firefighters know the most combustible tracts of land are those where a lot of deadwood and dry underbrush have accumulated. Over a period of years, a poorly tended forest floor can become a tinderbox. Then even a careless spark can create a dangerous inferno.

That analogy helps explain the devastation in Sam's life. In his case, the "floor" of his life became the unwilling target of an emotional napalm bomb.

That's how explosive anger works, too.

But where did Sam's violent anger come from?

Sam was angry because he was *hurting*. Outwardly, Sam was handling his wife's recent passing very well. He didn't display the usual signs of deep depression after such a significant loss. People said he seemed to be getting on with his life just fine. But beneath this sturdy facade, Sam was struggling with intense loneliness and pain.

The day these traumatic events took place was supposed to be a joyous one—the birth of his first grandchild. The truth was, it made him miss his wife more acutely than ever. This untended pain became powerful tinder to fuel his anger.

From Sam's own perspective, he was in great shape. But in reality, he was sitting squarely on Burner #1, unconsciously simmering.

Sam was also angry because he was *afraid*. When his car wouldn't start, Sam was suddenly afraid he would be prevented from fulfilling the promise he'd made to his wife, and to himself, to be present at the birth no matter what. He was afraid of failing his daughter and son-in-law. *Fear* fueled his anger by creating a false sense of do-or-die urgency, propelling him to Burner #2, where burning anger blurred his vision.

And Sam was angry because he was *frustrated*. Why did the car have to break down *that* day of all days? Why couldn't the shop have had a starter ready to install? How could the bus company be so incompetent? Why weren't things working the way they were supposed to?

With the stakes already so high in Sam's mind, ordinarily petty inconveniences grew in magnitude, sending him to Burner #3, where fiery anger consumed his common sense.

Sam's anger erupted when the insolent clerk treated him with disrespect. His fury was unleashed. He became infuriated over the unjust treatment, which, in turn, landed him on Burner #4.

In the end, the bus company reprimanded the rude clerk and refunded money to everyone involved in the mix-up. But no one could turn back the clock. Although Sam felt deep remorse, the damage had already been done. Once his fury was unleashed, the violent blaze of his anger took him down a path of embarrassing destruction.

Though Sam's anger was justified, his actions were not. The sources of anger had compounded together to create the *perfect firestorm* that raged through Sam. At Sam's expense, we can observe how the stages of anger progress from one burner to the other, rapidly becoming hotter with each stage.

Without a plan in place, we can see how a calm, rational person could get to Burner #4 with blazing anger, resulting in actions completely out of character for the person—actions later deeply regretted. That is why we need positive, proactive ways to keep anger from raging out of control. *Anger* is, indeed, one letter short of *danger*.

Escalating Anger: Burning Beneath the Surface[15]

Because there are different types of anger with varying intensities, people get burned in different ways. A spouse, child, or co-worker can be wounded by a harsh word or by a flying object that leaves a deep gash across the forehead.

Just as there are four intensities of anger, there are four types of burns that can damage skin in varying degrees, calling for minimal to maximum treatment. The least damaging to the skin are first-degree burns, usually characterized by sunburns that are superficial and can be treated with mild, aloe-based creams.

"Partial Thickness" burns, also known as second-degree burns, typically manifest themselves with blisters and require more medicated creams for healing. "Full Thickness" or third-degree burns stretch below the epidermis, often affecting muscles, bones, and tendons. The burn victim's skin takes on a shiny white, waxy hue, and he or she may require a skin graft.

Fourth-degree burns, the most severe, are characterized by black, shriveled skin and the suspension of all circulation. Grafting is not an option with such burns, and often amputation is the only way a life can be saved.

Just as you need to take every precaution possible to protect your body from physical burns, you need to be diligent about guarding your anger and ensuring that it doesn't intensify to the point that it severely burns you…and the people around you.

FUEL FOR THE FIRE
The Four Sources of Our Anger

"Fools vent their anger, but the wise quietly hold it back"
(PROVERBS 29:11 NLT).

BEAUTY TURNS TO ASHES when anger becomes a forest fire that incinerates everything in its path.

Take Philip, for example. How my heart hurt for him as we spoke during *Hope in the Night*, our live two-hour call-in counseling broadcast. He was in desperate need of help.

In a tense tone, Philip described how his father, a godly minister, had been murdered by his own cousin, Jack, 19 years earlier when Philip was a teenager. Philip's dad had taken in Jack's children, who had been sexually abused by their father. One day, after a church social, Philip's father returned home and was confronted by Jack, who was angry because he hadn't been included in the family festivities. A violent argument ensued. When it was over, Philip's father lay dead, shot to death just inside his own back door and surrounded by horrified, helpless family members.

Jack spent ten years in prison for his crime, and then spent the remaining five years of his life taunting and terrorizing Philip's family with ongoing threats of deadly retribution. When Jack died, Philip wondered if the gnawing anger that had come to define his life would be laid to rest, too. It was not. In fact, it steadily worsened.

Jack, it turns out, was buried just yards from Philip's "best friend"— his beloved father. Every trip to the cemetery rekindled the embers embedded in Philip's angry heart. Frustrated and exhausted, Philip told me he was desperate for change, but didn't know where to start. He wasn't even sure if help and healing were possible, given the severity of his wound. Could Philip's clenched fists unfold to form a bowl, and could the bowl possibly be large enough to contain all his angry memories so that one day he could release them?

Here's a portion of our on-air conversation:

Philip: "I've never been able to get over my dad's death...I can't get the anger out. Jack shattered our family. Now that I'm getting older, it's getting worse. I'm so angry inside."

June: "Are you saying you tend to overreact to things that should be fairly minor?"

Philip: "Oh, all the time."

June: "Philip, this is powerful pain you're describing. I especially appreciate your call because, often, what we focus on is *what we become*. Have you considered that the very thing that caused the death of your father—your cousin's anger—is what you're struggling with now? Do you want to be like your cousin?"

Philip: "No!"

June: "Of course not. But when we aim our resentment toward another person, our heart is not focused on what is good...we're just focusing on the bad. Scripture says, 'As a man thinketh...so is he.'[1] So we become bitter and unforgiving. We don't know what to do with our emotions because we haven't figured out a healthy way of handling the pain."

Philip: "I just don't feel like justice was served."

June: "In truth, many people want revenge after an injustice. They want to get even. So let me ask you: Is there anything you could do now that would make it 'even'?"

Philip: "Probably not."

June: "No. You're talking about the man you loved more than all others, the one who invested his life in you. There's nothing that could *ever* make that even."

The Four Sources That Fuel Anger's Fire

Clearly, Philip was being ravaged by his own smoldering anger. To quench the flame, he would need to examine the sources of his anger and deal courageously with each one.

Imagine that a chair in your home caught fire. You wouldn't apply water to the smoke or to the tops of the flames. No, you'd grab an extinguisher and aim squarely at the burning cushions—toward the source of the blaze.

That's the approach we must take to quench the fire of our anger.

Anger, you see, is a *secondary* emotion. It always comes from *somewhere,* but too often we can't see past the smoke and flames—a rude driver, a gossiping "friend," a procrastinating spouse, or tragically, in Philip's case, a horrible injustice—to identify the true source.

Unless we address our anger at its source: *injustice, fear, hurt,* and *frustration,* it will continue to burn us—and others. Unless we are able to release all the anger in our bowl, we'll never find lasting peace. So let's examine each of the four sources of anger, one by one, by getting to know the man in the Bible whom God used more miraculously than any other—a man "whom the LORD knew face to face,"[2] a man God considered His friend.

God's Hot-Tempered Hero

This man was humble, highly acclaimed, and *hot-tempered.* Can God use people with anger issues for His purposes? Consider the following verse: "No one has ever shown the mighty power or performed the awesome deeds that Moses did in the sight of all Israel."[3] And yet, even Moses experienced tragic consequences for combustible anger. Here's his story...

The day begins like any other day, but ends like no other—for on this day, Moses gives full vent to his anger. And, as a result, he finds himself running for his life.

Moses becomes part of a mistreated minority grievously persecuted not for doing something wrong, but for being perceived as a threat. Raised with privilege in the palace of a king, he had been spared the heartless treatment inflicted on his kinsmen. But watching the injustice day after day and year after year finally becomes too much for him to bear.

When Moses sees one of his own people suffering an inhumane beating at the hands of an Egyptian, Moses is filled with rage. He snaps. In an instant, he kills the Egyptian and hides the body in the sand. But his angry, impetuous act is not committed in secret. When news of the murder reaches Pharaoh, Moses fears for his life and flees.[4]

When you look at the life of Moses, you can see both the power and the problems inherent in anger. Has anger ever clouded your judgment to the point that you reacted rashly...and lived to regret it? Ultimately, you have the choice to *act* wisely or to *react* foolishly. In his lifetime, Moses did both. Like him, you too can face the fiery anger within and learn to keep it under control. In doing so, you will demonstrate wisdom because...

> *"A fool gives full vent to his anger,*
> *but a wise man keeps himself under control"*
> (Proverbs 29:11).

Source #1—How Can Injustice Ignite Anger?

Understandably, Moses felt anger over the unjust treatment of his Hebrew brothers, but what he did with that anger put him in danger. Moses allowed his anger to overpower him. Acting on impulse, he committed a crime—murder.

Although Moses was right about the injustice, he was wrong in his reaction. His hot-blooded volatility revealed how unprepared he was for the task God had planned for him. Consequently, God kept Moses on the back side of a desert for the next 40 years so he would realize that rescuing his own people *in his own way* would ultimately fail.

Moses needed to learn this vital lesson well before God would turn him into a godly leader—the powerful leader through whom God would accomplish His own will *in His own supernatural way.* In truth, Moses had tried to earn the Israelites' respect by coming to their rescue. Instead, his murderous rage earned only their disrespect.

> *"Moses thought that his own people would realize that God was using him to rescue them, but they did not"*
> (ACTS 7:25).

The novelist Charles Dickens wrote in *Great Expectations,* "In the little world in which children have their existence, whosoever brings them up, there is nothing so finely perceived and so finely felt as injustice."[5]

How true! Young children who probably wouldn't know the meaning of the word *rights* are very articulate when it comes to arguing for their right to a toy or their fair share of ice cream. We are born with a well-defined sense of the things and treatment we are entitled to—an awareness we never lose in life.

We who are part of Western society are among the most rights-oriented people in history. We have bravely championed civil rights, human rights, women's rights, animal rights, voting rights, and property rights. This includes the right to free speech, free assembly, and free religious expression—and rightly so! What, then, do we feel when our rights, or those of someone we care about, have been violated? We feel *angry*—and that's not necessarily a bad thing.

As with anything that fuels our anger, however, there is danger in letting our outrage grow to such proportions that it erupts like a volcano with a flow of regrettable consequences. There is an immense difference between mounting a campaign to legislate against an injustice and picking up a gun to shoot those who perpetuate injustice. Surrender your "right" to handle injustice in your own way to the Savior who *is* "the Way."

My Feelings of Injustice

While I despised my father, I adored my mother. She was everything he wasn't. When he tore into people with harsh, hateful words, she waited for the opportunity to say soothing words of healing.

To me, my father was the epitome of cruelty, and my mother was the epitome of kindness. I had a mountainous pile of angry memories of my father, and nary a one of my mother.

So, when he treated her unjustly, I would become indignant at the unfairness of it all and determined to make him see how wrong he was. After all, someone had to set him straight and come to my mother's defense!

Of course, my lofty aspirations were far above my nonexistent power to accomplish. And my feeble efforts served only to confront my father's infidelity and land me in boarding school, which only increased my mother's suffering. The lesson learned: Never confront my father again about his unjust treatment of anyone, not even my mother. Instead, I harbored hateful thoughts toward him for years.

Source #2—How Can Fear Ignite Anger?

Imagine leading some two million people through a desert with all of them looking to you to meet both their physical and spiritual needs. That was the case with the exodus of the Israelites from Egypt, which turned out to be the high calling of Moses. While Moses was setting up camp at the base of a mountain, God called him to climb the mountain and meet with Him because He wanted to give Moses the Ten Commandments and other beneficial laws.

While Moses met with God, unbeknownst to Moses, the very people God had instructed him to lead had turned their hearts away from God. They melted some gold, molded it into the shape of a calf, and merrily worshipped it! God interrupted this meeting with Moses to inform him of what had happened. Flushed with anger and fear, Moses rushed down the mountain to confront the people. Exodus 32:19 states, "When Moses approached the camp and saw the calf and the dancing, his anger burned and he threw the tablets out of his hands, breaking them to pieces at the foot of the mountain."

Moses reacted in anger because he was full of *fear*. He was afraid God's righteous anger against the disobedient people would result in their destruction. He knew they needed to…

> *"Worship God acceptably with reverence and awe,*
> *for our 'God is a consuming fire'"*
> (HEBREWS 12:28-29).

My Feelings of Fear

Money is power. That belief kept me in constant fear of my financially successful father. Whenever his multiple affairs and harsh treatment left my mother in tears, he asserted, "Tears are a sign of mental illness." On numerous occasions he took her to be evaluated by a psychiatrist.

Knowing mentally ill people were often hospitalized for long periods of time, I lived in constant fear of coming home from school one day and finding my mother had been taken away to be hospitalized by some doctor my father had paid off.

As a result, I made sure I never cried. And I began a "defense fund" for my mother in case my father ever had her declared mentally ill. I wanted to be ready, if necessary, to hire a lawyer to get her out of the hospital. I put in this fund every penny, nickel, dime, and quarter I could come up with—regularly stealing a few coins from the loose change my father left on his night table.

The fear of my father was balanced only by my anger toward him. And even though I never

> Fear is potent fuel for runaway anger, but our commitment to cling to God's fear-quenching love is more potent by far.

needed to use my defense fund, it was years before I would let myself cry or spend the money I had meticulously saved.

Fear is potent fuel for runaway anger, but our commitment to cling to God's fear-quenching love is more potent by far. The Bible explains it this way: "There is no fear in love. But perfect love drives out fear."[6]

Source #3—How Can Hurt Ignite Anger?

Betrayal by anyone certainly hurts our feelings, but betrayal by a friend deeply wounds the soul. Everyone expects opposition from those on the outside, but what do you do when opposition comes from within—from among your own circle, your closest confidants, your trusted few?

Moses was a national leader who knew the hurt of such betrayal. He had led wisely, demonstrated courage, and won the confidence of his people. He was there for them—and they knew it.

However, his authority was undermined by a subordinate who created such dissension that he successfully stole the loyalty of 250 others. Those whom Moses had trusted throughout the years, those who knew him best, those who should have been most loyal, turned against him. In response, however, Moses did not express his anger by taking personal revenge. He did not react impulsively. Rather, he appealed to the Lord to act on his behalf.

> *"Moses became very angry and said to the LORD,*
> *'Do not accept their offering. I have not...wronged any of them'"*
> (Numbers 16:15).

Although justifiably angry, Moses had learned how to face the fiery anger within and to *act* wisely rather than *react* foolishly. He restrained his rage, poured out his heart, and pleaded with the Lord to deal with his offenders. He released his bowl of anger before the Lord, and the justice of God purified the polluted political situation as with fire. God took up Moses' cause, destroyed his betrayers, and defended his honor. Moses refused to take revenge. Instead, he allowed the Lord to be his avenger because God had given this promise:

"It is mine to avenge; I will repay"
(Deuteronomy 32:35).

Think back to the last time you hit your thumb with a hammer or whacked your head on a low-hanging kitchen cabinet. I can guarantee your reaction was immediate—the intense pain you felt was quickly followed by a surge of anger.

Anger follows pain for one reason: to help you make the cause of the hurt go away. It's a useful and necessary response. If you accidentally hit yourself with the hammer, your momentary anger is directed *inward*. "I can't believe I did that! Be more careful! Watch what you're doing!" If someone else is attacking you with a hammer, your anger is focused *outward* in fear—preparing you to eliminate the threat by either fighting back or running away. That's called the fight-or-flight response.

The exact same anger reflex occurs when we are hurt *emotionally*.

The difference is that sometimes the cause (hurt) and effect (anger) are not so clearly linked. Physical pain is straightforward: "I'm angry— you just slapped my face! Don't you dare do it again!" But emotional wounds are more subtle, and we deal with them differently—less directly. Typically we try to ignore them, blame ourselves for them, or privately nurse them...for long periods of time.

Physical pain rarely makes us feel like a failure or a fool, but we're frequently embarrassed or ashamed of our emotional hurts. As a result, we are prone to leave our heartaches unattended, and then they start piling up like dry deadwood in the forest. There they become fuel for the kind of anger that is no longer beneficial, but dangerous and needlessly destructive. It sets the stage for explosive behavior we didn't even know was in us.

My Feelings of Hurt

My three siblings and I had virtually no personal relationship with our father. We never climbed up in his lap or reached out for his hand. We never heard "I love you," or "I believe in you." We were never tucked into bed or given a good night kiss by him. We never shared our hopes and dreams with him or sought his counsel or comfort when troubled.

We occupied the same house, but did not share a home.

Were it not for our mother, we would have been void of any emotional nurturing, spiritual encouragement, or physical affection. We had a father but never a daddy—a provider but never a protector, a critic but never a confidant, a bully but never a hero. The void I experienced was deadening, the hurt was demeaning, and the anger was damaging.

Emotional wounds come in many shapes and sizes and all too often leave us angry. Handling that anger in healthy, appropriate ways begins by first acknowledging our pain and then allowing God to bring healing.

Source #4—How Can Frustration Ignite Anger?

One hot, dry day, Moses' frustration reached a boiling point. He had led about two million people through a vast desert. But for all his efforts, they continually complained, criticizing his leadership and condemning him for their plight: "If only we had died when our brothers fell dead...! Why did you bring us up out of Egypt to this terrible place?"[7]

Now once again, they had no water. Earlier in their journey, God miraculously provided water by instructing Moses to strike a particular rock with his staff. When Moses obeyed, a stream of water—enough for all Israel—poured out of the rock.[8]

At this point, God intended to perform a similar miracle, but He told Moses to simply speak to—not strike—a certain rock. However, Moses was so frustrated with the people that his anger boiled over the edge. Rather than speaking to the rock, he forcefully struck the rock... not once, but twice. *Gushing water* is what God intended—not *gushing anger*. As a result, God disciplined His chosen leader by not allowing him to lead His chosen people into the Promised Land.[9]

At times, are you like Moses? Do you ever allow injustice, fear, hurt, or frustration to make you furious—for which you receive a painful repercussion? If so, what should you do when you are angry? The Bible says, "Refrain from anger and turn from wrath; do not fret—it leads only to evil" (Psalm 37:8).

Compared to the powerful emotions of injustice, fear, and hurt, the fourth cause of anger—frustration—seems relatively minor. But consider this: Each of us has a vision of the way life "should be." In other words, we have *expectations* of happiness, comfort, success, and security in life. Even in mundane matters we want blue skies and smooth sailing. Checkbooks should always balance, report cards should have straight A's, drains should never back up, and cars should never break down.

Of course, we all know life's not like that. Troubles seem to find us no matter how hard we try to avoid them. The problem arises when our expectations are consistently unmet over time. Then it's easy to find ourselves simmering on a slow burn.

After a while we stop *getting* angry at particular frustrations and start *being* angry as a lifestyle. And within every angry person is a bundle of kindling needing only a small match to ignite a blaze far hotter than the frustration ever warrants. Frustrated expectations and desires are volatile fuel for unrestrained anger.

My Feelings of Frustration

No child is a match for an adult, and I was certainly no match for my father. Yet I hoped against hope that someone would be able and willing to rise to the occasion and "take him down" a notch or two and rescue us from his tyrannical rule. But no knight of King Arthur's Round Table, no Superman, no defender of the people ever showed up to help us escape our prison.

I knew my father was wrong. But I also knew I was powerless to change him or the circumstances. Nevertheless, I knew right should prevail over wrong and good over evil, but that wasn't happening in my home, in my family, nor with my father.

Something had to be done, but nothing was being done. Nothing

I could conceive or contrive would help—nothing, that is, short of murder, the ultimate anger slip in my overflowing anger bowl.

As bizarre as it may sound to most people—not all—I was only trying to stop the pain. This was the only way I thought a "final solution" might be possible. When I approached my mother with the concept—"Mom, I have figured out a way to kill Dad." In my teenage mind, I was simply being loyal and using my human logic. However, she calmly assured me, "No, honey, I appreciate what you're trying to do, by that really won't be necessary."

Where did my morbid frustration come from? It was born out of my unmet expectations. I was a captive of my own making, a prisoner of my own unmet desires. But not until I was an adult would I realize that sobering fact.

We can keep from fanning the flames of frustration by surrendering all our unmet expectations to the perfect will of God, and recognizing He is in control of every circumstance and has a perfect plan for our lives. But until we let God's will for us reign over our own will—based on our own expectations—that compromise will remain elusive, and our anger will continue to burn.

In what I just shared, it's easy to find all four causes of anger at work. That is, a profound—and perfectly understandable—sense of hurt, injustice, fear, and frustration.

Emotional Debridement

As we revisit Philip's story, we see that friends, family, and a lifetime of Bible training told him he needed to let go of his anger and forgive. But thus far, he'd been completely powerless to do so. The death of his father had produced an ugly, oozing wound. Left unattended, it had festered for years—devastating his soul, draining his spirit, and threatening to decay his body. Total healing called for spiritual surgery.

When dealing with a burn wound, those charged with treating it have to carry out a painful and unwelcome process called debridement, in which the outer layers of crusty deposits are removed. This allows air to reach the innermost part—enabling lasting healing from the inside out. Debridement is anything but pleasant. It requires revisiting, exposing, and cleansing the wound. But if it's not done, a burn wound will never heal correctly.

With this in mind, I began to gently lead Philip through a process of spiritual and emotional debridement, prayerfully asking the Great Physician to bring healing.

June: "Philip, anger is actually a secondary response to one of four underlying injuries: hurt, injustice, fear, or frustration. I'd like for us to look at each one, beginning with hurt. How would you characterize the hurt that surrounded your father's death?"

Philip: "It was the absolute most you could ever hurt anybody. It was that bad."

June: "That's completely understandable. Now let's consider the second cause of anger, injustice."

Philip: "A ten-year sentence wasn't enough for premeditated murder. I can't reconcile it."

June: "Absolutely not. That is one hundred percent unjust. Your dad did not do anything to provoke this. What about fear? Did your ordeal bring any sense of fear of the future?"

Philip: "Jack sent letters from prison saying he was gonna kill all of us when he got out. He lived nearly five years after his release. During that time, my mother and I moved out of state because we were so afraid."

June: "Okay, so you're telling me you experienced hurt, injustice, and fear. What about frustration? Did you feel frustrated over the situation?"

Philip: "I still do. Every single day."

June: "Philip, I feel for you so deeply. And I have a better understanding now about why anger has taken root in your life. But holding on to this anger will only be detrimental to you. One question you must have considered is, 'Where is God in all this?' Have you been angry with God?"

Philip: "I've blamed God because my whole life, my father pastored and lived a godly life. I felt like God should have protected him. I started drinking and living a worldly lifestyle. But years later, I read my father's autopsy report. It said he was a severe diabetic who was probably on the verge of having a massive heart attack. I realized that God could have been protecting him from a heart attack...while getting a dangerous man off the streets. After that, I got back into church."

June: "I'm glad you recognize now that God's not the perpetrator. He is the One who gives us free will, and we can all choose to go against God's will, which is what the Bible calls sin."

Philip: "That's right. I don't blame God anymore for it. But I know I still have to find a way to deal with it."

June: "And that desire is great news. Hebrews 12:15 says, 'See to it that no one misses the grace of God and that no bitter root grows up to cause trouble and defile many.' You're giving the man who murdered your father the power to continue killing relationships—*yours*! This has to stop. And it can. Tell me, have you had a hard time forgiving Jack?"

Philip: "It's the hardest thing in my life."

June: "Why do you think it has been so hard?"

Philip: "Because he took away from me the one person whom I never wanted to lose. Everyone tells me, 'You need to forgive him.' But in my heart I can't find the justification. I can't see where he deserves forgiveness."

June: "Unforgiveness is going to keep you in prison just as surely as Jack was in prison. Forgiveness sets the prisoner free. I'm glad you used the word *deserve* because forgiveness is not based on what is deserved. Forgiveness means that you are giving what is not deserved. The Bible, in Colossians 3:13, says, 'Bear with each other and forgive whatever grievances you have against one another. Forgive as the Lord forgave you.'

> Forgiveness is not letting the guilty off the hook; it is moving the guilty from your hook to God's hook.

"Forgiveness is not circumventing God's justice; it is allowing God to execute His justice in His time and in His way. Forgiveness is not letting the guilty off the hook; it is moving the guilty from your hook to God's hook. Forgiveness is not excusing unjust behavior; it's acknowledging that unjust behavior is without excuse, while still forgiving. Forgiveness is not based on what is fair; it wasn't fair for Jesus to hang on the cross, but He did so that we could be forgiven. Is this making sense so far...?"

Philip: "It is. It really is."

June: "Think of it this way: Forgiveness is not a feeling; it is a choice. It's an act of the will. And the problem is this: If you do not forgive, the choice you have is to become bitter and angry, and then you become like the one who did the most damage to your life. You're finding you now have anger out of control. That's exactly what Jack had—anger out of control. Is that correct?"

Philip: "That is true."

June: "When Jesus hung on the cross, He said, 'Father, forgive them'— meaning He had a heart of forgiveness. Do you want to be like Jesus? Do you want to be Christlike? Is that important to you?"

Philip: "Oh yes, that's everything I want to be."

June: "That means you're going to need to find a way to forgive, and there's going to be a huge release when you do. Forgiveness not only means dismissing the debt, it means dismissing your demand that others owe you something. It means releasing your resentment. This has been tough for you, and I understand why. But it's releasing your right to hear, 'I'm sorry.' You release your right to be bitter, to get even, to dwell on the offense. You release your resentment toward the offender; you release the penalty you think he deserves."

Dousing the Flames Through Forgiveness

Philip and I talked for two hours that night, live, on the radio. During our remaining time together, I explained more about the biblical basis for forgiveness (which I cover at length in my book *How to Forgive...When You Don't Feel Like It*). I asked Philip to list as many specific hurts as he could that were related to his father's death.

Philip recounted each painful offense—representing his burdens and bitterness—the loss of his beloved father, his mother's resulting health problems, his inability to trust, his anxiety about the future, the strained relationship with his wife...one by one he listed them. There had been more that enough "fuel for the fire" for Philip to hold onto a lifetime of bitterness—even hatred.

Once he'd recounted every last grievance and hurt, I asked Philip two crucial questions: "Do you want to keep Jack closely tied to you for the rest of your life? Or are you willing to release him and to take this pain—all of your deep emotional pain—and give everything to God?" A long pause followed as Philip carefully considered the implications. Then he replied, "I want to be rid of him." As God's grace flooded in, Philip prayed the following prayer:

> Lord Jesus, thank You for caring for how much my heart has been hurt. You know the pain I felt because of Jack murdering my dad. How he threatened me...my mother...the whole family. Lord, You know the pain we've had because of his vengeful spirit. How he spewed anger...instilled fear...caused

sleepless nights…created distrust…and distanced some of our family. How he impacted my brother…made friendships difficult…and how he's worn me out.

Lord, I don't want to carry this pain any more. Right now, I release all this pain into Your hands. Thank You for dying on the cross for me…for extending Your forgiveness to me.

Now, as an act of my will, I choose to forgive my cousin. I take him off of my emotional hook…and move him to Your hook. I refuse all thoughts of revenge. And I trust that, in Your time, You will heal me fully. I know You will deal justly and fully with my cousin.

And Lord, thank You for giving me Your power to forgive. In Your holy name I pray. Amen.

In that moment, it was as if a cleansing flood of water washed over the raging fire within Philip's heart, dousing years of smoldering heartache. And, in that moment, he was free.

Finding What Fuels Your Anger

Philip's call clearly illustrates the kind of crippling confusion unresolved anger can create when we don't have a ready answer to the all-important question: Where does anger come from? For many people, any one of the fiery trials Philip faced would be more than sufficient to stoke the flames of fury. Perhaps you recognize one or more of the four sources of anger in your own life. But there's no need to live in dread of the next spark or to feel helpless to prevent another raging inferno. Know what fuels your anger. Sift through and clean up the emotional debris in your life, and you can prevent a harmful flare-up.

God indeed hears our anguished cries and heals our hurting hearts. All we have to do is humble ourselves before Him…and ask. Trust in His infinite love and care and in His promise: "We know that in all things God works for the good of those who love him, who have been called according to his purpose" (Romans 8:28).

With regard to the cause of my father's anger, it was many years after his death when I learned some eye-opening information from one of his nephews. I always found it curious that my father spoke little of his family or childhood, but it never occurred to me to ask him or my mother about it. All I knew was that he left home in his early teens and never returned.

Because he was more than twice my mother's age when I was born, I never knew his parents or siblings. I learned from his nephew that my paternal grandfather was extremely physically abusive, especially toward my father. On more than one occasion, my father sought refuge in the home of his older brother and spent numerous nights sleeping on a pew in a nearby church.

Needless to say, it was an "Aha!" moment for me. I felt a combination of sadness and relief. The mental imagery of any son being driven out of his home by an abusive father tore at my heartstrings. Now I had some understanding of his angry, hurtful ways. Hurt people *hurt people.*

For the first time, I saw my father as a hurting little boy in a grown-up body. Although I had forgiven him many years before, at that moment I felt compassion for him welling up in me.

How I thank God for caring enough about my healing journey to gift me with powerful insights into my father's past pain. Clearly, He is not finished with me yet.

The Sun: God's Kitchen

The weather forecast on the surface of the sun is always the same: *Hot!* The temperature there is around 10,800 degrees Fahrenheit. That's 100 times hotter than the most sweltering summer day here on earth, and 10 times more heat than it takes to melt solid rock into molten lava. In other words, it is hot enough to consume *anything* that comes too close.

But the destructive capacity of the sun is only one side of the coin. Flip it over and you'll see what astronomers have learned in recent decades: We need the sun—and other stars like it—for more than warmth on a cold winter day. Its blazing heat is essential for nuclear fusion, which turns abundant hydrogen into all the other elements in the universe. Without stars, there would be no oxygen, nitrogen, or carbon—upon which all life depends. Without the sun, there would be no Earth as we know it.

When the incendiary heat of anger has exploded in your life, it is easy to see only the threat of suffering and loss. But that same energy can be harnessed for positive change in your life. Trust God to show you how to put your anger to work—for good.

4

ASHES TO ASHES

The High Cost of Our Unresolved Anger

"Hot-tempered people must pay the penalty.
If you rescue them once, you will have to do it again"
(PROVERBS 19:19 NLT).

IF BURNING ANGER came in a bottle, no doubt we would bury it in
the deepest hole in the most remote place on the planet—but only
after sealing it and labeling it with multiple warnings. We might
stamp words such as *explosive, volatile,* and *combustible* all over the
bottle—or possibly *hot as blazes* and *active time bomb*—so sensibly
minded people wouldn't dare open it.

But rather than coming in a bottle, anger shows up in various sizes,
shapes, and shades without labels or warnings. And, like fire, it can
be dangerously mesmerizing. Who hasn't lit a candle and become
entranced by the flickering flame? As it dances on the wick, it's a
delight to see, but a danger to touch.

Anger is a lot like the flame of a candle—it's associated with "heat"
of varying degrees. Each hue of the flame is a different temperature,
but no matter the blues, yellows, oranges, and reds, the one thing we
all know is that the flame is *hot*—and if we put a finger into the flame
we will get burned!

And so it is with anger—there are varying degrees of it. And the
higher the degree of heat, the deeper the degree of hurt. And even
more so, the wider the area of hurt, the greater the severity of harm.

57

The book of Proverbs gives us this most graphic word-picture: "Can a man scoop fire into his lap without his clothes being burned?"[1]

What a scene! Obviously fire in and of itself is not bad—a campfire is wonderful, but a "lap fire" is dreadful!

Let me be clear about this: Anger in and of itself can be helpful, but anger out of control can be horrible.

The Victims of Anger

Few of us intend to hurt others—even when we are angry. We lash out, but hope there won't be any lingering effects. Few of us *want* to cause havoc and heartache for those around us. But the truth is, extreme anger is very much like a bomb—once it explodes, destruction is inevitable. It damages everything in its path, including relationships and reputations, people and professions, even property.

This isn't some abstract academic theory. By the time we reach adulthood, we've all seen it happen many times—on the playground, in the classroom, both at home and at work. Every time incendiary anger isn't snuffed out, the list of losses grows larger, the list of victims grows longer.

Counselors spend countless hours helping victims cope—the child of an angry parent, the spouse of an angry mate, or the target of an angry boss. Fortunately, with God's healing hand, those wounded by the flaming arrows of anger can move beyond *coping* to *healing*.

But it's just as important to remember the not-so-obvious victims of anger. I'm talking about the ones responsible for the emotional carnage. When surveying the "scene of the crime," we divide ourselves into victims on one side and victimizers on the other. But our all-seeing, all-knowing God sees each heart in need of help and healing—the hurting hearts of both the abused and the abusers.

I believe that is how God saw my family—not five victims of one angry man, but six victims of anger. We all needed help and healing.

Proverbs 22:24-25 warns, "Do not make friends with a hot-tempered man, do not associate with one easily angered, or you may learn his ways and get yourself ensnared." God is telling us that relationships with hot-tempered people always take a heavy toll—not just on those who are the target of rage, but also on those who feel powerless to stop the anger boiling up around them.

Plain and simple: You cannot stay around smoke without smelling like smoke. Likewise, you cannot stay around anger without taking on some characteristics of anger.

This principle was played out in my own life. My father's anger ignited my anger, which then resulted in anger controlling both of us. This is not the kind of healthy "sharing" God intends for dads and daughters. The very thing I hated in my dad took root in me, although I didn't see it at the time. Feeling totally justified in my anger, I didn't see any similarities between his anger and mine. I was right. He was wrong. But, in truth, we were both wrong. Neither of us allowed anger to accomplish good in us.

The High Price of Anger

Jesus said, "Each day has enough trouble of its own."[2] Life naturally brings us plenty of problems, and we can't afford to make matters worse with the self-inflicted hardship of unrestrained rage. Let's examine six ways that we pay a high price for our anger:

1. Anger Destroys Relationships

"I want a divorce" was the last thing Rob expected to hear after returning home from a three-day Promise Keepers conference. But that evening Rob's wife, Judy, was unusually quiet. When he asked her why, her anguish poured out.

Judy explained that during the days Rob had been gone, a new sense of peace had settled over their household: "During the past three days, I've felt better about myself than I've ever felt during our marriage." Missing were his explosive outbursts of anger—and the anxiety they caused. For Rob, this painful moment of truth cut deeply.

Soon afterward, a marriage counselor identified the "pressure cooker" issue: Rob had a problem with unresolved anger that fueled his frequent rages. His verbal rantings had left Judy feeling wounded and fearful—not only for her own well-being, but for that of their young son, Tyler, as well.

Rob's reaction? "I got angry at the counselor!"

Several months later, unable to resolve their differences, the couple divorced. But by the grace of God, while Rob's marriage had ended, his journey of healing had just begun.

Uncontrolled anger is deadly to relationships because it undermines the very conditions necessary to create and maintain trust between people. Couples can ride out the storms of life together so long as trust rides with them, but unbridled anger destroys trust and makes the storms too threatening.

Healthy relationships require freedom from fear. To open our life to another person is, by definition, to make ourself vulnerable. Like a fire victim being asked to jump from a rooftop above a raging inferno, we must be able to trust the one who says he is ready to catch us and break our fall.

If that person periodically lets go and we get hurt, the inevitable fear and uncertainty we feel will rob us of the strength and confidence we need to stay committed through tough times.

Random outbursts of raw anger can be terrifying. They create an environment in which everyone is guarded and ready to either fight or flee. This constant state of alertness saps vital trust, energy, and spontaneity from our lives. And its impact on our relationships? "Ashes to ashes."

After his divorce—through circumstances only God could orchestrate—Rob met Jack, one of our enthusiastic Hope for the Heart team members. Learning of Jack's part in our ministry, Rob eagerly related how God had used Hope for the Heart to change his life. Humbled and inspired, Jack invited Rob to come to our weekly staff devotions. There, our team had the privilege of hearing the rest of Rob's story.

During a sleepless night a few months after his divorce, Rob turned on the radio. Our *Hope in the Night* radio program was airing, and the topic just happened to be anger. "I'd never heard the topic of anger approached from a biblical perspective. That broadcast was God-sent... no doubt about it."

Rob listened intently, then ordered our set of audio recordings and Biblical Counseling Keys on anger. With those in hand, he reserved an extended stay in a hotel room for a time of intense reading, listening, and praying. His goal was to grasp God's principles on how to uproot his past anger and handle his present hostilities. Faithfully, God began to reveal the severity of Rob's problem.

"It hit me like a ton of bricks: I responded to people—especially my ex-wife—with rage, just erupting like a volcano." At 2:00 Sunday morning, Rob penned this journal entry: "Just like the eruption of a volcano, the hot lava pours down the mountain, scorching everything in sight. It changes the composition of the rock by its heat forever. Its damage is lasting and leaves black, ugly, scarred rock. My explosive anger scorches everyone in sight—my ex-wife, my son, my mother, employees—it scars them for life and leaves our relationships black and ugly. However, Christ can scrape away…scrape away the black outer covering through me as I forgive those who have made me angry and as I work to restore my relationships."

Rob said that over the next several months and years, "God gradually revealed to me the source of my anger, which was hurt and rejection from my childhood and teenage years. When I raged at Judy, I'd been trying to control her so she couldn't reject me. But in reality, I was making things worse."

Rob did the difficult work necessary to tame his toxic anger, and he continues to reap the rewards. His relationship with his son is blossoming in an atmosphere of trust and loving discipline. Though Judy has remarried, the two are now able to communicate openly so they can parent productively. In fact, Judy recently wrote Rob a letter, thanking him for his compassionate and Christlike attitude in the years following their divorce.

"I'm a work in progress," Rob told our team, concluding our inspirational visit. "I still get angry, but now I'm able to process my pain. Had it not been for your Biblical Counseling Keys, I wouldn't have changed. They brought healing through the application of God's Word. After years of burning others with my out-of-control anger, I finally know how to express my feelings constructively. Your ministry gave me the tools I needed. My dream now is to help others, along with their families, who are suffering just like I was."

Although it took the loss of his marriage, Rob finally got the message. He sought help from God, enlisted the support of a Christian counselor, and took responsibility for winning back the trust and respect of those he loved. He did this by rooting out unresolved anger and gaining control over his temper. As good as that is, how much better it would have been had he faced his anger earlier and spared others the scars they now carry as a result of his out-of-control tongue.

Like a bridge subjected to repeated earthquakes, relationships will *always* suffer damage in the presence of unrestrained anger. Chronic anger inevitably weakens the foundation of trust. And this foundation needs to be unshakable so that close relationships can withstand life's unpredictable tremors.

2. Anger Destroys Harmony at Work

Many people are unhappy these days and often take it out on others.

A study by Erickson and Williams-Evans (2000) revealed that 82 percent of emergency room nurses surveyed had been assaulted during their careers, and that many assaults go unreported. Only 3.6 percent of nurses surveyed felt safe from the possibility of patient assault at work.[3]

Anger and aggression in the workplace are increasing, making colleagues anything but congenial. This issue makes the evening news only when anger turns to horrible violence—which, sadly, is becoming increasingly commonplace.

But for many people, low-level frustration at work—anger they feel themselves or must deal with in others—is a daily way of life that drains the workplace of the joy and satisfaction that a good day's work should bring. In fact, American companies spend billions of dollars on legal fees, medical expenses, lost employee time, and related expenses every year dealing with the consequences of workplace anger that turns violent.[4]

Yet even without physical aggression, unresolved anger among employees diminishes productivity, inhibits creativity, and limits personal success. Left unchecked, it usually costs the angry person both a good job and good references, not to mention the loss of potentially meaningful work relationships. Managers and corporate bosses certainly don't want their company to be the next to make headlines because they allowed a conflict to turn ugly.

Dave is a good example. This retired military man—now in his second career—became a project manager at a prominent software design company. His job was to oversee the development of a new program that would help streamline accounting tasks for small businesses. He had a staff of 20 programmers working around the clock, but as the project deadline approached, it became increasingly clear something was wrong. The software failed every important test run, and each attempted correction only made things worse.

When senior managers decided it was time to take a closer look, it didn't take long to identify the trouble: Staff communication and trust had been completely broken. The troubleshooting process of pinpointing problems and solving them as a team had ceased to function. The programmers were afraid to report glitches and failures—a necessary part of testing and improving the product.

It turned out that when they did speak up, Dave often exploded in a terrible rage. By shouting put-downs and slamming doors, he made it clear he would not tolerate bad news. So his employees stopped giving it to him...with disastrous results.

Dave was a smart, competent man. But he was used to giving orders to soldiers and pushing for the results he wanted, no matter what. The corporate model of consensus and team-building didn't make sense to him. As a result, he mistakenly saw every problem as a breakdown of "discipline" that needed to be quashed.

The more Dave's management style failed, the more angry he became. The angrier he became, the more his management style failed. It was a downward spiral that repeated itself again and again when anger gained the upper hand. Eventually, the company had no choice but to replace Dave with someone more skilled in communication and problem-solving...and less likely to erupt in anger.

Dave's story brings to mind a therapeutic camping program for troubled youth, where a close friend of mine worked. Three counselors would take ten teens camping in the wilderness for twenty-six days at a stretch. The goal: to teach them how to talk their problems out rather than fight them out or run away from them.

Needless to say, problems were easy to come by in the hot, dry Chihuahuan Desert of southwest Texas. And there was definitely no place to run away to. Before leaving Dallas, by prior agreement with all ten teens, when tempers flared, everything came to a screeching halt. No one could fix a meal, hike to water, go to sleep—not until the problem was resolved.

Immediately the group would circle together (called a "huddle up") to clarify the problem and come up with a workable solution—agreeable not only to the parties involved, but to the *entire group*. Then it was back to the challenge of climbing mountains and surviving in the desert. It's amazing how quickly hot tempers cool down when the stakes are high enough—such as eating!

> Your health is powerfully affected by what you think and feel.

Dave's story might have had a different ending if his team had chosen to come around him, identify the problem caused by his management style, and then talk it through with him to an agreeable end. Instead, he chose to keep silent and to sabotage an important company project.

Let's face it: Work can be very stressful. Many people feel pressured by deadlines, bullied by bosses, frustrated by missed promotions, and impatient with underachieving co-workers or demanding clients. But allowing anger to boil over into intimidating outbursts not only makes things worse, but offers no help to everyone involved.

As in Dave's case, excessive anger can result in unemployment—then you can add *unemployment* to the list of reasons to be angry. Who can afford that kind of costly anger?

And what society can long survive such self-destructive behavior? That's why God's Word says, "Refrain from anger and turn from wrath; do not fret—it leads only to evil. For evil men will be cut off."[5]

3. Anger Destroys Our Health

One of the most important ideas to emerge in medical science is also the most often ignored. In its simplest form: Your health is powerfully affected by what you think and feel. This fact is presented throughout the Bible, now those in the field of science finally "get it."

The traditional model held that good health depends only on external factors such as rest, nutrition, and exercise. Yet when it comes to health, intangible influences are powerfully at work as well. Researchers have discovered that our thoughts directly affect the creation of real biochemical compounds—such as adrenaline and endorphins—which have a significant impact on how our bodies function.

Here's a simple demonstration: Imagine you've just come home from the grocery store with a carton full of ripe, plump strawberries (or your favorite fruit). You can't wait to take a bite and slowly savor its sweetness on your taste buds. You wish you could hold on to that succulent flavor forever.

If you are like me, your mouth is watering in anticipation as you read these words. Why? The beautiful, delectable fruit exists only in your mind as a thought, but your body reacts nonetheless with a very real physical response. This happens frequently, whether you are aware of it or not. Many thoughts and emotions have a tangible effect on our bodies, and anger is one of the most potent.

Dr. Redford Williams, director of the Behavioral Medicine Research Center at Duke University, has spent much of his career studying the effects of sustained hostility on the human body. He says:

> There is some evidence that the immune system may be weaker in hostile people. According to a study of more than 1,000 people at a Western Electric factory in Chicago over a 25-year period, those with high hostility scores were at a high risk of dying not only from coronary disease but from cancer as well.[6]

In other words, living in a constant state of angry frustration is physically harmful. In fact, *it can kill you*. Here are some findings from similar studies:

- According to the American College of Cardiology, sudden cardiac death accounts for 400,000 deaths each year in the United States.

- In 2009 a group from Yale University studied 62 patients with heart disease and implantable defibrillators that detect dangerous heart arrhythmias and deliver an electrical shock to restore a normal heart beat. The subjects were put through an exercise in which the patient recounted a recent angry episode while the electrical activity of the heart was measured. The study found that *anger increased electrical instability* of these patients. The study followed these patients for three years and suggests that anger impacts the heart's electrical system *in ways that can lead to sudden death.*[7]

- A study of men found those "generally hostile and contemptuous of other people" are *30 percent more likely to develop a heart condition* called atrial fibrillation—a "flutter" that signals an *increased risk of stroke.*[8]

- Increased heart rate and blood pressure when a person is angry cause "micro-tears" in the lining of the arteries, making it *easier for blockages to form.*[9]

- A study begun in 1983 concluded that medical students with high "hostility" levels while in school were *seven times more likely to die before age 50*—of any cause—than their calmer peers.[10]

- People who already suffer from heart disease nearly *triple their risk of a heart attack* when they become extremely angry. The increased vulnerability lasts for at least two hours.[11]

- A survey of nearly 2,500 emergency room patients who had been injured in some way found that "people who described themselves as feeling irritable have a 30% increased risk for getting injured, while those who are feeling hostile *double their risk of injury.*[12]

Researchers acknowledge there are many factors that contribute to ill health. And it is increasingly clear an angry disposition is one of them. Psychologist Ernest Johnson put it this way: "In the end, for many people who have problems really expressing and dealing with their feelings, there's early mortality—dropping dead from a stroke or a heart attack, kidney disease or breast cancer."[13]

It's hard to get more blunt than that. No wonder God tells us to guard our hearts (minds) and give careful thought to our ways. And no wonder He warns us regarding anger and angry people.

The Bible says, "Everyone should be quick to listen, slow to speak and slow to become angry, for man's anger does not bring about the righteous life that God desires."[14]

4. Anger Causes Irrational Thinking

When people get angry, their problem-solving ability plummets. Consider the case of my normally even-keeled assistant, Elizabeth, who recently shared this story with those attending at our monthly Hope Biblical Counseling Institute.

"Many years ago, I was driving to a corporate planning conference, where I was to serve as a presenter for the opening session. Hoping to arrive early, I instead became ensnarled in a terrible traffic jam. With each passing minute, I became more frantic.

"My hands gripped the steering wheel…my jaw tightened…I could hardly take my eyes off the clock on the car dashboard. My heart raced as I scanned the horizon looking for a way—any way—to escape the gridlock. I began tailgating. Soon I was eyeing the median, wondering if I could somehow sail across it in the family minivan and find another route."

As her anxiety mounted, Elizabeth had no way of knowing that important chemical changes were also taking place inside her body. Here's what happens when circumstances stress us:

- Epinephrine (adrenaline) is released by the adrenal glands,[15] immediately preparing the body for a fight-or-flight response. However, if fight or flight does not occur, the highly energized body has difficulty calming down. (This is why angry people experience a racing heart, shaking hands, and fast breathing.)

- The angry person's hormones then travel from the brain to the adrenal glands, signaling the need for tension reduction by the release of cortisol. However, cortisol raises blood pressure above the norm, which makes *rational thinking more difficult.*

Elizabeth continued her story:

"As I sat there stewing, the thought crossed my mind that I had done everything but pray and give thanks to God in my situation. I realized the Bible says, 'Do not be anxious about anything, but in everything, by prayer and petition, wth thanksgiving, present your requests to God.'[16] However, I was so anxious I could barely comprehend the thought. But still it persisted. So in a very sarcastic, very loud voice, I blurted out, 'Okay, God, *thank You*! Sitting in this traffic jam...being late for the big conference...is *just great*! I mean I'm *really thankful*, God. In fact, if I were any more thankful, I just don't know what I'd do!'

"Just hearing myself be so irreverent, angry, and sarcastic with my wonderful, loving, patient heavenly Father jolted me. I felt convicted and saddened by my disprespectful attitude. After a minute or two, my heart began to soften and I began, again, to talk to God: 'Lord, I'm sorry I have such a terrible attitude...that I'm so impatient and angry. I commit this drive and this day to You. Thank You for waking me up this morning...for giving me a car to drive and a job to drive it to. Thank You for taking such good care of me. Thank You that I'm not the one involved in the accident that's slowing us down this morning. Please help those involved in the crash. I trust this drive to You and ask You to get me to the conference in Your perfect time. I love You, Lord! Amen.'

"Unexplainable peace seemed to envelop every square inch of my car. It's like I was driving a joy bubble. Instead of feeling anxious and angry, I felt calm and at perfect ease. I relaxed, sat back, and drove safely. I even begin to sing. The traffic began to open up, and I arrived at the meeting in time to start my presentation on time."

It's as though Elizabeth took her bowl full of anger and tilted it outside the car window, its contents fluttering away in the wind—and in turn, she experienced a welcome return of her equilibrium. This should come as no suprise to us because after we do what the Bible says—sincerely pray about our problems with thanksgiving—then we receive what is desribed in the very next verse: "And the peace of God, which transcends all understanding, will guard your hearts and your minds in Christ Jesus."[17]

5. Anger Undermines Mental and Emotional Well-Being

There is a big difference between occasionally getting angry and being an angry person. Getting angry when circumstances call for it is a natural response, whereas being angry most of the time is a precursor to a psychological enemy that stalks millions of people: chronic depression.

In fact, numerous studies confirm anger and depression go hand in hand, particularly when we get angry with ourselves.

What a sad and self-destructive price we pay for anger. The truth is that anger and depression feed each other in a relentless downward spiral of despair. The angrier you become, the more depressed you feel. The deeper you sink into depression, the angrier you feel.

Fortunately, God has provided a way to clear up this convoluted concoction. Jesus said, "Come to me, all you who are weary and burdened, and I will give you rest. Take my yoke upon you and learn from me, for I am gentle and humble in heart."[18] What do we learn from what Jesus has modeled for us? To let go and to forgive.

The evidence is clear: Unresolved anger is toxic to the human heart, mind, and body. To live the life God intended, your anger simply *must* be poured out into the Refiner's fire. Allow God to burn away the damaging dross that has accumulated from years of anger, resentment, and bitterness.

6. Anger Hinders Our Christian Walk

God gives you permission to be angry. He never says, "Thou shalt not ever be angry!" He made you in such a way that expressing anger is a natural, spontaneous part of being human—like laughing or crying. What He does say is don't sin and don't *stay* angry. Specifically, "In your anger do not sin. Do not let the sun go down while you are still angry, and do not give the devil a foothold."[19]

Why is it important to resolve anger before you lay your head down at night? What opportunity does prolonged anger give the enemy of our souls? Just how does nursing hostility leave the door open for evil to creep in on us?

Imagine you are visiting the home of a dear friend. You both look forward to an evening of laughter and conversation. In the living room is a fireplace with a raging fire.

The fire is too hot for the small room, and right away, you start to sweat. It's hard to breathe. You move your chair as far from the flames as you are able, but before long you can't focus on a single word your friend is saying. All you can think about is that fire and how uncomfortable you are.

That's exactly what raging anger does to our relationship with God—it *dominates,* while our spiritual vitality *diminishes.* As long as our anger burns, it's next to impossible for us to concentrate on anything else. The raging fire in our anger bowls becomes the center of attention.

The Christlike walk comprises in part love, forgiveness, humility, and prayerfulness. There is no place for unresolved anger in the mix. Here are three reasons why:

- *Anger suffocates our motivation to love our enemies.* It is okay to be angry—on our way to forgiving our offender. Unresolved anger drives us toward revenge, not reconciliation—toward hatred, not love. However, Jesus unequivocally says, "Love your enemies" (Matthew 5:44). (This is not emotional love. The

Greek term Matthew 5:44 uses for love is *agape,* which refers to a commitment to doing what is best for the other person.)

- *Anger smothers our motivation to pray for our enemies.* The longer we fume over some offense, the harder it will be to pray for those who have hurt us. In fact, typically, the last person we want to pray for is the one who has hurt us. Yet Jesus, who understands your anger, says, "Pray for those who persecute you."[20]

- *Anger stifles our motivation to surrender to God's will.* Rage is an attempt to control the people and events in our lives and make them bend to *our* desires. It's necessary to tame the flames before you can expect to sincerely say to God, "Not my will, but Yours" (Luke 22:42).

So...what is God's will? Even when we've been unjustly wronged, Jesus commands us to forgive and to cancel the offender's debt, just as our debts have been wiped clean by the Savior. The Bible says, "Love for God" is "to obey his commands."[21] Don't allow anger to drive a wedge between you and your love for God.

So...the bad news is chronic anger is costly, taking a tremendous toll on our physical, emotional, and spiritual well-being. It wields the power to ruin our relationships, impair our employment, damage our health, and interfere with our being in the will of God—and that's just the short list.

The good news is we are not doomed to a lifetime of lament. The Bible says, "If anyone is in Christ, he is a new creation; the old has gone, the new has come!"[22]

If you are in Christ, you are a new creation. This means the past is wiped clean. God has made this possible, and He makes it possible— "as far as it depends on you"[23]—to know peace, healing, and hope in all your relationships and circumstances.

Matches: Fire on a Stick

It seems magical: You can actually make fire leap from a tiny piece of wood. But it doesn't take a wizard to strike a match and light a fire, as if it were some supernatural feat. It's a simple matter of assembling the right ingredients and applying the right forces at the right time. Here's all you need:

- a matchstick coated on one end with red phosphorus and finely ground glass

- an abrasive surface

- friction

The heat of friction turns a small amount of the red phosphorus into its chemical cousin white phosphorus—a substance that bursts into flames in air. Other chemicals in the mix release oxygen in small amounts to feed the flames. Then—presto!—the wooden or paper match catches fire.

Of course, a match by itself doesn't provide much light or heat. For that you need something to fuel the flame—a candle, or firewood.

To ignite anger also requires just the right combination of emotional ingredients—and friction caused by some hurt, injustice, fear, or frustration (or any combination of the four). Even then, however, what size fire you wind up with depends on the fuel you provide. So before the sparks fly, work to clear the kindling—the underbrush of bitterness—from your life.

5

THE FIRE EATERS

The Harm of Holding In Our Anger

*"Careful words make for a careful life;
careless talk may ruin everything"*
(PROVERBS 13:3 MSG).

"SO THAT'LL BE A CHEESEBURGER—hold the onions—one large
order of fries, and a supersized bowl of anger. Anything else?"

Had a restaurant server attempted to confirm such an order in my
younger years, I would have quickly corrected him. *Never* would it have
been my intent to down a big, steaming bowl of fiery anger. But for a
number of years, anger had become a staple in my emotional diet.

Growing up in an unpredictable home that fostered anger, I frequently chose silence when fiery eruptions occurred. Going underground
with my feelings seemed the only way to survive in the presence of my
painfully punitive father, who tolerated *no anger* but his own.

"Eating" my anger felt less dangerous than allowing it to surface.
But over time, I've learned that when we bury anger alive, it's only a
matter of time before it comes raging back to the surface—only hotter
and more harmful. I was subconsciously heaping my hurts into what
appeared to be a bottomless pit. But every bowl has a bottom.

Fear Evokes Fire Eating

If you consistently internalize your anger, it doesn't take a rocket
scientist to figure out why—the reason is *fear*. Either you're afraid of

what *you* will do if you express your feelings, or you fear what *others* will do (as in my case).

I constantly evaluated my situation: What will it cost me to be candid, to be honest? Security? Safety? Survival? I didn't risk showing anger without calculating my potential losses. And from my fear-based perspective, the cost seemed to always exceed the gain.

Unfortunately, when fear is the dominant decision-maker, the idea that you might gain something by expressing your anger appropriately never enters the equation. Soon, you conclude it's *always* safer to just "stuff it."

That may sound cowardly, but in truth, many of us "anger eaters" have had good reasons to run from conflict. To survive we've had to find a way to endure relationships in which anger was truly threatening. Once in place, these patterns of behavior became reflexive, a kind of subconscious survival instinct that governed our relationships from then on.

> It's never too late to bring your fears to God and leave them there.

Realize that whether you indiscriminately detonate your anger in public or swallow it in private, you will end up scorched—possibly scarred for life. The good news is it's never too late to stop stuffing your anger. How comforting it is that the Lord says, "Do not fear, for I am with you; do not be dismayed, for I am your God. I will strengthen you and help you; I will uphold you with my righteous right hand" (Isaiah 41:10).

The Six Kinds of Anger Eaters

There are many ways to avoid confronting your anger. They run the gamut from total denial to clandestine counterattacks. That is why honestly identifying *your approach* is a great place to begin getting control over the smoldering and sometimes blazing fires in your life. Consider these common types of *anger avoiders* and see if you recognize yourself:

1. Stuffers: "Who, me? Angry?"

Everyone who knew Joan marveled that she seemed completely

unflappable. She never raised her voice or lost her composure, even when tempers flared all around her. In her position as the office manager of a large church, Joan's restraint served her well.

Coordinating the activities of eight full-time pastors and a dozen other staff members was enough to challenge anyone. But not Joan. She was calm and competent to a fault. A prominent church member once joked that if Joan had worked for Moses, she'd have served Pharaoh tea and cookies and had the children of Israel peacefully on their way before lunch.

It was a reputation Joan enjoyed and cultivated. Imagine her surprise, then, when the senior pastor began a private meeting with her by asking a startling question.

"Joan," he said, "I wonder if you'd be willing to share with me why you are so angry?" She was floored. What? Had she heard him correctly?

"But I'm not angry," she said with a serene smile. "I deal with angry people all the time, but I'm never one of them."

"I'll agree with you that you never lose your temper," the pastor said. "But that isn't the same thing as not being angry." Having observed Joan at work, the pastor noticed a formidable line of emotional defenses just beneath the surface of her even-keel demeanor that kept everyone at a safe distance.

True, no one got under her skin enough to provoke her anger. But neither did they get close enough to enjoy her friendship or trust. Furthermore, he noticed her placid approach to life masked the harsh, punitive core of the high standards she set for her subordinates.

Stuffers are people who hide their anger well. They are fearful of its negative consequences. They convince themselves—and sometimes others—that it never existed in the first place. They stuff it down inside and forget all about it, like the fuming, slightly smoldering firecracker relegated to the bottom of the fireworks box. Out of sight, out of mind...*for a while*.

On the surface, the strategy appears to work just fine. Like Joan, these folks often project a soft, magnanimous personality in public—even when enduring a painful offense that would infuriate most people. They simply smile and get on with life as if nothing is wrong.

But anger exists for a reason and doesn't just disappear because you tell it to. Anger tells *you* when something needs your attention. Ignoring it doesn't make it go away. No matter how deeply you hide your anger—even from yourself—it will eventually make its way back to the surface of your life, often with a vengeance.

Joan left her pastor's office that day truly baffled. But she took his gentle suggestion that she ask God to show her any hidden anger she might secretly harbor. She went home and adopted David's prayer in Psalm 139:23-24:

> *"Search me, O God, and know my heart;*
> *test me and know my anxious thoughts.*
> *See if there is any offensive way in me,*
> *and lead me in the way everlasting."*

It didn't take long for Joan to find an answer—she had deeply entrenched anger. Instead of releasing her anger to God, she had been harboring her anger...at God.

Ten years earlier, Joan and her husband tragically lost their first baby suddenly to a rare kind of respiratory infection. Joan had never resolved her seething rage at God for allowing the tragedy to strike her family. At the time, Joan was devastated and so overwhelmed with grief that denial became an iron curtain of forgetfulness falling over her thoughts, shielding her from molten emotion that threatened to spread and destroy everything else in her life.

Now, aware of it once again, she suddenly realized her pastor was right. In spite of her determined denial, the heat of hidden anger had silently seared her relationships all these years. Freedom came as she prayerfully acknowledged each hurt, and then gratefully released them all to God.

If you are a "stuffer" and want to be free, take heart. Nothing is hidden so deeply God can't reach down and make it right. I know because He reached into the depths of my being, uprooted the bitterness, and extinguished the anger burning there toward my father. Be assured He can and wants to do the same for you.

2. Sulkers: "Just leave me alone."

Unlike Joan, some people know very well they are angry, but have no intention of risking more pain and hardship by confronting it head-on. Rather than deny their anger, they simply pull down the shades of their heart and hang a "Do Not Disturb" sign on the door. From within this sullen fortress they resist all attempts from others to confront their anger and resolve it. The very last thing they want to do is *talk* about it.

Clearly, we all deserve privacy and the right to deal with anger in our own way. But sulkers usually aren't just taking a time-out, or pausing to count to ten before proceeding. These are people who completely withdraw from relationships and can nurse a grudge in silence for *years*. Sadly, they allow a past wrong to burn up any prospect for joy in the present, and to destroy any hope for joy in the future.

Withdrawing is a breeding ground for bitterness that is practically guaranteed to inflame your anger, not tame it. Cut off from other points of view, you are much more susceptible to error and exaggeration in your thinking. In your mind, you replay the anger-producing offense again and again until it grows out of proportion.

Living with a Turtle

Lee wanted his wife's forgiveness. Uncharacteristically, he'd had too much to drink at Jana's office Christmas party and became overly loud and obnoxious. To make matters worse, he blatantly flirted with two of his wife's co-workers. When Jana told him it was time to go, he said he was sick of her "mothering."

The next day, Lee was horrified at his own despicable behavior. He was desperate to communicate how sorry he was and to begin repairing the damage done. There was just one problem: Jana refused to listen to what he had to say or even share her feelings about what had happened. Obviously humiliated and embarrassed, she wore her hurt like a suit of armor and withdrew behind its cold, hard exterior.

You see, Jana's grandfather was an alcoholic with a long history of ruining family events, especially holidays, by drinking too much. Lee's behavior struck a tender nerve in Jana's heart. She responded to her fear and anger the same way her mother and grandmother had: She retreated to a "safe distance" and silently fumed. Her anger was plain to see, but completely inaccessible.

By the time Lee called me on *Hope in the Night*, he was desperate to break through the firewall of Jana's closed-off emotions. "She's a turtle. She pulls her head inside her shell and won't come out. There's absolutely nothing I can do or say!"

"Lee, I hear your frustration. Sulking keeps anger alive by slamming the door on honest, direct communication. Yet communication is the essential ingredient of eventual forgiveness and reconciliation. Sulking denies passage even to the most sincere apology. It's one of the behaviors the apostle Paul had in mind when he wrote: 'Do not let the sun go down while you are still angry, and do not give the devil a foothold.'[1]

"You already know you can't *force* Jana to open up. But I believe there are steps you can take to strengthen your relationship with your wife. Would you be willing to explore what *you* can do in this situation and forget, at least for a moment, what you want *her* to do?"

Refocus on What Can Be Controlled

Lee seemed skeptical, but agreed to hear me out, enabling me to direct his attention to what he could control. Since Jana's trust had been violated, reconciliation would require time, a behavior change, and consistency to prove to Jana that Lee was worthy of her trust. He could not expect her to re-extend trust without his demonstration of a true understanding of what he had done wrong, how deeply it had hurt her, a godly sorrow over his actions, and sincere repentance.

I probed Lee's decision to drink too much at the party and to make passes at Jana's colleagues. It became clear that Lee had deficits in his own life that would require his focused attention: Always being over-shadowed by a high-achieving older brother had left Lee with some deep-seated wounds of his own. By addressing these, Lee could grow emotionally and become a healthier person.

Demonstrating his genuine desire to make God his priority and to become a man of integrity would also be life-changing for him and a huge factor in the possible restoration of his marriage.

"Lee, I'm going to recommend you involve a godly man, or even two or three, in your life—to provide support, prayer, and account-ability on your journey toward reconciliation. Is there anyone in your life who could come alongside you?"

"I know one man who is a really strong Christian. I could ask if he'd be willing to help me."

Develop a Dialogue of Integrity

"Good! Ask him. And in the meantime, I'm going to recommend some things you can say when you talk to Jana about this issue. Of course, these words won't do you a bit of good unless they come from your heart. But if you can say this and mean it, consider communi-cating something along these lines:

"'Jana, my actions at the party were completely wrong—I have no excuse. And, I realize I opened up that old wound from your grand-father when I got out of control. I acted like him.

"'I know you are feeling hurt, betrayed, embarrassed, and fearful. And I don't blame you one bit. I pray that someday you'll forgive me. But I know I can't demand your forgiveness…and I must earn your trust. That's what I want to do, no matter how long it takes.'"

Because Lee had committed his life to Christ, he needed to tell her that and state, "With God's help, I am going to do everything I can to become a man of integrity. As a Christian, that's my deepest desire. And as my wife, that's what you deserve."

Lee and I talked long into the night. After our call, I sent him our ministry's resources on reconciliation, along with my prayers that he would experience new hope for his heart.

Many men (and women) in Lee's situation—people who had "blown it" then had to face the consequence of living with a sulker—*have* contacted me with glowing reports of restoration. But they had to take the necessary steps to address their *own* issues, and live a life of total integrity before their loved ones.

3. Snipers: "Can you believe what she did to me?"

While some people hide behind an impenetrable shield of silence, others are more than willing to talk about their anger—to anyone except the person who sparked it. They avoid owning up to their rage by diverting its energy into making sure everyone knows their version of events.

The payoff in using this approach is twofold. First, in playing the aggrieved victim, why do the strenuous work of resolving the conflict when you can bask in an outpouring of pity instead? Don't misunderstand me—we all appreciate genuine compassion when a painful event has caused us harm. That's a natural and healthy role friends and family can play in our lives. The problem arises when we begin to crave the "camaraderie" inspired by our anger—so much so that we stay stuck there.

Second, by engaging in gossip about the people who made them mad, snipers often succeed in *imparting* their anger to others—empowering them to also fire their angry bullets. Shared anger means shared responsibility for action. In this way they enlist surrogates willing to take the lead in confronting the "offender" on their behalf. In other words, the snipers' fear of anger leads them to create a human shield around themselves, behind which they hide for as long as they're able to keep the collective fire hot.

When you are angry, don't hesitate to call on the support of wise friends. But remember that your anger is *yours,* and solidarity with others is a stepping stone toward receiving God's gift of freedom and healing—not a destination in itself.

4. Schemers: "I never get mad—I just get even."

Recently I heard about a husband who questioned his wife, "How can you be so calm when I lose my temper so much?" She answered, "I clean the toilet." Still confused, he asked, "Well, how does that help?" She replied sweetly, "I use your toothbrush."

A humorous story, perhaps, but real-life issues aren't quite so laughable.

Shirley was already angry with her husband, Neil. She had felt for some time that she did far more than her share to keep their household running smoothly. Both had demanding jobs that contributed income to the family. But when it came to doing the laundry, making dinner, cleaning the bathrooms, or getting the kids to bed on time, the responsibility wasn't distributed evenly. There seemed to be an unspoken assumption that *all* those responsibilities belonged *only* to her.

"At times I felt guilty for being irritated," Shirley told me. "An image would pop into my head of my mother—the perfect, happy homemaker. She never complained or got angry about all she did for us. So neither should I."

But when Neil announced he had joined a fitness center and planned to work out for an hour a couple of evenings a week, it was too much for Shirley. She became furious. Couldn't Neil see she was already stretched to the breaking point? Of course, that would have been a perfect time for Shirley to openly confront her anger, but that's not what she did. She was unable to escape the memory of her mother's voice saying, "God can't hear you when you grumble, dear."

So, instead of acting on her anger directly, Shirley channeled it into a series of less risky hit-and-run attacks—a campaign of emotional guerrilla warfare. She intentionally "forgot" to include Neil's clothes in the laundry one week. She fed the kids early some nights and told Neil to "fend for himself" with leftovers. She went shopping and spent more than usual on new clothes for herself. The problem was, none of these actions eased her anger. The more she got even, the worse she felt. "Then Neil started getting angry, too, but not knowing *why* I was behaving the way I was," she said.

Cultivate Clear, Credible Communication

"Shirley, you haven't been candid with Neil. Is it possible you are expecting him to read your mind?" I asked when we spoke on *Hope in the Night.*

"He's a smart man. Shouldn't he be able to figure out something so obvious? We've been married for twelve years. This doesn't take a mind reader."

"But *you* already know what's in your head and heart. True communication occurs when there is *shared understanding.* It's a process of revealing our values, assumptions, beliefs, and expectations.[2] It involves listening, clarifying, and many other important tasks. Deep, meaningful communication doesn't just happen. It takes work. Let me ask: So far, what's been the result of assuming Neil should *simply know* how you're feeling?"

"I've been wrong."

"Shirley, have you ever heard that great Albert Einstein quote: 'Insanity is doing the same thing over and over again and expecting different results'?"[3]

"Now *that's* funny! I use that line with my kids all the time."

"Could it also apply to the way you and Neil are attempting to communicate with each other?"

"The way we've been living since Neil joined the gym has me tied up in knots."

"Well I've got some good news for you. You can begin today to untie those knots—the ones in your heart, and the ones in your marriage. Would you be willing to set aside some time this weekend to talk to Neil...to tell him how you're feeling, and share your heart with him? Even if you have some fear of his response, it is the truth, and speaking the truth in love sets you free! Are you ready to make that investment in your marriage?"

The Sandwich Technique

"I'm seeing that, to turn our marriage around, I probably have no other choice." Thankfully, Shirley decided to face her fears about openly communicating with her husband. Heartened by her courageous decision, I encouraged her to ask for what she needed emotionally from Neil. I also suggested she position any criticism as though it were a piece of meat in the middle of a sandwich. That is, to surround the "meat of correction" first with the "bread of praise" (a positive statement about Neil, a sincere compliment, or statement of genuine care) on the top side, and the "bread of encouragement" (a statement expressing Shirley's confidence and assurance of the future success of their marriage) on the bottom side.

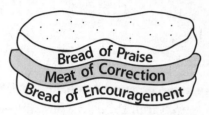

After Shirley and Neil had their talk, things improved dramatically. He saw her point of view and agreed to make appropriate changes in his behavior—like sharing some of the responsibilities at home. Likewise, she continued practicing her new communication skills. Rather than scheming to get even when Neil disappointed her, Shirley gradually began to feel better about herself—and her marriage.

When God said, "It is mine to avenge; I will repay,"[4] His purpose was not to reserve for Himself the pleasure of getting even. He was warning us to avoid the perils of letting our anger lead to a destructive escalation of conflict. If you've handled anger by scheming ways to get back at someone, try God's plan for a change: "Do not repay anyone evil for evil."[5] Rather, give God your bowl of vengeful anger, and let His healing comfort fill your heart.

5. Sweeteners: "Thanks for being there...when I needed you here!"

The writer of Proverbs tells us "a gentle answer turns away wrath."[6] That is certainly true. But have you ever noticed that a gentle answer can also be used to *conceal* wrath? That a compliment can become a weapon?

For years, my nonconfrontational mother would say, "If you can't say something nice, don't say anything at all." Well, in truth sweeteners are anger-avoiders who have rewritten the adage to read, "If you can't

> Let anger serve its rightful
> purpose of drawing attention
> to a problem that needs to
> be solved.

bring yourself to say what's really bothering you, say something 'nice' instead."

Trying to be nice when you are really angry is like camouflaging a time bomb with ribbons and bows. It looks pretty enough, and people on the receiving end have a hard time turning it down. But, in truth, the disguised explosive is meant not to delight, but to punish and wound. It is a sneaky way to lash out at someone who has made you angry while hiding behind a shield of plausible denial.

A sweetener will say, "You did a good job" when he is thinking, *You should have known not to do it this way!*

Or, she will say, "I appreciate your help so much" when she is thinking, *I can't believe you handled it that way!*

Here's the bottom line: A bomb with a pretty bow on top is still a bomb. Sooner or later, you'll have to quit passing it off as a present and detonate or diffuse it (that is, blow up because of it or honestly talk about it). Chances are, those with whom you are in conflict aren't fooled anyway. Why not be honest from the beginning? Why not let anger serve its rightful purpose of drawing attention to a problem that needs to be solved, rather than creating another problem to pile on top of the existing one?

6. Self-blamers: "It's all my fault."

Counselors who work with victims of domestic violence for any length of time get used to hearing them say, "I brought it on myself. If only I hadn't..." You can fill in the blank with any number of perceived failings on their part as justification for the actions of abusers. These victims create endless shades of grey in any situation, whereas objective people will clearly see the stark black and white—the obvious right from wrong. And victims blame themselves rather than risk facing the fact that they are in a troubled, abusive relationship. For them, the truth must be avoided at almost all cost.

Some anger-avoiders operate the same way, even without the threat of physical violence. For them it feels far safer to plead guilty for sparking a conflict than to ever utter the words, "You hurt me. I am angry."

These overly submissive self-blamers have been emotionally battered by angry, controlling people who consistently have found a way to successfully transfer their fault onto others. Therefore, the names in the anger bowls of the self-blamers are their *own*. After repeatedly being falsely accused and repeatedly failing to "win" their case, "Why not save a step, avoid a fight, and just succumb to the inevitable?" reasons the self-blamer.

I personally know about this type of anger avoider. For years, it seemed smarter to give in than to fight a losing battle. After all, I found that acquiescing (and sometimes admitting guilt—falsely) ended the conflict sooner and momentarily appeased my accuser. Plus, it prompted peace—but not peace within me, and not peace with God.

The truth is, taking blame that doesn't belong to you can lead to all sorts of self-destructive beliefs and behaviors. Your anger is still there, sending the message that "there is something wrong." However, you've come to believe that what's wrong is *you*.

Self-blamers label themselves as guilty, stupid, foolish, and worthless. The distorted assumptions result in low self-worth, self-rejection, and false guilt. And it can lead to eating disorders, drug and alcohol abuse, sex and pornography addictions, dependence on antidepressants, and even suicide. In other words, blaming yourself to avoid your anger— or someone else's—becomes a dangerous, self-fulfilling prophecy.

When something happens to make you angry, do you find yourself fanning the flame of self-blame? If so, find healing for your seared emotions through the power of God's Word:

> *"Who will bring any charge against those whom God has chosen? It is God who justifies. Who is he that condemns? Christ Jesus, who died—more than that, who was raised to life—is at the right hand of God and is also interceding for us."* [7]

If the Son of God Himself doesn't condemn you, then surely it is safe to face your anger without condemning yourself. Take it to Him and see.

Once I began to see the destructive effects of self-blaming, I diligently searched the Scriptures to find out how God sees me, and then learned to line up my thinking with His. I came to understand my worth and value to Jesus and to trust His Spirit within me to use the gifts He had given me to accomplish His purpose for me.

There are many ways to avoid facing your anger—but absolutely no good reasons for doing so. Anger is energy meant to flow through us like electricity turning the motor of positive change in our lives. Sometimes it forces us to look honestly at ourselves and admit where we need work. At other times, the message is that it's okay to stand up to unjust treatment in our relationships and to stop being a doormat for angry people.

Here's the truth: Anger we deny or deflect will burn and leave scars on the inside—just like the damage explosive anger leaves on the outside. Freedom comes for "the fire eaters" when we let our true feelings surface and we seek to deal with them in a timely, straightforward, constructive way. With the power of the Lord, you can learn to address, not avoid, anger in your life.

Let's face it—fire eating is no way to live!

Fire Eaters: Who Are They Fooling?

Fire eaters are common attractions at circuses and sideshows. They mesmerize thrill-seekers with their life-threatening feats. Contrary to popular opinion, fire eaters don't literally swallow or eat fire. Instead, they skillfully use their mouths to extinguish a flame.

Many assume that fire eaters coat their mouths with fireproof chemicals before displaying their death-defying craft. However, that is not the case. Another assumption is that fire eaters use "cold flames" not hot enough to burn the mouth. Wrong again!

The success of fire eaters is based on the law of physics: both hot air and flames rise upward. When a fire eater tilts his head back, takes a deep breath, opens his mouth wide, and lowers the flaming torch into his mouth, he then exhales slowly, blowing the flames upward. Nevertheless, in the course of mastering this daring art, fire eaters inevitably receive multiple burns.

One of the most critical skills of fire eaters is controlled breathing. When they lower a flaming torch toward their tonsils, they never, ever inhale! Doing so could cause serious burns, collapsed lungs, or the inhalation of poisonous vapors that could potentially kill them. Instead, fire eaters snuff out the flame—either by a quick exhaled breath or by enveloping it inside their mouths, depriving it of oxygen.

Fire eaters use a variety of fuels to ignite the wick of their torches. A popular combustible for this purpose is lighter fluid. Unfortunately, no matter how careful they are, fire eaters who work with lighter fluid end up ingesting small amounts of the fuel each time they perform. And it's no small matter that the containers carry the warning "Harmful or fatal if swallowed." Tragically, over time, the effect of such ingestion can be cumulative, building up in the liver and potentially causing lasting damage—and worse.

Similarly, those who continually ingest their own fiery anger can suffer lasting damage from the cumulative effects of a lifetime of fire eating. The adage "Play with fire and you'll get burned" is true for fire eaters of every variety—whether under the big top or the rooftop.

Swallowing your anger is harmful to relationships. And, it's hazardous to your health.

THE FLAMETHROWERS
The Damaging Displays of Our Anger

"Short-tempered people do foolish things"
(PROVERBS 14:17 NLT).

HE WAS CAUTIONED...counseled...commanded. He was warned, and well aware of the danger. He received repeated instructions to leave as Mount St. Helens quivered and quaked. But 84-year-old Harry Truman stood his ground near the volatile volcano.[1]

As the shifts beneath the earth's surface were regularly recorded—seismic activity logged day after day—Harry repeatedly turned a deaf ear to the evacuation orders. He had gained quite a reputation over the years for holding out when everyone else was heading out.

The former bootlegger had left his rebellious life of running Canadian whiskey to California during the Prohibition years, but there was still plenty of rebel left in him. Harry wasn't about to budge from his lodge near Spirit Lake in Washington State. In 1929, he staked a 40-acre claim. And in the spring of 1980, he staked his life.

Known as a cantankerous wilderness guide—as rough and rugged as they come—Harry had already withstood 100-mile-an-hour windstorms, a fire that engulfed his house, and numerous earthquakes. If the crater should start spewing out lava, Harry assumed he would have enough time to escape into an old mine shaft he had stocked with food and whiskey.

Despite ongoing eruptions of steam, harmonic tremors, and even a summit explosion, bullheaded Harry refused to budge. Although the number of eruptions lessened through March and April, the evacuation mandates continued.

However, Harry Truman had a tenacious stubborn streak, much like his presidential namesake, who quipped, "If you can't stand the heat, you better get out of the kitchen!"[2] As conditions worsened in the vicinity of the volcano, most people in proximity did "get out of the kitchen"—but not tough ole Harry.

In fact, Harry gained national notoriety after a Portland, Oregon, television station interviewed him. People from one news show even visited him via helicopter. Harry could have literally been lifted out of harm's way, but he remained unwilling to leave.

Years ago I remember reading about "holdout Harry" in the newspaper. I also remember seeing the televised interviews featuring his overconfident bravado: "I'm gonna stay right here...I've stuck it out 54 years and I can stick it out another 54!"[3]

On May 18, 1980, a 5.0 magnitude earthquake sent a blistering ash cloud up in the air—a blast clocked at 300 miles per hour. The powerful eruption triggered an avalanche of devastating, fiery debris—the largest ever recorded to that time.[4] That fateful day, 57 people lost their lives—including Harry, who was buried deep beneath a massive flow of ash and lava.

Evacuate Before the Volcano Erupts

Like live volcanoes, hot-tempered people steam and stew below the surface. When the inner pressure builds to the boiling point, their molten rage explodes—burning and scarring those around them. They vent their volcanic wrath and cause widespread devastation.

> Anger, in and of itself, isn't a sin—nor does it necessarily have to lead to sin.

As I've thought about the volcanic people in my life, I've wished I had heeded this clear, direct warning from the Bible: "Do not make friends with a hot-tempered man, do not associate with one easily angered."[5] Unequivocally, God's Word instructs us to *leave* the presence of hot-tempered people. If we don't, we—just like Harry—will be burned…and possibly buried! Harry died because he *ignored the warning.* Thus, he died needlessly.

The volcanic eruption not only took the life of Harry, it also forever changed Mount St. Helens. It laid waste to itself! The warning bears repeating: Explosive anger should not be ignored, overlooked, or minimized.

Of course, those who have this kind of explosive temper need to know that their volatility cannot help but damage and sometimes destroy their most meaningful relationships. Their anger bowls are more like basins, with every name and every painful event etched *in molten red.*

The people I call fire eaters—those who swallow their anger—can't keep their anger hidden. Eventually it will flare up in harmful ways. But, people with the opposite problem are what I call flamethrowers—those whose anger flares openly, those who too easily torch and scorch others. Rather than smother their emotions within, they spew their emotions outwardly onto others.

As I've said before, anger, in and of itself, isn't a sin—nor does it necessarily have to lead to sin. But clearly, anger can be the precursor to sin. Uncontrolled anger is *always* wrong and all too often results in offensive words, wrong behavior, even criminal acts.

Flame-throwing anger takes many forms: put-downs and name-calling, profanity and intimidation, property damage and vandalism, personal assaults and murder.

Let's not get the wrong impression, however. Explosive anger isn't necessarily characterized by the screamer shouting insults at strangers, or the mother cruelly mistreating her child for a minor wrongdoing, or the mean neighbor creating noise just to be a nuisance.

Those the Bible describes as hot-tempered can also cause damage in more discreet ways. They might display their anger through constant criticism, behind-the-scenes bullying, intense intimidation, or surreptitious sabotage. Yet regardless of the way a volatile temper is displayed, the Bible doesn't mince words about hotheaded flamethrowers.

Proverbs 14:17 says, "A man of quick temper acts foolishly, and a man of evil devices is hated." [6]

The Four Types of Human Flamethrowers

The first step in dealing with flamethrowers is to recognize the four different types and how their anger is exhibited. Let's take a look at *exploders*, *seethers*, *blamers*, and *abusers*.

1. Exploders: Those prone to sudden eruptive anger

A familiar example of explosive anger and its resulting repercussions is found in Genesis 4:1-16—the biblical account of brothers Cain and Abel. Each man gave an offering to God, each presumably expecting acceptance. As it turned out, one offering was accepted and one wasn't. Abel gave what God wanted to receive. Cain gave what he, himself, wanted to give.

- *The reception?* No surprises here—God received Abel's acceptable offering and rejected Cain's unacceptable one.
- *The reaction?* Cain grew angry and sullen.
- *The remedy?* Simple—God inquired as to the cause of Cain's anger, then told him to do what was right. In doing so, Cain would be accepted.
- *The reality?* If Cain didn't do what was right, sin was waiting to devour him.
- *The result?* Cain invited Abel to go out to the field, where Cain exploded into murderous rage and killed his brother.
- *The repercussion?* Cain left the presence of God, lost his home and livelihood, and lived the remainder of his life as a restless wanderer.

Exploders lash out and behave recklessly. They might normally be reasonable and responsible people, but sometimes their emotion overshadows their thought process and they blow a fuse.

Although the exploder can find no consolation in the account of Cain, he can find assurance and caution in the previously explored story of Moses' (see pages 39-47). He can take solace in the fact that God used—in magnificent ways—a man who was flawed with a violently explosive temper. If the Lord can use Moses, whose fiery rage caused him such trouble, then He can use others who have the same problem. The warning, however, is clear: Actions have consequences, and uncontrolled anger has unwanted repercussions. For months or even years, we might be on our best behavior—cool and controlled—only to have just one explosion cause disastrous results.

2. Seethers: Those who simmer until their anger boils over

Seethers hold in their anger for long periods—nurturing it with grudges and fantasies of revenge. Their festering emotions also lead to an unforgiving heart toward a past offense or offender. Unforgiveness eventually results in resentment and deep bitterness that harms relationships. When I think of seethers, I recall the words of Frederick Buechner:

> Of the seven deadly sins, anger is possibly the most fun. To lick your wounds, to smack your lips over grievances long past, to roll over your tongue the prospect of bitter confrontations still to come, to savor to the last toothsome morsel both the pain you are given and the pain you are giving back—in many ways it is a feast fit for a king. The chief drawback is that what you are wolfing down is yourself. The skeleton at the feast is you.[7]

When anger is allowed to ferment over a long period of time, it becomes that much more potent. A little bit can do a whole lot of damage. That's why the writer of Hebrews said, "See to it that no one misses the grace of God and that no bitter root grows up to cause trouble and defile many."[8] Seethers are those who have permitted bitterness to take root in their heart, to the detriment of themselves and others. They go through life with a chip on their shoulder and rancor in their spirit, never knowing when their simmering anger is going to boil over.

For these reasons, the Bible instructs us to resolve our conflicts as quickly as possible. Jesus said if you're worshipping at church and remember you have a lingering dispute with someone, you should leave and go take care of it: "Settle matters quickly with your adversary."[9] In a famous admonition we saw earlier, the apostle Paul declared, "Do not let the sun go down while you are still angry, and do not give the devil a foothold."[10] The link here is inescapable: Seething over past offenses opens the door for Satan's influence in our lives.

How grateful I am for the example my mother set for me in this area. Were it not for her refusal to harbor hurts and rehearse wrongs, my seething anger toward my father might easily have turned me into a resentful, bitter person. My mother kept her anger bowl empty by releasing offenses to God almost immediately upon receiving them.

After totally yielding her life to the Lord, my mother realized how deeply she had been forgiven by the undeserved grace of God. How then could she refuse to forgive others? Over the years, she had realized the danger of holding on to anger, and so she doggedly refused to let it take root in her heart.

3. Blame-shifters: Those who blame others for their faults

In our society, shifting blame to others has been elevated to an art form. People caught speeding tell the traffic cop it is the car's fault for having too much horsepower. Shopaholics blame their massive debt on retailers for displaying irresistible goods. Democrats blame Republicans for America's woes, and Republicans blame Democrats.

We shouldn't be surprised, then, when angry people blame their explosive tendencies on others. Blame-shifters are the exact opposite of self-blamers (those who say, "It's all my fault" to every conflict that arises). In contrast, blamers say, "It's *not* my fault! I'm mad because *you* made me mad. It's your fault!"

Have you ever heard the term *blame speak*? Perhaps you've heard these statements come out of someone's mouth—or maybe even your own:

- "I wouldn't have gotten mad if you hadn't made me." *Translation: I'm not responsible for my outbursts—you are.*
- "I can't help it. This is just the way God made me." *Translation: The Creator gave me my temper, so blame Him, not me.*
- "I'm Irish, and we all know the Irish are famous for their fiery temperaments." *Translation: Blame it on my genes.*
- "I didn't mean it." *Translation: I should be let off the hook because my intentions were good, even if my behavior wasn't.*
- "I was just joking. Don't be so uptight." *Translation: You are to blame, not I. You're too sensitive. If you're hurt by my humor, you need to grow thicker skin.*
- "I had lousy role models. Mom and Dad never showed me a better way." *Translation: I shouldn't be held accountable when my parents didn't teach me properly.*
- "Hey, everyone loses their cool now and then." *Translation: I don't take my temper seriously, and neither should you.*

There's an obvious theme running through these statements: I'm not responsible for my actions. Blame-shifting is a strategy used by those who are determined to take their own anger and heap it onto someone else. By refusing to acknowledge their anger, explore where it really comes from, and take responsibility for it, the emotions of blame-shifters stay raw and ready to explode. The apostle John challenged this kind of blame-shifting:

> "If we claim we have no sin, we are only fooling ourselves and not living in the truth. But if we confess our sins to him, he is faithful and just to forgive us our sins and to cleanse us from all wickedness. If we claim we have not sinned, we are calling God a liar."[11]

Clearly, God can bring healing and freedom, but we must be willing and courageous enough to face the truth about ourselves and own up to our imperfections. "You will know the truth, and the truth will set you free."[12] The Lord is eager and willing to wash out all the soot that's piled up inside us—but we have to come clean about our anger problem before He can cleanse us.

4. Abusers: Those determined to control others through anger

"He had his hands around my neck, squeezing tighter and tighter," Kayla told me, her voice trembling. "It was the first time I seriously thought, *He's going to kill me. My husband is going to kill me.*"

I had known Kayla for several years and had heard bits and pieces about her background. When I asked her to share her story with me in detail, she was remarkably open. Kayla came from a loving home, but one that always bordered on poverty. Her dad was a hardworking man who didn't make much as a mechanic at the local repair shop.

By the time she was 18, Kayla was ready to leave behind all the financial worries and the constant tension they caused. About that time, a good-looking guy named Mitch appeared riding not on a white horse, but on a refurbished motorcycle. Still, Kayla convinced herself he would whisk her away all the same.

Soon came a starry-eyed romance, promises of a blissful future together, a short dating period, and then an even shorter engagement. Before you knew it, the happy couple was married and living in a run-down duplex, which didn't matter—they were *in love.*

But it wasn't long before this young couple discovered marriage was harder to live than dream about. "I do" meant sacrifice, compromise, and hard work. Disillusionment quickly set in. Mitch couldn't hold down a job. When at home, he whiled away the hours watching television or playing video games. Kayla grew weary of waiting on him hand and foot.

A baby joined the family, then another. Mitch soon lost all interest in playing the role of dutiful, loving father and husband, and his selfish character began to emerge. He also began to drink heavily. He recklessly spent what little money they had, and flirted with other women. Then things went from bad to worse.

"Five years into our marriage, Mitch's temper became violent," Kayla recalled. "Our fights had always been heated, but then they got physical. At first, he would get mad and shove me. After a while, he started punching me. On a couple of occasions, I really did think he was going to kill me. These violent episodes became more and more frequent, and went on for several years."

My heart ached as I heard Kayla's sad story. It's hard to believe this kind, sensitive young woman could end up in an abusive marriage. And she said as much herself.

"You hear about battered wives and read about domestic violence, but that always happens to someone else," she said. "It wasn't supposed to happen to *me*. I was never unfaithful. I was conscientious about housework and parenting. But still…"

But still many good people like Kayla find themselves unexpectedly and undeservedly suffering the consequences of another person's bad temper. We hear sad tales like this, and our indignation prompts us to ask, "Why did you stay? Why didn't you just leave?" I posed those questions to Kayla.

"Looking back now, I know I should've left much sooner," she said. "But it was complicated—not just a matter of picking up and moving on. We eventually had three children, and their safety and protection were my biggest concern. Mitch had become so irrational and unpredictable that I didn't know if he'd try to take the children from me—or hurt them—if I left. I didn't want those beautiful little children to end up in his custody. Not to mention my terror at what he might do to *me*."

There were practical matters as well. Kayla had no real job skills and couldn't have supported the children on her own. Moving in with her parents or other family members—which she did occasionally for short stints—was not a long-term option. She felt trapped.

Of course, Kayla unwittingly contributed to this tragic drama. She realizes now she lacked boundaries and a biblical view of her own self-worth. Her fragile self-esteem prevented her from speaking up or walking out when she should have. Her strong need for security clouded her judgment and justified her decision to stay in a terribly troubled relationship far too long. Still, nothing about her inaction warranted the mistreatment she received.

Fearing for her life, Kayla faced a heart-wrenching decision. Should she leave her husband, or could she stay in the relationship while trying to establish healthy boundaries and ensure her own (and her children's) protection? She prayed, seeking the Lord's guidance. She searched Scripture for direction. She took to heart the Lord's promise in Psalm 32:7-8:

> *"You are my hiding place;*
> *you will protect me from trouble*
> *and surround me with songs of deliverance.*
> *I will instruct you and teach you in the way you should go;*
> *I will counsel you and watch over you."*

Growing Through Ghastly Pain

As Kayla sifted through the rubble of her relationship with Mitch, she learned a number of important lessons. Thankfully, she realized she couldn't manage such difficult transitions on her own—she needed help. She enlisted a mentor, an older woman in her church, who provided sound advice and plenty of encouragement. Together, the two of them developed a plan that, if diligently followed, could give Kayla's marriage a good chance of surviving. They decided Kayla needed to...

Understand the consequences of codependence. If she permitted her husband to continue his disrespectful and damaging behavior, choosing to overlook mistreatment or to acquiesce to his unscriptural demands, she would be contributing to the problem. She memorized a key verse: "A hot-tempered man must pay the penalty; if you rescue him, you will have to do it again" (Proverbs 19:19).

Correct the confusion. Kayla realized that the woman who wants to please God but is not grounded in the Word of God can become captive to an incorrect understanding of biblical submission. All too easily she accepted abuse, thinking it was right even though God says it is wrong. Kayla recognized she needed to study God's Word and seek wise counsel so she could accurately understand the Lord's design for healthy marital relationships.

Build healthy boundaries. This meant clearly communicating acceptable limits of behavior, stating what she would do if her husband crossed the line into inappropriate territory, and following through on her established consequences for boundary violations.

Prepare strategies for safety. Kayla and her mentor knew that abusive cycles do not change overnight. Most often, improvement—if any—is incremental. Therefore, if Kayla were to stay in the marriage, she needed a plan to ensure her physical and emotional safety. She devised a clear-cut strategy for the times when she felt threatened: confide the seriousness of her situation to trustworthy people; be alert to cues that tension was escalating; establish an "escape route" for dangerous situations; and have trusted people on standby to provide help and intervention, if needed.

In an ideal world, I could report that these and other strategies transformed Kayla's marriage into a storybook romance. But of course, life is rarely ideal. Despite her efforts, Kayla couldn't piece together the fragile fragments of her broken marriage alone. Without Mitch's cooperation and commitment to change, she was forced to make the painful choice to live apart from Mitch, knowing that to stay would put her own life, and the lives of her children, in grave danger.

As is so often the case, Mitch didn't let her go easily. He harassed, stalked, and stole from her—employing devious weapons from his anger arsenal. But Kayla's story does have a happy ending. Her Christian friends and caring church community provided resources and shelter when she needed help. A family-law attorney at her church offered advice and helped Kayla navigate the legal system. She called upon law enforcement officials to provide protection for herself and her children.

It took several tense and trying years for Kayla to finally feel free of fear. Today she understands her God-given worth and appreciates the respect, care, and love she now expects, receives, and deserves. Her children, though not without wounds of their own, are thriving in a safe and stable environment. And Kayla is using her hard-won wisdom and insight to help other women find freedom from abuse.

Domestic Violence: A Worldwide Epidemic

We have to wonder how many women and children (and even men) don't experience a happy ending, since, sadly, the kind of mistreatment Kayla suffered is epidemic:

- Around the world, at least one in every three women has been beaten, coerced into sex, or otherwise abused during her lifetime.[13]

- Nearly one-third of American women (31 percent) report being physically or sexually abused by a husband or boyfriend at some point in their lives.[14]

- In a nationally representative sample of Head Start programs serving low-income children ages three to five, researchers found 17 percent of the children studied had been exposed to domestic violence.[15]

I've heard terror, resignation, helplessness, and hopelessness in the voices of countless callers to *Hope in the Night*—precious people in an emotional prison, who feel trapped and alone with nowhere to turn for help, no one to turn to for protection, and no feasible avenue to freedom. "The Flamethrowers" had deeply wounded and left us no hope for healing.

I've also been privileged to paint the picture for them of a loving, saving God who is able to overcome any obstacle standing in the way of their walking in the freedom Jesus purchased for them...and becoming the person God created them to be.

I've introduced them to their true Need-Meeter and shared His promises with them. And like Kayla, many have found freedom by trusting God and relying on His strength and guidance. They have experienced healing by finding forgiveness in Christ and extending that forgiveness to their abusers.

The statistics are grim...and endless. No one would argue that abuse—physical, sexual, spiritual, emotional, or verbal—is a colossal problem in our society and in our world. Whereas exploders are overcome with rage and lash out, abusers have *chronic, ongoing* rage issues. To be sure, both have an anger problem, but abusers take theirs to an entirely new level.

> If your genuine desire is to overcome explosive anger, remember: True transformation begins with true repentance.

These people are in critical need of intervention and treatment from qualified mental health professionals. Their rage is so far out of control it's unlikely they will learn to contain it without significant intervention, accountability, and help.

Overcoming Explosive Anger

So what to do about all of this out-of-control anger? In Part Three of this book, I will provide numerous practical ways to handle anger by identifying and releasing wounds from the past, preparing ahead of time for anger flare-ups, and managing anger in the heat of the moment. For now, let me give a few ideas to ponder if you (or someone you know) have an explosive temper:

Repent. This means agreeing with God that your anger crosses into sinful territory, and committing to turn away from your wrongdoing. Without rationalizing or excusing your behavior, ask for God's forgiveness and grace. As Paul said, "Godly sorrow brings repentance that leads to salvation and leaves no regret...See what this godly sorrow has produced in you: what earnestness, what eagerness to clear yourselves, what indignation, what alarm, what longing, what concern, what readiness to see justice done."[16] If your genuine desire is to overcome explosive anger, remember: True transformation begins with true repentance.

Recognize your responsibility. It's painful to admit our faults and failings to ourselves and others. But if we're ever going to conquer destructive anger, the process must involve clear-eyed and candid honesty. It must start by telling ourselves, our loved ones, and our Lord the truth. Diminishing the magnitude of the problem or discounting the damage it inflicts will only keep you stuck in unhealthy patterns.

Realize the effects of anger. Unless explosive anger is used to confront injustice and correct some wrong, there is nothing good that comes of it. An uncontrolled temper erodes trust in close relationships, creates an atmosphere of fear, thwarts intimacy and communication, and tarnishes your witness and reputation. Until you truly grasp the impact of anger on others—and yourself—you probably won't be motivated to do the work necessary to prevail over the problem.

Request help. Few of us can triumph over significant personal challenges on our own. We need others to provide support, encouragement, and accountability. James tells us, "Confess your sins to each other and pray for each other so that you may be healed."[17] Trying to make changes while going it alone rarely works. God has designed us to draw strength from one another. Success in correcting our deficiencies comes not in isolation, but in the community of fellow sojourners.

Regain trust. When trust is tarnished by the smoky soot of burning anger, this precious treasure can be restored, but it takes some elbow grease—hard work and a determined effort—to reclaim its beautiful luster.

Those you've scorched need to hear you take full responsibility for wrong choices and how your wrong choices are going to become right choices.

- Verbalize that you were totally wrong for reacting in anger. Admit your harshness is totally your fault.

- Confess your harshness was selfish and an attempt to control.

- Ask for a willingness to truly forgive you. (This may take time, so do not be demanding.)

- Demonstrate the depth of your remorse by the strength

of your resolve to change. (Promises and tears won't build trust, but actions will.) Develop a plan to act differently when you are angry.

- Share your plan, and *be consistent* in carrying it out.

The way to gain trust is to prove, over time, you are trustworthy not just when the relationship is easy, but when it is hard—when you feel frustrated, when getting your way has failed. Consistency is the key. Consistently responding without any harshness can, over time, change hearts and restore trust.

> *"Love your [spouses] and do not be harsh with them"*
> (COLOSSIANS 3:19).

Unresolved anger is one of the most vexing problems plaguing our society—and the repercussions reverberate across all socioeconomic lines. At this very moment, anger bowls are bursting in homes, in the workplace, at schools, and even in churches. Thankfully, God has not left us to feebly cope on our own. Through the power and the resources He supplies, anger can be managed and used in a healthy way.

Volcanoes: A Not-So-Mysterious Force

For much of human history, people thought volcanic eruptions were the work of malevolent spirits or a vengeful god. What else could possess the power to shake the ground and bury whole villages in molten rock? Elaborate ceremonies were held to appease these supernatural forces in hopes of silencing the shuddering mountains.

Naturally, twentieth-century scientists did not subscribe to such superstition—but that didn't mean they fully understood why volcanoes exist or what causes them to erupt. That is, not until unrelated research in the 1960s and 1970s introduced us to plate tectonics. In short, the surface of the earth is covered by enormous slabs of continental and oceanic crust, and these slabs are *moving* relative to one another. But the movement is imperceptibly slow.

Suddenly things made sense. Earthquakes and volcanoes around the world are mostly concentrated at the edges of these plates, where they grind against each other in various ways. The pressures and friction are often great enough to melt underlying rock and send it to the surface in the form of a lava explosion.

Sometimes anger lies deep beneath the surface in your heart and mind, and it periodically erupts for no apparent reason. But God knows why—there is always a reason. Ask Him to help you delve deep to discover the source of your anger, and then allow Him to help you excavate it.

Part Two

DETECTING
UNQUENCHABLE FIRES:

*Why We Stay Stuck in
Unhealthy Anger Patterns*

BLAST FROM THE PAST
How Childhood Hurts Kindle Current Anger

"Refrain from anger and turn from wrath;
do not fret—it leads only to evil"
(PSALM 37:8).

HOLLY CALLED ME at *Hope in the Night* the day she got a startling ultimatum from her husband, Tim. He said she had to get help for her hair-trigger temper or he was going to take their two daughters and stay with his parents for a while. They needed a break from her frequent tantrums.

"I know I have a short temper, especially where Tim is concerned," she told me. "I'm not sure why. He just pushes my buttons, and I go off without even thinking. I convinced myself it's a good thing—particularly as a woman—to stand up for my rights and needs, even if it means a fight. 'Never give an inch,' my mom used to say. But for the first time, I saw real pain and desperation on Tim's face, and I knew I was hurting someone I love—and who loves me. Something has to change, but I have no idea where to begin."

Holly's "short fuse" was characterized by slammed doors and thrown objects. She confessed to being the "queen of the silent treatment" and to using stinging sarcasm. Knowing anger always comes from *somewhere* and usually is signaling some kind of underlying issues, I asked Holly to tell me about her husband and their relationship.

Tim was a high-ranking sales manager for a prosperous electronics company. He supervised employees in five states, which meant he was away from home two or three nights a week, sometimes more.

Between trips, he was a reasonably attentive father to their daughters. He did his share of household chores. He was conservative with their money, but not stingy. He hardly ever drank and never gambled. However, Tim had an "annoying" fondness for watching sports on television, and Holly thought he spent a little too much time and money restoring an old motorcycle he rescued from a salvage yard. He wasn't the best listener in the world, though he was making a concerted effort to improve.

After Holly told me all this, I responded, "Sounds like a pretty good guy. He may not be perfect, but who is?"

Holly chuckled in agreement. Then I asked, "So what triggers your temper?"

Holly thought for a moment. "It gets under my skin every time he chooses something else over spending time with our family. It's like he's got a secret life he'd really prefer. If the phone rings around the time I expect him home, I'm angry even before I pick it up. I know it's him saying he has to work longer. But does he really? He goes to the gym a few times a week, and I just seethe. I accuse him of being prideful about how fit he is. He says it's a good thing to stay in shape, but I can't help it—I get angry. It just comes over me."

The stress and anxiety were steadily rising in Holly's voice. Clearly, we were coming close to whatever was fueling her anger. She had trouble trusting that all was as it seemed in her marriage. She doubted Tim's word and suspected he had a secretive side. Certainly I was in no position to say whether or not she had adequate cause for her feelings. But one thing was certain: Holly was angry, and the unhealthy way she expressed it was making matters in her marriage that much worse.

I gently explained to Holly that anger is a *secondary* emotion, meaning it doesn't arise by itself, but is a natural response to anything we perceive as painful or threatening. It is our body's way of preparing us to do what is necessary to protect ourselves from harm. We most often get angry when we are hurting, afraid, frustrated, or confronted with an injustice. It seemed obvious which of these was the primary source of Holly's present anger.

Prisoner of Past Pain

"I'm going to ask you something, and I want you to answer with the first thing that pops into your mind," I told her. "In your opinion, what is the worst thing that could happen in your marriage? What do you *fear* the most?"

"Betrayal," she blurted out instantly. "Infidelity."

"And has Tim given you tangible reasons to believe he is unfaithful to you?"

"I'm not sure," Holly said. "How would I know?"

I suddenly heard Holly gasp on the other end of the line. Then there was a long pause, during which I silently asked God to reveal the healing truth to Holly so she could take steps toward freedom. Finally, when she spoke again, it was apparent she had begun to cry. I realized she was experiencing "a blast from the past."

"Oh, June, I *do* know where my anger comes from," she said quietly. The pain was choking her voice to nearly a whisper. "How could I have not seen it before? What I fear most is that Tim will turn out to be like my *father*."

For the next few minutes, Holly poured out the story from her childhood that had been feeding the flames of her anger at Tim. By all appearances, her father was a loving husband and a good dad. He never missed one of Holly's gymnastics meets, and helped her design the winning science fair project two years in a row. He was a church deacon and served on the board of the local retirement home. No one in the family noticed there had been a sudden increase in board committee meetings or that they lasted longer than before. And no one gave it much thought when he spruced up his wardrobe, lost 20 pounds, and changed his hairstyle.

It's a Family Affair

By now you've probably guessed the truth: Holly's father had an affair—with a member of the retirement home staff. His act of betrayal devastated her mother and cast a dark shadow over the whole family. When the truth came out, her father terminated the illicit relationship immediately. There was no divorce, but neither was there true reconciliation. Peace and trust never returned to the marriage, or to the household in general.

"I remember being so angry at him for how he had deceived us all, and for what it did to my mother. But I didn't realize until just now how mad I was at Mom for letting it happen and for not doing more to hurt him. She just withdrew into her shell...distrustful and removed. I swore it would never happen to me."

The more we talked, the clearer it became to Holly that she had indeed achieved her goal: Her husband had not been unfaithful. It had not "happened" to her. But neither was she free to fully commit to the relationship and be happy. She was fearful that she was being fooled, just like her mother.

Holly's chronic anger was a legitimate attempt to keep those fears at bay by showing she was not someone you could hurt without paying a price. The problem was, none of it had anything to do with Tim. Holly's wounds predated his presence in her life by 15 years. He was just an innocent bystander and the victim of her unresolved childhood wounds.

"I've been angry at Tim, making him serve a sentence for crimes he didn't commit," Holly concluded.

In doing that, she was certainly not unique. Christian counselor Gary Chapman tells us,

> Whenever we have experienced a series of wrongs over a long period of time, our emotional ability to absorb these wrongs is stretched beyond capacity...We begin to express this anger not toward the people who perpetrated it through past years but toward other people in our present setting. The purpose of our anger is to motivate us to take constructive action with the person who has wronged us, but if we fail to do this, unresolved anger becomes a dark cloud over our lives.[1]

For Holly, the cloud finally lifted, and the path to anger resolution and peace was suddenly clear to her: She would free Tim from unfair judgment by working to free *herself*—by God's grace—from unforgiveness and bitterness toward her parents.

By the time our conversation ended, Holly had not only emptied her anger bowl, but she had given her life to Christ. In her voice I heard lightness and hope, which I suspect had been missing for a long time. I assured her that God would not fail to provide a new heart in place of her old one. As the apostle Paul wrote, "If anyone is in Christ, he is a new creation; the old has gone, the new has come!"[2]

> When it comes to childhood wounds, it is common to have smoldering embers of which we may not even be aware.

When it comes to childhood wounds, it is common to have smoldering embers of which we may not even be aware—remnants we would never suspect could actually spark present-day anger. But when it comes to anger, *out of sight* definitely is not the same as *out of mind*. In fact, hurtful childhood emotions can smolder for decades, be stoked by a current circumstance, and then engulf the unsuspecting in seething rage long after the events that triggered them are forgotten. Let's look at some reasons this happens.

Bonfires from the Beginning

By the time we come of age, most of us have forgotten what a vulnerable state childhood is. At birth we are a bundle of insistent needs and wants, but without the means to meet them on our own. From day one, our dependence on others is absolute. Gradually, we gain both the abilities and the skills we need to fend for ourselves, but our needs are no less real as we grow older. If anything, we become more complex, progressing from simple needs like food and shelter to the need for significance and self-esteem or for moral certainty in the world.

Psychologist Abraham Maslow identified specific needs he found common to all humans, and subsequently developed a "hierarchy of needs" consisting of five categories: physiology, safety, love and belonging, esteem and respect, and self-actualization.[3] The higher up Maslow's ladder a particular need lies, the more psychological and even spiritual in nature it becomes—but no less vital to our well-being. There is something that rings true about admitting people need—really *need*—more than just the basics of survival in order to thrive. We also need acceptance, affection, and the freedom to be who God created us to be.

Here's the most important part of Maslow's ideas: If *any* of our needs go unmet, even the more abstract ones, we suffer harmful psychological and emotional effects. To a child who endures chronic verbal abuse, for instance, it simply does not help to say, "Sticks and stones will break my bones, but words will never hurt me." The hurt takes the form of an unmet need for safety, dignity, and respect. In other words, many of the deepest wounds we receive in life, especially in childhood, are not just a matter of what was done to us, but also what was *withheld* as a result.

To a child, such "crimes of omission" can be just as damaging and threatening as overt acts of abuse or oppression. Why? Because in our state of extreme vulnerability to those who have been called by God to care for us, unmet needs add up to the possibility we might be abandoned altogether. If we grow up carrying these childhood hurts and fears, we can easily become fearful and angry adults.

Incensed for the Innocent

Never will I forget walking toward the exit of a large store and noticing a mother—probably in her late twenties—walking with a shopping cart a few feet in front of me. Toddling along behind her was a cute, curly-haired tyke obviously trying his best to keep up with her. But his little legs were far too short to match her long stride.

Suddenly she whirled around and barked at him in a hateful voice, "If you don't hurry up I'm going to chop your legs off!" With a look of terror, he rushed to get beside the cart.

I was shocked...stunned...I couldn't believe my eyes and ears. Of course, the little fellow's frightened face said it all.

Immediately, I felt angry that any parent would use such an unjustified fear tactic—or in this case, terror tactic—to motivate a child. I picked up my pace and approached her. "Excuse me," I said, intentionally speaking slow and quietly, "I don't know if you realize that children are literalists and what you just said could be terrifying."

My face was flushed and my eyes were wide open from the adrenaline rushing through my body. I was definitely in a fight-or-flight mode, with flight being the furthest thing from my mind.

I had no idea how the woman would respond, and it didn't matter to me. I could no more hold my tongue than she apparently could hold hers.

As we stood there looking at one another, her countenance communicated surprise but also showed genuine embarrassment. She apparently heard my words and hopefully "got it." To my surprise, she sheepishly took the toddler's hand and, without saying a word, turned and walked off toward the exit.

As I watched them leave, I prayed the Spirit of God would work in the woman's life and fully convict her of the need to permanently change her parenting style. I knew if the mother did not change, that precious little one would carry fear and anger into his adulthood. But then it would be detached from its true origin so that even he wouldn't know where it came from.

It would become what psychologists call free-floating anger—it's disconnected from its cause and purpose. Childhood pain can stoke smoldering embers into a raging blaze in adulthood.

As we attempt to discover why we stay trapped in patterns of anger, it helps to know where the skeletons from our childhood may be hidden. Here are the most common burial grounds:

Emotional Archaeology: Unearthing a Heritage of Heat

Most often, if we retrace the tracks of our unresolved anger back into the past, the trail ends at our parents' doorstep. Who else had such power over our lives? Who more than Mom and Dad shaped our view of God, the world, and our relationship to both? It is often said parenting isn't for cowards. It's a big job—one that can't be mastered, only practiced. Along the way there are bound to be failures, mistakes, and lapses, even among the most well-intentioned, loving people. That's why, for many of us, the first names ever scrawled across our slips of paper—forming the deepest layer of our anger bowls—read *Mommy, Daddy*, or both.

In fact, many incidents in which a child may feel wounded by parents are inevitable and necessary. A kindergartner might feel abandoned on the first day of school as mother walks away. Yet change and unfamiliar situations are an inescapable part of growing up.

It was our parents who had the ability to either provide or withhold what we needed to survive and thrive. As our immediate role models, it was they who, perhaps unwittingly, taught us how to handle our emotions, especially anger. There is truth in the old adage "With children, more is caught than taught." What we learned spans the spectrum from an inability to express our anger (because our parents wouldn't allow it) to expressing our anger in destructive ways (because our parents did). We also learned to *be* angry—like Holly—in response to ill treatment we may have received from them.

Like emotional archaeologists, we must often excavate long-past childhood relationships to answer the question, "Why am I so angry?" The purpose here is not to blame parents for our problems nor bash them for their shortcomings; it's to understand the basis, the foundation, of our emotional makeup so we can identify and correct wrong beliefs we formed about life and how to live it. We need to know and understand *why* we are the way we are so we can have the wisdom to know *how* to change the way we are.

In fact, here's an important thing to remember: Our parents were not—and are not—machines. They were not unpacked fresh from the factory floor the day we were born, made specifically to serve our needs. They are people, just as vulnerable and just as fallible as anyone. If they are angry themselves, it is surely in response to their own hurts, fears, frustrations, and struggles with injustice.

Chances are, the attitudes and behaviors you have adopted from your parents didn't originate with them. You may be wearing a cloak of unresolved anger that has been passed down in your family for generations.

Knowing this will help you unearth the connections between your past wounds and your present anger without falling into the common trap of pointing fingers and laying blame. The point is not recrimination, but to obtain God's healing.

Finding the Family Fire

Let me tell you about Ryan, a young man who learned in dramatic fashion how to see past his father's angry exterior. Ryan grew up in constant conflict with his father, who he described as a "fuming, withdrawn, cynical alcoholic." Everyone in the family had tried various ways to reach out to him, but they could never get past the wall of his deep pessimism about life and his mistrust of everyone. He kept his wife and children at bay by adopting a menacing, unapproachable posture at home.

Years later, Ryan began to see in himself evidence of his own anger. Girlfriends told him more than once that he was too sarcastic and brooding. His volcanic temper frightened them when all-too-frequent arguments erupted. Ryan quickly recognized his father's imprint on his life, which made him even angrier. He felt helpless to overcome the effects of his upbringing, and he began to blame his past for everything in his life that wasn't going according to plan.

Then one day, he got a rare and healing glimpse into his father's painful past.

"I was riding in the car with my dad, something I hadn't done for years," Ryan told me. "We were listening to news on the radio when a story came on about a local man who had just been arrested for molesting several neighborhood boys. It made me really sad, and I said I couldn't even imagine what those boys must be feeling."

Suddenly, Ryan noticed his father's knuckles were white and his arms were shaking as he struggled to keep a tight grip on the steering wheel. His breathing grew labored and his face turned red. The car hurtled down the highway, faster and faster. Ryan began to fear his father was having a heart attack, which was not far from the truth. Long-buried fear, pain, and anger had swiftly surfaced...and all-consuming rage was now coursing through his body.

"I *know* how it feels," Ryan's father uttered through clenched teeth. "It feels like you want to die, or kill the guy. It's worse than dying. It feels like you'll never be clean again. *Ever.*"

Ryan's father knew all too well what victims of abuse feel because he had been abused as a boy.

Ryan sat in stunned silence, looking at the man he had feared and sometimes even hated, but had never understood until now. His father was no longer just the *perpetrator* of all that angry malice within his family, but also the *victim* of wounds so deep and painful he had stuffed and buried them for 50 years. Ryan experienced compassion for his dad and empathy he'd never felt before, and that became the key to eventually dealing with his own anger. He began reaching into his bowl of anger, releasing to God one tear-stained slip of paper after another...

> God presents Himself in the Bible as the Refiner—the One who refines us so that we come forth as purified silver.

The truth is, we start feeding on conflict, woe, and disappointment long before we grow up to become men and women. Like children playing with matches, we learn early in life what it feels like to get "burned." And though parents are sometimes responsible for childhood hurts and unmet needs, they are by no means the only source. Children can be wounded by any number of people in any number of ways. Hurt people *hurt* people.

Some of those wounds can, and do, lead to deep-seated anger later in life. We can feel just as abandoned or mistreated by siblings, peers, teachers—even society at large. Although the severity can vary greatly, it seems virtually impossible for anyone to go through life and not at some point need to release pain into the purifying fire of God. God presents Himself in the Bible as the Refiner—the One who refines us so that we come forth as purified silver.

"See, I have refined you, though not as silver;
I have tested you in the furnace of affliction"
(ISAIAH 48:10).

Carrying Childhood Coals

Bonnie was a beautiful young woman, a smart and talented graphic artist with a bright future. She was also lonely and miserable. The older she got, the more estranged she became from her family, especially from her sisters, all of whom were married and starting families of their own. It wasn't that her sisters excluded Bonnie—far from it. She was invited to every family event, but rarely participated. To make matters worse, she had endured one dismal dating experience after another. None of the men she was interested in stuck around very long.

"Why don't you want to spend time with your family?" I asked her, sensing the answer to her unhappiness lay in those troubled relationships.

"Oh, it isn't them," Bonnie replied. "It's their kids. For as long as I can remember, I haven't been able to tolerate being around kids for more than a few minutes at a time. Everything they do irritates and annoys me."

"Considering that our anger is always present for a reason, why do you think kids make you mad?" I probed.

"I don't know," she said. "Maybe it's because they can be so *mean* to each other, really cruel. I hate that."

I decided to venture a guess. "Maybe there was a time when a kid or group of kids was really mean to *you*," I said.

"I don't think so," she replied. Then she thought about it. "Well, maybe there is something to that."

Bonnie then relayed an incident that occurred when she was seven years old. Her family had moved to a new town a few months earlier. For some reason a group of kids in the new neighborhood took an instant dislike to Bonnie. They excluded her from games, pestered her at school, and yelled names anytime they rode their bikes by her house.

One day the family planned a birthday party for Bonnie's younger sister. Her mother decorated the front yard with streamers and balloons.

"Before the guests arrived, those kids sneaked into the yard and tore down all the decorations," Bonnie said, still outraged after all this time. "They shredded everything. When my mother confronted them later, they told her they thought the party was for me, as if that would make it okay."

By the time Bonnie finished the story, she was in tears. Obviously, she had never gotten over the pain and injustice she suffered as a child at the hands of a few bullies. The revelation rekindled powerful emotions. Twenty-five years later, the traumatic event was almost as real—and as infuriating—as it was the day it happened. She conceded it was unfair of her to assume the same mean spirit was present in *all* children, particularly in her own nieces and nephews. Ultimately, that insight led her to see the high cost she had been paying for unresolved anger, and motivated her to get to know her nieces and nephews and even invest in their lives in some way.

You Can Transform Your Tomorrows

Without exception, we *all* receive wounds in childhood. We all bear emotional, physical, or spiritual scars. There is no way to turn back the clock and undo what has been done. We must live with the experiences we've been given. But *how* we live with them is entirely up to us. We can nurse our wounds, or ignore them and continue to suffer. Or we can take them to God and be healed by His infinite love and grace. Scripture makes clear which path will lead to healing:

> *"I waited patiently for the LORD; he turned to me and heard my cry.*
> *He lifted me out of the slimy pit, out of the mud and mire;*
> *he set my feet on a rock and gave me a firm place to stand.*
> *He put a new song in my mouth, a hymn of praise to our God.*
> *Many will see and fear and put their trust in the LORD"*
> (PSALM 40:1-3).

When we travel back in time to find the source of unresolved anger, the journey will lead to incidents we thought we'd long since forgotten. But undeniably they still have the power to shape our emotions in the present. No experience, no event, should be dismissed as trivial or childish.

Take each hurt, even the seemingly tiniest, to the Lord, and allow Him to apply His healing salve to your soul.

Firestorm: From Ember to Inferno

A *firestorm* is a conflagration that attains such intensity it creates its own wind system. The heat of the original fire draws in more and more of the surrounding air. This kind of raging blaze causes widespread damage and destruction.

Anyone caught in a firestorm would have great fear, as would anyone thrown into a blazing furnace. And yet, in the book of Daniel, we read the unusual account of a powerful king who makes a golden image of himself and orders his subjects to bow down before it. Three friends of Daniel refuse to bow because their allegiance was to the true King of kings, the living God.

Enraged, King Nebuchadnezzar gives them an ultimatum: bow or be thrown into a fiery furnace. But the three stand firm in their convictions. "If we are thrown into the blazing furnace, the God we serve is able to save us from it, and he will rescue us from your hand, O king. But even if he does not, we want you to know, O king, that we will not serve your gods or worship the image of gold you have set up" (Daniel 3:17-18).

You probably know how the story ends. The three men are thrown into the furnace—a literal *conflagration*—yet they remain unharmed. They walk around in the blazing heat and were joined by a fourth figure— generally regarded as an angel of the Lord or the pre-incarnate Christ. God indeed rescues them.

When you find yourself in one of life's "fiery furnaces," remember the three godly friends of Daniel—Shadrach, Meshach, and Abednego. May your prayer be, "God, I know you are able to rescue me, but even if You choose not to, I will serve You wholeheartedly."

How then can you withstand the heat from life's inevitable firestorms? By resting in the knowledge that *all things* will work together for your good. God is unfolding a perfect plan for your life.

Too Hot to Handle

How Being Defensive Heats Up Past Anger

"A hot-tempered person starts fights;
a cool-tempered person stops them"
(Proverbs 15:18 nlt).

If human beings were plants, many of them would belong to the hot pepper family.

You know the kind of people I mean: those who defend their every action with hot, breathing fire, ready to strike at the slightest question. Everything about them says, "Don't get near—or else!" For them, their defensiveness is not just a response to a specific situation, it's a perpetual state of being. Even a simple hello can sound like a stern warning to not cross "the dividing line."

Why is it so easy to get stuck in unhealthy anger patterns? For those who are "pepper people," the answer is clear: Getting caught in habitual, hair-trigger defensiveness is the result of *hanging on to hurts* rather than *handing them over to God.* They nurse their wounds, feed their grudges, and cultivate a victim mentality that walls off their pain from God's healing touch.

Somewhere along the way they were deeply hurt, afraid, frustrated, or offended. Maybe the injury is decades old, dating back to childhood. And maybe something happened just this morning that irritated the wound. In any case, they get angry—a typical response to anything they perceive as threatening.

Processing the "Pepper People" in Our Lives

Just as hot pepper seeds can burn for hours after eating them, the problem develops when pepper people *stay* angry. By refusing to forgive, they remain trapped in a destructive cycle of chronic defensiveness, perpetually poised for "fight or flight."

Several years ago, such a person unexpectedly entered my life. As the newness of the relationship began to wear off, I noticed the quick-to-please behavior also turned into quick-to-anger defensiveness.

After bearing the brunt of several explosions, I became aware of my hypervigilance. Never knowing when an eruption might occur, I began to maintain an almost constant state of expectation. Rather than being able to relax and enjoy an activity together, I was always on high alert.

I felt like a bank guard who stands vigilant, continually looking in all directions for any signs of danger. Never letting your guard down is emotionally draining!

From that experience, I gained some insight and some empathy for pepper people. They never allow themselves to completely trust, to completely relax, to completely be themselves. They falsely think that to let go of their pain is to invite even more pain—or worse, to suffer total defeat. They treat everyone as a potential threat. What a lonely and exhausting way to live!

If we have this defensive anger, we set up a firewall around our lives, and we create a forbidding no-man's-land where chronic anger scorches everyone who enters. Others quickly get the idea it isn't safe—steer clear!

Who wants a relationship with someone surrounded by emotional barbed wire, guard dogs, and searchlights—someone who "lets 'em have it" first and asks questions later? Is our ironclad defense really worth the price we pay in lost intimacy and love? Most people would answer no; yet many of us continue to fall prey to our own disastrous hair-trigger defensiveness.

Diffuse Defensive Anger

If you are trapped in constant defensive anger, chances are you feel you have no choice. It's as if every challenge or insult is a do-or-die fight for survival. All it takes is a harsh tone of voice, a critical comment, getting cut off by another driver, or any one of a thousand other perceived "violations" of your personal rights. Under these conditions, the often-quoted saying "The best defense is a good offense" becomes "The best defense is to decimate your enemies."

That's hardly God's way of looking at things. Jesus said, "In everything, do to others what you would have them do to you, for this sums up the Law and the Prophets."[1] He did not say, "Smash others first before they have a chance to smash you."

If you want to escape the anger snares holding you captive, start by assessing your personal state of alertness. Are you ready—at a moment's notice—to demonstrate God's love and forgiveness for others, lay down your "rights," and declare peace? Or are you prone to reach deep into your anger bowl and retrieve a bitter memory, only to vow you'll never forgive *that* incident? The difference between these two responses is what Jesus had in mind when He said,

> *"You have heard that it was said, 'Eye for eye, and tooth for tooth.'*
> *But I tell you, Do not resist an evil person. If someone strikes you on*
> *the right cheek, turn to him the other also. And if someone wants to s*
> *ue you and take your tunic, let him have your cloak as well.*
> *If someone forces you to go one mile, go with him two miles"*
> (MATTHEW 5:38-41).

Here's the point: Being excessively defensive is as hazardous as building your house in a minefield. If the constant stress doesn't get you, sooner or later an explosion will. And chances are, your explosions will do the greatest harm to those nearest and dearest to you.

Never a Story More Full of Woe

It seems the legendary playwright William Shakespeare understood the high cost of defensive anger. For proof we need look no further than his tragic tale of Romeo and Juliet.

At the beginning of the play, we learn that two wealthy families in

Verona, Italy—the Montagues and the Capulets—are embroiled in an angry feud. Some long-ago offense sparked their fiery emotions, and neither side is in the mood to forgive or forget. The slightest insult is all it takes to bring out the clubs and swords. Both sides say they *must* fight to defend the honor of their name; thus a wall of contention continually divides the two families. By the time the curtain falls at the end of Act V, it is clear just how costly that anger turns out to be.

Romeo (Montague's son) and Juliet (Capulet's daughter) have grown up in this toxic atmosphere of warfare between their families. But like most young people, deep down they are more interested in the joys of love and romance than the sorrows of fighting and feuds. One night they meet by chance at a celebration and fall in love. In this moment, nothing else matters to them but the power of their feelings for each other.

The lovers decide to marry in secret. The day after the wedding, as proof of his new commitment to peace between the families, Romeo refuses to fight a young Capulet named Tybalt (Juliet's cousin). Love has already begun to alter the war-torn landscape of Romeo's life. But defensive anger often has a life of its own. In a tragic turn of events, Romeo's best friend later picks a fight with Tybalt and is mortally wounded, and dies in Romeo's arms. Enraged, Romeo slays Tybalt and is banished for life from Verona—cut off from his family and, worst of all, from Juliet.

The friar who married the lovers then concocts a way to reunite them by faking Juliet's death. The plan goes horribly awry when Romeo believes her death to be genuine—he kills himself rather than face life without her. Upon waking, she discovers his dead body and, in turn, ends her own life.

All Are Punished: The True Cost of Rage

The two families lived a long time with defensive anger—with a seething mentality, with an "eye for an eye" endless repetition of violence. With the loss of their children, they now have to count the true cost of their rage. The prince of Verona says to them: "See what a scourge is laid upon your hate...All are punish'd."[2]

That about sums it up: *All are punished* by unbridled anger that bursts forth from deeply entrenched defensiveness. All are at risk, the angry ones and the innocent bystanders alike. As Proverbs 29:22 reminds us, "An angry man stirs up dissension, and a hot-tempered one commits many sins."

There's no way around it: defensiveness—focusing only on what we want to *protect*—just compounds whatever painful and possibly legitimate reason we had for being angry. Becoming defensive makes matters far worse by searing our relation-

> The longer we don't allow God to pry our fingers off our anger bowls, the less opportunity there will be for Him to use our hands for good.

ships and blocking our ability to grow through adversity. And the longer we don't allow God to pry our fingers off our anger bowls, the less opportunity there will be for Him to use our hands for good, to reach out and help those in need.

Something's Got to Give

When Jimmy called me at *Hope in the Night*, he reluctantly—almost apologetically—described himself as shell-shocked in his marriage to Diana. He explained that, by most measurements, he had little to complain about in the relationship. Diana was a brilliant and successful professor at a prominent university. She was a good mom and a reliable partner in family affairs. After ten years of marriage, Jimmy and Diana were still "deeply attracted to each other" and often joked about having had the world's longest honeymoon.

"So what's the problem?" I asked.

"Maybe I am just an overly demanding person, but I honestly don't think so," he said. "Diana has always been sensitive to criticism, but lately it has come to the point where she reacts like she is under full-scale attack over the smallest things. She raises the drawbridge and goes into siege mode. Then there's no way to go near her without getting an arrow through my chest."

Jimmy's vivid choice of words is a perfect description of life with a defensively angry person. In response to any perceived threat, the person withdraws behind formidable fortifications erected around his heart—and fires flaming arrows at anyone within range. Diana had simply become "too hot to handle."

"It's like she's got to prove to the whole world that she is smarter, stronger, and better than everyone else," Jimmy said sadly. "It breaks my heart to think about what may have caused her to feel so insecure in who she really is. But it's also sapping the life out of our relationship. Now *I* am starting to feel like I'm on the defensive all the time. Something's got to give."

Jimmy rightly recognized Diana's struggle with defensive anger as the result of some past wound that caused her to feel afraid and insecure. When people are angry, there is a reason. Jimmy also discovered he was more than just an innocent bystander—he had become a regular target of Diana's unresolved anger, or the bull's-eye, if you will.

The truth is, defensively angry people are often hardest on those who love them the most. Their dearest relationships frequently come under intense stress and strain. Why? Let's take a look.

The Downsides of Defensive Anger

1. Defensiveness Stifles Communication

It is hard work to talk through the many thorny issues arising in the normal course of any intimate relationship, even when both people are open and willing to listen. A delicate balance of give and take, advance and retreat is required. But when one or both consider any "give" to be tantamount to treason, conversation can quickly turn combative, and vital compromise grows vastly more difficult.

Chances are, someone will have to surrender unconditionally before peace can return to the household. And guess which person usually waves the white flag? Right—not the defensive one with the angry red face.

Over time our family and friends grow tired of constant capitulation and simply stop talking to us about sensitive matters. This much is certain: When communication starts to break down, divisions develop and relationships are in trouble.

The antidote for defensive division is letting God's healing love bring reconciliation, and then passing that love on to others. The Bible sums up love's restorative power:

> *"Love is patient, love is kind. It does not envy,*
> *it does not boast, it is not proud. It is not rude, it is not self-seeking,*
> *it is not easily angered, it keeps no record of wrongs.*
> *Love does not delight in evil but rejoices with the truth.*
> *It always protects, always trusts, always hopes, always perseveres"*
> (1 Corinthians 13:4-7).

When we give up defensiveness as a way of relating to others, communication flows more freely and loving relationships grow stronger and healthier.

2. Defensiveness Preempts Accountability

Here is an unavoidable truth: No one is perfect. Each of us is a work in progress, with room to grow and much to learn. Every day is a new opportunity to gain maturity and wisdom. For that reason, the world is our classroom, and our relationships are among our most valuable teachers. They serve as mirrors in which we can see ourselves more clearly. In countless ways, those closest to us help hold us accountable for our words and actions.

The problem with our defensiveness is that it throws a monkey wrench into the process. We dodge responsibility, missing out on the opportunity to learn from our mistakes. The clamor of combat may drown out the people who we think could possibly hurt us, but it also prevents us from hearing God's gentle corrections through those He would use to help change us.

Solomon wrote, "He who listens to a life-giving rebuke will be at home among the wise. He who ignores discipline despises himself, but whoever heeds correction gains understanding" (Proverbs 15:31-32). That's great advice for anyone who uses defensive anger to keep accountability at bay.

3. Defensiveness Makes a Mountain out of Every Last Molehill

Over the years, I have learned to trust the deep wisdom in this simple phrase: *Choose your battles carefully.* This is never more true than when I am angry. To follow this advice, I try to stop before acting on my anger and ask myself:

—Am I in the right?
—What benefit will come from fighting this battle?
—Even if I succeed, will it do more harm than good?
—How would Jesus respond to this situation?

Believe me, I don't always get it right. But more than once I've avoided making a costly mistake by counting the cost before initiating a confrontation. As Jesus said, "Suppose a king is about to go to war against another king. Will he not first sit down and consider whether he is able with ten thousand men to oppose the one coming against him with twenty thousand?" (Luke 14:31).

It's just common sense, really. Yet when you are ensnared in endless cycles of defensive anger, this kind of strategic thinking is next to impossible. When every offense, no matter how small, feels like a matter of life and death, it is unthinkable to simply let it go. When you haven't surrendered your past pain to God, you may feel compelled to react to every new threat with fresh anger whether it makes sense or not. Unable to really afford another fight, you are convinced you can't afford to pass it up either.

A king like *that*, I'm sure Jesus would say, is doomed to defeat—or at least to poverty from constant warfare. The only solution is not confrontation but rather submission...submitting our anger wounds to God's healing touch. Then we can seek the wisdom of God, surrender all our battles to Him, and trust Him to bring peace and reconciliation.

4. Defensiveness Keeps You from Dealing with the Cause of Anger

After our conversation, Jimmy told Diana he was tired of living in a war zone. He invited her to participate in "peace talks" with him and a counselor who would mediate. It wasn't easy for her to see past the feeling that she was once again under attack. But she eventually agreed.

Months later, I spoke with Diana about the experience. She said, "The breakthrough came when I realized being defensive and fighting with Jimmy over every little thing was preventing me from seeing the truth: He wasn't the source of my anger at all. It was like being so focused on the smoke, that I had no idea where the fire was."

As it turned out, her hidden fire had been burning for a long time. Growing up with three highly competitive older brothers, Diana came to believe she had to work ten times harder than most people just to be considered "good enough." By the time she went to college, she was already on high alert. But it was there her habit of expressing razor-sharp defensive anger really took hold. As a young graduate student in a field dominated by men, she felt she had been "dropped behind enemy lines." Unfortunately, her advisors all seemed to be cut from the same chauvinistic cloth, and their critique of her work was often belittling, sarcastic, and overly personal.

"I decided no one would ever treat me that way again," Diana told me. "The sad thing is I turned into the very sort of angry person I was trying to protect myself from."

By building impregnable walls out of hyperdefensiveness, Diana had prevented herself from getting to the bottom of why she was mad in the first place. Hardly a day went by when she didn't find some petty reason to project all her pain and anger onto Jimmy. It was unfair to him and kept her stuck in a self-reinforcing cycle of unresolved anger. Thankfully, she finally realized this negative cycle and began addressing it.

Civil rights leader Martin Luther King, Jr. once said, "Darkness cannot drive out darkness; only light can do that. Hate cannot drive out hate; only love can do that."[3]

A life of angry defensiveness cannot drive out pain and fear. Only

God's healing grace can do that when we surrender ourselves into His care. Let Him take responsibility for your defense as you retreat into His arms.

Underground Fire: Invisible Sparks

In 2002, an unusual brush fire erupted in western Colorado. Before firefighters contained the blaze, it destroyed more than 12,000 acres of forest, two dozen homes, and came dangerously close to the scenic resort town of Glenwood Springs. Drought conditions across the state made fighting the fire especially difficult.

What made the fire out of the ordinary was not the damage it caused in the end, but how it actually began.

The spark that triggered the inferno didn't come from a campfire, or a lightning strike, or a carelessly discarded match. In fact, the fire had already been burning for more than three decades—*underground*—in a smoldering seam of coal. There are many such unseen fires burning around the world, in subterranean coal seams and peat deposits. They can suddenly erupt unexpectedly at the surface, threatening homes and lives.

It is equally possible for anger to simmer away beneath the surface of your life—out of sight, out of mind—until one day it surfaces and consumes you. With God's help, you can excavate those past wounds that have been there since childhood and allow His love to bring hope and healing to your heart.

FIRE AND ICE
How a Controlling Spirit Fuels Chronic Anger

"A gentle answer turns away wrath,
but a harsh word stirs up anger"
(PROVERBS 15:1).

BECAUSE OF OUR unprecedented access to technology, to some degree we all have control issues—so much so that we are unaware of its influence on how we think and the role it plays in our problems with runaway anger.

At the touch of a button or the flick of a switch, we exercise a level of command over our environment that our ancestors would never have imagined possible. We have thermostats to regulate room temperature, light bulbs to "extend" the day, timers on everything from coffeepots to automatic sprinkler systems, and cars and planes that can condense months of travel by foot into a few hours' journey.

Kids and adults alike play home video games and watch what happens in the world using a device called a "controller." We *order* our food, *manage* our careers, *master* our money, and *secure* our retirement. The list could go on and on. Clearly, we've made control a way of life.

The Cop Who Copped an Attitude

One Christmas holiday years ago when I was a youth director, a family in the church I served invited me and two friends to their vacation home in Crested Butte, Colorado—they wanted to teach us how to ski! What a perfect place to spend time with friends and celebrate the season...or so I thought.

On Christmas evening, with great excitement, Sandy, Barbara, and I packed my car and headed out from Dallas, taking turns driving the long stretches of open road. About three-fourths of the way into our trip, I was behind the wheel when we were coming down mountainous Raton Pass into Colorado. I looked in the rearview mirror and saw what sparks apprehension in most of us—the flashing lights of a patrol car.

"Oh, no!" I nearly shouted. "I can't believe it!" Barbara and Sandy looked back and saw the pulsating bursts of the police lights. In unison, they let out a groan.

Immediately I looked at the speedometer. I breathed a huge sigh of relief when I saw I wasn't exceeding the speed limit. (I've been known to say, "I don't drive fast; I just fly low." Fortunately that morning, I wasn't flying!)

"I know I wasn't speeding," I said confidently and guilt-free as I pulled onto the shoulder of the highway. After the police car came to a stop behind me, I opened the driver's side door and hopped out.

"Lady, get back in that car!" the officer barked. He punctuated his command with a pointed finger stabbing the air in my direction. "Now!"

Feeling scolded, I retreated back into my car. The officer sat in his car for a long time, doing who knows what, while the three of us waited in silence. Finally, he swaggered up to the car in his uniform—knee-high boots, pants flaring at the thighs like British hunting breeches, and sporting the kind of hat forest rangers wear.

He leaned over to survey the car's occupants, then growled, "License and registration." After handing him the papers, he looked at them and said matter of factly, "I'm going to ticket you for speeding."

Though surprised, I tried to sound cooperative. "Sir, I'm sure I wasn't speeding."

For several long seconds, he just glared at me as if I'd said the stupidest thing he'd ever heard. Finally, in a tone dripping with condescension, he said, "Lady, with these hazardous road conditions, you should have dropped your speed by ten miles per hour. That's the law."

"Officer, I'm sorry. I've never heard of this law."

He had his quick retort in place. "Ignorance of the law is no excuse! You were driving recklessly, endangering yourself and others. I'm going to issue you a citation. Don't blame me—blame yourself."

I was incensed. *A ticket for not slowing down, even though I was going the speed limit? That's ridiculous!* But I still tried to explain, "Well sir, in Texas..."

Mid-sentence, he turned on the heels of his shiny boots and strutted back toward his car. Immediately I felt my cheeks get hot, my heart start pounding, and my blood pressure soar.

Let me point out I have tremendous respect for law enforcement officers, but this one had a bad attitude to match his big ego. "I think he needs to read *How to Win Friends and Influence People*," I muttered sarcastically.

"He must have had a nasty fight with his wife this morning!" Barbara quipped.

Sandy—never at a loss for words—upped the ante. "No, I think he's in a foul mood because his uniform makes him look like Dudley Do-right!" I mustered a chuckle even though I was fuming. Then things got worse.

Returning to our car, he demanded, "Follow me back into town. You have to pay your fine now."

"But...can't I just send a check in later?"

"No," he insisted. "Follow me—*now*."

My "Go Directly to Jail" Card

I couldn't believe it! We had no choice but to drive about 15 minutes to the police station. Upon arrival, the officer didn't say a word. He just pointed with obvious disdain. I felt like I had just drawn the orange "Go Directly to Jail" card in the game of Monopoly.

With a hard stride, I marched in, paid the fine, and marched out. I opened the car door—with unusual strength—and uncharacteristically slammed the door shut. Barbara and Sandy fell silent.

During the entire time of our detour, my teeth were clenched and beads of perspiration formed on my forehead even though the temperature outside was an icy 20 degrees Fahrenheit. When we finally resumed our northward trek, I noticed my knuckles were white from clutching the steering wheel so tightly.

> Discerning our own anger cues can help us avoid trouble.

After my encounter with that haughty, arrogant officer, I kept replaying the incident over and over in my mind, and each time I did so, my pulse would quicken and my stomach would tighten.

What I learned (besides the need to reduce my speed in snowy conditions if I don't want a ticket!) was just how much my angry feelings impacted me physically. For a person who thought she didn't have any anger issues, I exhibited *all* the symptoms of someone who had them! (Well, almost.)

What Are "Anger Cues"?

At those times when we really are angry but won't admit it, everyone else around us knows it! That's because we give off "anger cues." Our anger may be *internal*, but its expression is *external*.

Anger and volcanoes have similar symptoms. Before an eruption, there's a gurgling beneath the surface, a swirling series of events that creates pressure. In fact, scientists look for cues that a volcano is about to erupt, including the release of steam and gases, small earthquakes and tremors, and the swelling of a volcano's slopes.

Similarly, the human body has physical reactions when it experiences anger. These anger cues alert us to when we begin to feel angry.

Discerning our own anger cues can help us avoid trouble. Likewise, being aware of the signs of anger in others can alert us to avoid an angry response—allowing us to "don fire-retardant clothing," if necessary.

A biblical example of an anger cue is Jonathan's loss of appetite when he was hurt and grieved over his father's unjust, shameful treatment toward his close friend David: "Jonathan got up from the table in fierce anger…he did not eat, because he was grieved at his father's shameful treatment of David."[1]

We may not all experience the same feelings, but once we have identified our anger cues, we will be in a better position to quickly identify anger in ourselves as well as in others. Then we can take the steps necessary to prevent an explosion of anger we would undeniably regret.

Anger Cues

- churning stomach
- clenched fists
- clenched teeth
- decreased appetite
- dry mouth
- fast/hard breathing
- fast/hard walking
- flushed face
- inappropriate language
- harsh/coarse/sarcastic language
- increased perspiration
- loud sighing/groaning
- racing heart
- rapid/high-pitched speech
- shutting down verbally
- tearful eyes
- tense muscles
- twitches/anxious behaviors (such as tapping a pencil, shaking a foot)
- becoming unusually hot or cold

Of course, there is nothing wrong with a desire for order and structure in our lives. For example, I'm grateful for refrigeration that preserves food and systems of hygiene that control disease.

Letting go of control doesn't mean we have to take a debilitating step back into the Dark Ages. But with such immense power at our disposal, it's easy to see how we learn to take for granted our ability to master just about every aspect of our lives. When control is curtailed, it can be *catastrophic*—for those who struggle with anger, and for those all around them. Control, it turns out, is a dangerously addictive commodity.

The Bible says,

> *"What causes fights and quarrels among you? Don't they come*
> *from your desires that battle within you? You want something but*
> *don't get it. You kill and covet, but you cannot have what you want.*
> *You quarrel and fight. You do not have, because you do not ask*
> *God. When you ask, you do not receive, because you ask with wrong*
> *motives, that you may spend what you get on your pleasures...*
> *But he gives us more grace. That is why Scripture says:*
> *'God opposes the proud but gives grace to the humble'"*
> (JAMES 4:1-3,6).

Problems break out like scattered brush fires in our lives. Trying to contain and control them on our own only leaves us ultimately sitting in an ash heap, smoldering in angry frustration and sometimes giving God the silent treatment.

Why does that happen? There's no one better qualified than Jonah to answer that question.

An Ill-Advised Power Struggle

Poor Jonah. He's held up to Sunday school children everywhere as an example of how *not* to behave. It's true he tried to defy God's will and got a couple of painful object lessons for his rebellion—time spent in the belly of a fish and time under a blistering sun.

Indeed, he was a stubborn, angry man.

But I think we, of all people, shouldn't be so quick to judge Jonah. What he wanted in life, after all, was something we are conditioned to expect from earliest childhood: to have things our way, to call the shots, to be in the driver's seat, to determine our own fate.

In other words, Jonah just wanted *control* of his life, the right to decide for himself what was best. When he couldn't have it, he grew angry, stalking off to stock his anger bowl. Then when he tried to deal with his indignation, he did something that probably sounds familiar to most of us: He grabbed for *more* control and wound up *more* angry when that didn't work.

In the Bible, the story ends before we find out whether Jonah ever caught on that his solution didn't work so well. Maybe we can pick up where he left off and connect the dots for ourselves. Here's his story:

I'm Not God's Man for the Job

In those days, there was an important city called Nineveh. It was full of wickedness, and God decided it was time to give the people there an ultimatum: "Repent within forty days, or watch as your city is overthrown."

We tend to focus on the thundering threat of wrathful destruction in these words, but there is amazing grace here as well.

Clearly, God didn't want punishment for the people, no matter what they had done. He wanted redemption and reconciliation. Forty days is ample time to reflect on a life of sin and turn to righteousness.

To convey this message, God selected His servant Jonah. All we know about this prophet comes from his description of himself: "I am a Hebrew and I worship the LORD, the God of heaven, who made the sea and the land."[2] He sounds like the perfect man for what God had in mind, except for one detail: Jonah didn't want the job.

Unlike the Lord, Jonah *did* want punishment for the inhabitants of Nineveh, because they were considered enemies of Israel. In his view, they didn't deserve the opportunity to escape the harshest possible judgment.

The last thing Jonah wanted was for God to let them off the hook. After all, these were a people known for their excessive cruelty to prisoners of war and for idolatrous worship. Jonah was fully aware of the graciousness of his God, and the thought of forgiving the Ninevites made his blood boil.

I'm Outta Here!

So when Jonah got the call from God to pack up and head for Nineveh, Jonah decided to take matters into his own hands. He ran away—in the opposite direction!

I imagine he thought, *If God wants to go easy on those heathens, He can use someone else to do it. I have a right to choose what I will and won't do.* To prove it, he bought a ticket on the first boat out of town. Bad idea.

> *"Then the LORD sent a great wind on the sea, and such a violent storm arose that the ship threatened to break up. All the sailors were afraid and each cried out to his own god. And they threw the cargo into the sea to lighten the ship. But Jonah had gone below deck, where he lay down and fell into a deep sleep. The captain went to him and said, 'How can you sleep? Get up and call on your god! Maybe he will take notice of us, and we will not perish'"*
> (JONAH 1:4-6).

Jonah told his fellow travelers that he was running away from God, which terrified them even more. Even they seemed to understand what Jonah had evidently forgotten: You can't run, nor hide, from God.

Jonah convinced the sailors that to save themselves, they must throw him overboard. As the storm intensified, the sailors reluctantly agreed.

They begged God to forgive them, then threw Jonah into the water. It worked—the wind and waves immediately began to calm.

A Frightening Fish Encounter

What happened next is the part everyone knows: "The LORD provided a great fish to swallow Jonah, and Jonah was inside the fish three days and three nights."[3] Apparently, that was just enough time for Jonah to think things over.

In the terrifying dark and stench of the great fish's belly, he cried out to God:

"When my life was ebbing away, I remembered you, LORD,
and my prayer rose to you, to your holy temple.
Those who cling to worthless idols forfeit the grace that could be theirs.
But I, with a song of thanksgiving, will sacrifice to you.
What I have vowed I will make good. Salvation comes from the LORD."
(JONAH 2:7-9).

That sounds pretty good, but it needs a bit of translating to get Jonah's true meaning: "Those Ninevites still don't deserve Your love, but if you'll let me out of here, I'll go tell them what You said."

That's a long way from sincere surrender to the wisdom of God's will, but it was enough for the Lord to cause the fish to spit Jonah out upon dry land. In spite of the fact that his heart wasn't fully in the mission, he went straight to Nineveh and delivered God's message.

Then, from Jonah's perspective, things went from bad to worse. The people of Nineveh actually believed God and repented. They fasted and prayed. They put on sackcloth and sat in the dust, both signs of humbled and repentant hearts.

And yes, God had mercy on them. "When God saw what they did and how they turned from their evil ways, he had compassion and did not bring upon them the destruction he had threatened" (Jonah 3:10).

Repentance and Resentment

That must have been some powerful preaching! The irony sent Jonah's blood pressure soaring, figuratively speaking. He had secretly hoped the wicked sinners would prove him right by refusing God's offer and inviting destruction. Instead, an entire city answered a call that Jonah never wanted to give.

The Bible says this "displeased Jonah exceedingly, and he was angry." [4]

"O LORD, is this not what I said when I was still at home?
That is why I was so quick to flee to Tarshish. I knew that you are
a gracious and compassionate God, slow to anger and abounding in

love, a God who relents from sending calamity. Now, O LORD,
take away my life, for it is better for me to die than to live"
(JONAH 4:2-3).

Now here's a man with control issues. When things didn't turn
out the way he wanted, Jonah left Nineveh and sat down in a shady
shelter outside the city and waited, probably hoping that God would
change His mind.

It is tempting to laugh at Jonah's foolishness and dismiss him as
someone who should enroll in an anger-management program. But
the truth hits much closer to home than we comfortably care to admit.
The fact is there is a lot of Jonah in *us*.

Many of us are just as bent on control, and react with irrational
anger when we don't get our way.

The Freedom of Relinquishing Control

Anger can run high in a significant relationship in which you
know what *could be*, or *should be*, yet *won't be*. I know the frustration
of being unable to change any of the painful dynamics in my family
life when I was growing up. Neither the "fire" of my white-hot anger
nor the "ice" of seething resignation ever once helped me resolve a
conflict. Thankfully, my relationship with the Lord enabled me to
release my family, my father, and my future to Him.

Then years later as an adult, I came face-to-face with another situation I wanted desperately to change but couldn't. It seemed the Lord
wanted to give me a refresher course in trusting Him in all circumstances, but on an entirely different level and in another situation.

How well I remember my hurt and disappointment at having one
failed attempt after another to persuade an estranged friend to reconcile with me and re-establish our relationship.

I did everything I knew to do and absolutely nothing worked. I
sought forgiveness for my mistakes and failures, I supported my case
with biblical injunctions, I made requested changes. I did all I could
to prevent the demise of our friendship, but to no avail.

The hurt was deep and, to this day, I sometimes miss the camaraderie we once shared. But God has long since healed my heart regarding that relationship, and He has blessed me far beyond what I deserve or expected with a handful of forever friendships.

God has faithfully met my needs and taught me to trust His control over my life, my relationships, and my circumstances. True freedom involves no longer fighting God for control but completely relinquishing it to Him!

The Truth About Control

If we really want to find freedom from destructive anger, a good place to start is relinquishing control of anything and everything around us. Here are a few points to remember about control:

Control is impossible. It is an inescapable truth that everything in God's creation is in a state of constant motion. Nothing remains the same. Even in the depth of frozen winter, spring is already present in seeds beneath the ground. As the tide flows out to sea, it's already gathering itself to return.

The tallest mountains experience erosion, and all that remains of many great civilizations of the past are a few stones stacked together. Indeed, life is a flowing river that sometimes thunders in flashfloods and other times meanders lazily through broad meadows—but it never stops changing the landscape as it moves.

Some people are called "control freaks." They try to control everything and everyone. However, attempting to control events and circumstances and people—to step into that current and command it to turn right or turn left or be still—is futile. It simply cannot be done. When we approach life as the absolute sole masters of fate and controllers of destiny, we are doomed already to failure, frustration, and anger.

It doesn't have to be that way. We can admit we've been mistaken and have invested ourselves in an impossible task.

It's time to let God heal us of this need to be overcontrolling and the anger that comes with it when we don't get our way. We must surrender our wishes and wants, our desires and demands to the sovereignty of our loving and compassionate God.

Control is a heavy and unnecessary burden. In the Bible, we see an example of one sister's attempt to exert control over her siblings. Martha was angry with her sister, Mary. Jesus had come to stay at their house, so there was work to do and food to prepare.

The Bible says Martha was "distracted with much serving," and she perceived Mary as no help at all. She felt abandoned to do the heavy lifting while Mary sat listening to Jesus speak.

Finally, Martha had had enough. It was time to force Mary into the kitchen. She approached Jesus and said, "Lord, don't you care that my sister has left me to do the work by myself? Tell her to help me!"[5]

Oh, how my heart goes out to Martha. How many times have I tried to enlist God in my efforts to control something I didn't like? I can feel the familiar weight of responsibility on her shoulders, can't you? Her face was probably flush from frustration as her voice rang with indignation.

Jesus responded to her put-upon attitude this way: "Martha, Martha... you are worried and upset about many things, but only one thing is needed. Mary has chosen what is better, and it will not be taken away from her."[6]

Some might hear stinging censure in Jesus' words, but I interpret them as a compassionate invitation for Martha to lay down her needless burden of worry and control. I can imagine Him saying, "There is a better way. Mary has chosen it, and so can you." That way is called trust, putting God first and allowing Him to guide your life. Martha needed to empty her personal anger bowl, place it at the back of a cabinet, and leave it there for good.

Control is God's business, and not having this heavy responsibility is His gift to us. As Jonah discovered, our God is sovereign. The earth is His and everything in it.

Assuming the right to control our lives according to our own will is dangerous arrogance—and sinful pride. Job learned the same lesson. When he assumed too much, God replied,

"Who is this that darkens my counsel with words without knowledge?
Brace yourself like a man; I will question you, and you shall answer me.
Where were you when I laid the earth's foundation? Tell me, if you
understand. Who marked off its dimensions? Surely you know!
Who stretched a measuring line across it?"
(Job 38:2-5).

It was a well-deserved rebuke. But like an earthly father who refuses to give a little child the keys to the family car, God's authority and sovereignty are intended for our protection and well-being.

> God wants you to seek His answer for anger quickly before it singes your heart and burns the bridges of your relationships.

No, it is not possible for us to control every facet of life. But the good news is that the Creator of the whole universe has promised to do it for us.

Jesus said, "Do not worry about your life, what you will eat or drink; or about your body, what you will wear. Is not life more important than food, and the body more important than clothes?"[7] You can't control it anyway, so trust your Father to provide.

Jesus also said, "Who of you by worrying can add a single hour to his life?"[8] Let go, and release the stress and tension that accompanies the need to control.

Furthermore, Jesus said, "Come to me, all you who are weary and burdened, and I will give you rest. Take my yoke upon you and learn from me, for I am gentle and humble in heart, and you will find rest for your souls. For my yoke is easy and my burden is light."[9]

There is nothing light about the burden of control. Give it to God, and end your angry turmoil.

What Is the Quick Answer to Anger?

Few people know the importance of a quick answer more than the members of a First Response T.E.A.M. (Tactical Emergency Asset Management). When disaster strikes, they rapidly deploy communications technologies to the scene, ensuring that voice, video, and data capabilities are fully functional among the attending agencies.

When you sense a surge of anger, it's just as vital that you too learn to respond quickly. If not, your anger can blaze out of control.

The possibility of anger remains ever present. A spark of irritation can be ignited intentionally by hurtful people or even unintentionally by those who love you. God wants you to seek His answer for anger quickly before it singes your heart and burns the bridges of your relationships. "A gentle answer turns away wrath, but a harsh word stirs up anger."[10]

Many people try to make the solution for anger more complex than it should be. Of course, there will always be multiple approaches and steps to managing anger (and I will detail many later in this book). However, at the risk of sounding too simplistic, I will present here what for decades I have called...

The Quick Answer to Anger

If I boiled down managing anger to the most basic steps, I believe you could reduce the solution to two points: one question and one action step.

> Step 1: Ask—Can I change this situation?
>
> Step 2: Action—If you *can*, *change* it. If you *can't*, *release* it.

Let's start with the first step: Can you change what angers you? Answer yes or no—that's it.

Now consider the second step: If you answered yes, you are angry about something you *can* change—so change it.

- If the door squeaks, oil it.
- If the faucet leaks, fix it.

If you answered no, you are angry about something you *cannot* change—so release it.

- If your house burns down, release it.
- If your loved one dies, release that person.

If your house does burn down, only by emotionally releasing the pain of your loss can you rebuild your life, and possibly your home. Being angry with a burned house or a buried body—or anyone who caused either—will not change the situation—it will only make matters worse.

But How Do I Surrender?

Here's the point: God has provided an antidote to poisonous anger that comes from trying to be in control all of the time. All it costs us is *surrender to His will*.

More than 300 years ago, a French priest named Jean-Pierre de Caussade put it this way:

> "[True surrender to God is] a state in which one discovers how to belong wholly to God through the complete and total assignment of all rights over oneself—over one's speech, actions, thoughts and bearing; the employment of one's time and everything related to it. There remains one single duty. It is to keep one's gaze fixed on the master one has chosen and to be constantly listening so as to understand and hear and immediately obey his will."[11]

Yes, we are conditioned by culture and coaxed by human nature to believe we can achieve control over our lives. And yes, it makes us angry when our efforts to keep things and people in line don't work as we intended.

The more energy we pour into the impossible task of control, the more we place ourselves at the mercy of runaway rage. Let go. Release control. Allow God to reign over every aspect of your life, and you'll soon see the dam of damaging rage give way to streams of calm.

Lightning: Fire in the Sky

True or false: Lightning is the hottest thing in our solar system.

True! The temperature of an average bolt of lightning reaches well over 50,000 degrees Fahrenheit—nearly five times the temperature on the surface of the sun—and can contain 100 million electrical volts. That's a lot of juice—enough to instantly fuse ordinary silica sand into solid glass. There are approximately 1,800 thunderstorms in the earth's atmosphere at any given time. In the United States alone it is estimated there are 25 million lightning strikes every year, many causing significant damage from resulting fires and power outages.

Lightning forms when an electrical imbalance develops within thunderclouds or between clouds and the ground. When the difference between positive and negative charges becomes great enough, the natural resistance of the air is overcome—and electricity flows suddenly and without warning.

Anger is like that too. It can build unnoticed in the atmosphere of your life until one day it strikes with full destructive force. With God's help, you can learn to pay attention to the gathering clouds—in yourself and in others—and take shelter in His loving arms before the damage is done.

SELF-INFLICTED FLAMES
How Guilt and Shame Ignite Harmful Anger

*"Be quick to listen, slow to speak, and slow to get angry.
Human anger does not produce the righteousness God desires"*
(JAMES 1:19-20 NLT).

DO YOU KNOW SOMEONE who struggles with any of these burning questions?

> Why do I feel so angry at times?
> Why do I lash out at others over little things?
> What can I do before my anger does lasting damage?

If you, at times, are the questioner, consider this: In the best-case scenario, finding an answer is a simple matter of analyzing cause and effect. You retrace your steps in a nice, straight line back to the spark that ignited your anger, then you set about addressing the root cause.

The same can be true when you try to uncover the deep-seated source of your anger. The answer isn't always obvious. This chapter is devoted to exploring one possibility especially easy to overlook. It goes like this:

If your anger has ever erupted in disproportionate hostility toward another person, it may be the intended victim of your anger was really *yourself.*

Typically, anger toward yourself comes from personal failure, personal disappointment, or being taken advantage of—all with painful consequences. These include living in a way that's far from God's ideal and your own.

Whatever the cause, anger at yourself can easily detonate like a bomb and damage those around you.

Collateral Damage

When I met Lily, she was on top of the world. A vivacious woman in her late twenties, she was hired as a full-time member of the youth ministry team at a growing, dynamic church.

She talked a mile a minute about her new position, bursting with ideas and energy. It was obvious she cared deeply about young people and the problems they face in our permissive culture.

Neither of us could have guessed, when we spoke again a few months later, that she would have fallen from the top of the world to the bottom of the barrel.

"I quit my job," she told me abruptly, fighting back tears. Her spirited enthusiasm was gone, replaced by a defeated demeanor. "I let everyone down, and I haven't got a clue how to fix it."

Lily's pain was palpable, and my heart went out to her.

"Well, first things first," I said, gently. "Do you agree with me there is no such thing as a hopeless situation when we trust in God?" I reminded her of what the apostle Paul wrote in Romans 8:31: "If God is for us, who can be against us?"

After thinking for a moment, she said, "Yes, I believe that."

"Good," I said. "Now tell me what happened that has caused you so much distress?"

She took a deep breath and plunged into her story.

"I have a lot of anger inside that gets out of control sometimes," she confessed. "I've always thought people who criticized my temper were just too touchy and thin-skinned. But I can't run from it anymore. Now I *know* I have a problem."

Not long after she started working at the church, a troubling pattern began to emerge in Lily's relationship with some of the young people in the group.

She took a few especially troubled ones under her wing and made it her mission to guide and disciple them. Perhaps because of this investment, she began to take it personally anytime they broke the group's rules. Naturally, it was part of her job to be sure the teens adhered to expected standards while at church.

The problem lay in how angry she became when one of "her kids" failed to live up to those expectations. On several occasions, she publicly yelled at them in a rage.

"I convinced myself tough love was the way to get through to them… to save them from themselves," Lily said. "I thought I was doing them a favor in the long run."

She was forced to change her mind after a traumatic incident during the youth group's weeklong summer camp. One night, after lights out, she caught three girls drinking from a whiskey bottle one of them had smuggled from home in a suitcase.

"When I think about that night, I can't explain why I got so mad," Lily admitted. "Something inside me just snapped."

Enraged, Lily berated the girls. And then the unthinkable happened. She grabbed the bottle of alcohol and hurled it against the wall. A shard of glass rebounded and struck her in the head, leaving a gash on her scalp that bled profusely.

The terrified teenagers ran for help, and soon the entire cabin, counselors, and staff turned out to see what had happened.

"I thank God I was the one who got hurt and not one of them," she said. "I feel like some kind of monster. I know I looked like one, too, standing there with blood pouring down my face.

"Even though they shouldn't have been drinking, my reaction was over the top. How could I get so angry with them?"

"Perhaps they weren't the reason for your anger at all," I suggested. "Maybe they were only standing in for the *real* target of your disappointment and outrage."

"What target?" she asked skeptically.

"Well, is there something in the kids' behavior that reminds you of someone else? Yourself, perhaps?" I was only probing, but apparently I had struck a nerve.

Lily began to cry in earnest. When she regained her composure enough to speak, the rest of the story emerged.

"I was a pretty wild teenager," she said. "I know a lot of kids go through a rebellious phase, but I was worse than most."

Lily had a long list of offenses from her high school years she could pin on herself: experimentation with drugs and alcohol, promiscuous sex, and flagrant disobedience toward her parents. One incident stood out above the rest and haunted her mercilessly.

On her eighteenth birthday, Lily's friends threw her a party when she was supposed to be at soccer practice. Their "gift" to her was a six-pack of beer and a few bottles of tequila pilfered from parents' liquor cabinets. By dinnertime, Lily was in a drunken stupor and she staggered home.

What happened next became a nuclear explosion of pain and self-loathing that still burned through every fiber of Lily's being. When she stumbled through the front door of her house, everything was quiet. It appeared no one was home. She felt immediate relief to be able to sneak upstairs to her room unnoticed. Until—

"Surprise! Happy birthday!"

"Suddenly, the house was full of happy, laughing people all looking at me," Lily recalled. "My grandparents and aunts and uncles were there. Church people. My *pastor*.

"I'll never forget the look on my mother's face when she realized the state I was in. I reeked of booze, my eyes were bloodshot, and every word that came out of my mouth was slurred.

"All the lies I'd been telling them—and myself—were on vivid display.

"I blurted out a terrible obscenity and tried to run up the stairs, but had to be carried instead. There was nowhere left to hide after that."

Thankfully, the humiliation that night became a turning point in Lily's life—evidence of God's capacity to transform any defeat into victory.

Lily abandoned the rebellious, self-destructive path she had started down and devoted herself instead to a life of service to God. Her family forgave her and helped her form new values and habits.

There was just one problem. Through it all, Lily never forgave *herself.* Years later, her anger still burned at her unwise choices and actions. And her anger was hot enough to scorch anyone who got in its path.

The misbehaving teenagers in Lily's youth group became unwitting "mirrors" who had reflected Lily's own troubled past and fanned the flames of her longtime anger at herself.

Arson Investigation 101

Here's the lesson in Lily's story: Unresolved rage directed at yourself is like a pressure cooker without a relief valve—as the underlying source continues to add heat, the pent-up force continues to build until it explodes.

Even after the explosion, superhot anger spills into chronic depression, self-sabotage, broken relationships, or inexplicable anger toward others that blows scorching steam at the slightest provocation.

When these things happen, there are two questions you need to ask that will lead to help and healing: Why am I so mad at myself? And, why can't I forgive myself? Here are four flammable possibilities:

1. Good-Guilt Gary and Shame-Filled Shannon

Justifiable guilt is a *good* thing. Yes, that's right—there is such a thing as "good guilt." It is that shrill alarm that blares in your conscience and warns when you've strayed off course.

In fact, admitting you are guilty of sin and in need of God's forgiveness is the first step you must take to receive the salvation He offers through faith in Christ.

Think about it: No one seeks a pardon for a crime he doesn't believe he committed. In order to be free of guilt before God, you must first take full responsibility for what you did wrong. As the apostle John wrote: "If we claim to be without sin, we deceive ourselves and the truth is not in us" (1 John 1:8).

What happens when you get stuck somewhere between confessing your sins and receiving the freedom of God's forgiveness?

That's what happens to Shame-Filled Shannon. What if she can't take the next step and let go of her guilt, leaving it in God's hands where it belongs? The answer is that her healthy guilt will become distorted into something God never intended His children to feel: shame.

The difference between Good-Guilt Gary and Shame-Filled Shannon is enormous. Consider these contrasting statements:

Gary: "I know what I did was wrong."

Shannon: "I am a terrible person because of what I did."

Gary: "I ask God to forgive me and show me how I can
          make amends."

Shannon: "No amount of punishment can repay what I owe."

Gary: "I have a lot to learn from my mistakes."

Shannon: "If I were a good person, my mistakes would
          never have happened in the first place."

You can easily see that proper feelings of guilt open the door for repentance, restoration, and right living.

Shame, on the other hand, leads only to more shame—with no way out—and leaves you with a lifetime of considering yourself a terrible person.

Shame isolates you in a circle of fiery self-loathing thoughts—like an eternal flame burning continuously in your mind—over and over and over again.

Here's the problem: Eventually shame makes you angry at yourself for failing so miserably to be worthy of God's love. In fact, shame and anger go hand in hand, beginning in earliest childhood.

Shame creates this cycle of anger whether we receive it from someone else—a teacher, parent, spouse, or boss—or mercilessly heap it on ourselves. Most important of all, anger you direct inward rarely stays there—it usually fights its way into the open.

Lily learned these things the hard way. In letting her guilt turn to shame, she lit the fuse on a volatile bomb of anger aimed at herself, and it inadvertently spewed on innocent bystanders when it finally exploded.

The apostle John said, "If we confess our sins, he is faithful and just and will forgive us our sins and purify us from all unrighteousness."[1] If shame is the source of your anger, own up to your guilt, agree with God that you are forgiven, and then...let it go!

2. Perfectionist Patty

Someone once remarked, "Perfectionists are the only people on earth who fail 100 percent of the time." At first glance, this statement seems absurd. After all, no group of people works harder at success than perfectionists. They take pride in their high standards and never rest in the quest for excellence.

Failure? Not an option for the perfectionist.

But look again, and you'll see a tragic truth in the saying. By definition, perfectionism is a pattern of thinking that demands all areas of life be flawless. Anything less than perfect is unacceptable.

Take Perfectionist Patty, who *never* accomplishes precisely what she sets out to do. Why? Because flawless perfection in this world is always an unattainable fantasy. It can't be had at any price. Her achievements may be excellent or optimal—but they are never always *perfect*. Therefore, she can't help but feel like a failure.

If Perfectionist Patty fails to understand this crucial fact, she is doomed to spend life chasing a mirage, running ever harder and faster to win a prize that doesn't exist. No matter what she achieves in life, it will never be good enough.

And *that* is a ticking time bomb—one that is ready to detonate from unavoidable repeated defeat.

Of course, if you are a demanding perfectionist, who are you most likely to blame for your constant frustration and failure? That's right— yourself! You'll conclude you simply *are* a failure, and imagine God judging you as harshly as you judge yourself. And then you become consumed by your own self-diagnosed insufficiency.

But let's be clear: God doesn't share our illusions of human perfection. He knows better than anyone that His children are a work in progress and always will be. As Isaiah 40:6-8 tells us:

"All men are like grass,
and all their glory is like the flowers of the field.
The grass withers and the flowers fall,
because the breath of the LORD blows on them.
Surely the people are grass.
The grass withers and the flowers fall,
but the word of our God stands forever."

Oliver Wendell Holmes once said, "The secret of my success is that at an early age I discovered I was not God."[2]

3. Condemnation Carl

Perhaps you live at the opposite end of the spectrum, among people who need no evidence that they'll never be perfect. Maybe you are painfully aware of your seemingly innumerable flaws already. That's because barely a minute goes by when you aren't reminded of them by a relentless critic—your own thoughts. It is as if a two-bit judge has set up court in your mind, banging the gavel all day long and handing out harsh verdicts left and right.

- Lost your car keys? *Bang! You haven't got the brains of a turnip!*
- Burned the lasagna? *Bang! You are a sorry excuse for a cook!*
- Ate a donut in the break room at work? *Bang! You are a glutton!*
- Had a lustful thought? *Bang! You're a lukewarm hypocrite!*
- Tripped over the rug? *Bang! You're a klutz!*

The point is, we take a lot of abuse from inside our own heads—perhaps far more than we would if someone were following us around shouting insults.

And if you grew up with a critical parent, it may be especially difficult for you to tune out the voice of condemnation in your conscience.

This daily torrent of negativity can lead to self-blame, self-loathing, and self-combustion. Such all-consuming anger can't help but singe and scorch those nearby.

Freedom lies in asking yourself, *Is this the way God sees me? Are these labels He would attach to me: loser, moron, failure, rotten, hopeless?* The answer is obvious: Never! His thoughts toward His children are rooted in His unfathomable love. The proof is in His sacrifice for your sake. This is how the Bible describes His love for you:

> Anytime the voice of condemnation in your conscience berates you, answer it with scriptures describing God's view of you.

> *"This is how we know what love is: Jesus Christ*
> *laid down his life for us…This then is how we know that*
> *we belong to the truth, and how we set our hearts at rest in his*
> *presence whenever our hearts condemn us. For God is greater*
> *than our hearts, and he knows everything"*
> (JOHN 3:16,19-20).

Anytime the voice of condemnation in your conscience berates you, answer it with scriptures describing God's view of you. In the light of His Word, hateful "self-inflicted flames" will dissipate and a strong sense of self-worth will emerge. Let God's exclamations of love drown out those whispers of accusation and condemnation.

The Importance of Seeing Yourself Through God's Eyes

A few days after *Hope for the Heart* began airing on March 3, 1986, I received a letter dated March 11—a letter I still have to this day. I've kept it because it's the voice of countless others who struggle with low self-esteem and who have no idea of their value to the One who created them and died for them.

The letter was from a former high school beauty queen who grew up with a father who repeatedly told her, "You'll never amount to anything. You're nothing!" And a boyfriend who berated, "You dingbat… you miserable slut!" I remember hurting for her as I read the letter.

She was writing to say she felt like she had little value. Although she had become a Christian, the tapes from the past kept replaying in her mind.

In the providence of God, she married a man who was, in her own words, "a wonderful, fruit-bearing Christian." Then she wrote, "But he has the same problem." Ending her letter, she asked, "Could you help us?"

My first thought was, *I wish I could have a month with her, going over what it means to have her identity in Christ.* But that wasn't possible, so I immediately drafted a response reassuring her of Christ's presence in her life, of her being a new creation in Him, and of the transforming work being done by His Spirit living within her.

And then I spent what spare time I had over the next three years mining the Scriptures and studying what it means to have our *identity in Christ*—what He did for us through His death, burial, and resurrection; what He does for us day by day, month by month, year by year; and what He will do for us when we die.

My study culminated in writing a 31-day devotional, *Seeing Yourself Through God's Eyes.* The concept is simple. I thought, *If it takes 21 days to form a habit, 31 days should be long enough to form a new belief about how God views us.*

This is now our ministry's best-selling book and has been translated into over 20 languages. Why is it so vital we know our identity in Christ? If we don't know who we are, then we don't know our resources, we don't know our purpose, we don't know our inheritance, and we don't know our destiny. It is like living with amnesia. Just imagine not knowing who you are!

The Only Defense for Lies Is Truth

Not knowing who we are as Christians makes us easy prey for those who would fill our heads and hearts with lies about our value and worth. The only effective defense for lies is truth. If you know the truth, you will be set free from the lies. God loves you and established your worth by dying for you—now that is the truth!

4. No-Chance Charlie

Poor Charlie Brown. Right now, I can hear him sigh, "There is no heavier burden than great potential."

Poor, frustrated Charlie—there's no chance he will succeed. He is considered the classic example of "the great American unsuccess story" because he seems to fail at everything. No one expects him to win anything.

It's easy to see poor No-Chance Charlie standing on the pitcher's mound with his well-worn baseball cap and glove and a forlorn look in his eyes. Everyone who's read the *Peanuts* comic strip knows why this scene is so poignant—Charlie Brown has never won a game. His potential for greatness is still only an abstract possibility.

Maybe you know how that feels. Most of us begin life with great expectations of ourselves and the possibility of grand accomplishments that lie ahead. Potential is a powerful force that can indeed propel us to do great things.

But what happens when, like Charlie Brown, you don't achieve all you expected of yourself? When the very dreams that lifted you skyward become a burdensome weight pulling you down?

Many people—along with Charlie—get angry about that.

They don't have the wealth they wished for, the house they hoped for, the recognition they reached for, the love they longed for, the position they prayed for, the years they yearned for. Their teenagers are in trouble, their marriage is miserable, and their physical health is failing.

So…they blame themselves. *What's wrong with me? How could I have squandered my potential?*

The fact is, life happens! And you are to yield your will to God's will—to let your plans be based on His plans, which have nothing to do with earthly accumulations, accolades, and achievements.

When His purpose includes hardship and disappointment—as it so often does—the Bible tells us to consider ourselves fortunate because reward is coming: "Blessed is the man who perseveres under trial, because when he has stood the test, he will receive the crown of life that God has promised to those who love him."[3]

Although No-Chance Charlie is considered a loveable loser, there's nothing loveable in God's eyes about always losing. In fact, God intends for us to utilize the gifts and talents He has given us, and then leave the results to Him. He desires for us to offer our potential in humble service to Him, not use it as an excuse to beat ourselves with angry self-recrimination.

Your Value to God: He Paid the Ultimate Price for You

My brother's family was excited about moving into their new home. The carpet was down, the curtains were up, and the furniture was in. Only a few remaining items needed to be moved.

Then in the early morning just before the family was to take up residence, a fire broke out and their possessions went up in flames. Personal items, precious mementos, and priceless pictures—all were lost.

When I arrived at the house's charred frame, I had expected to see Ray and Nancy Ann. Instead, to my horror, I learned they had gone to the homes of two firemen who had lost their lives in the blaze. The cry of all our hearts was, *If only they could have been saved!*

Only against such a tragic backdrop can we fully grasp the significance of salvation.

Firefighters especially understand the gravity of life and death—of what it means to be saved.

Saved...who wouldn't want to be saved? Obviously, the word *saved* implies being saved *from something.* If only every person could comprehend what Scripture says they can be saved from: a present life of emptiness, the void of not being all that God created them to be, and a future destiny of fiery, eternal torment. Who wouldn't want to be rescued from such a destiny?

Recently I visited the fire station at Love Field Airport in Dallas to learn what is necessary to know in order to save lives. Jay (the husband of one of our ministry team) and his fellow firefighters shared numerous points that can be applied to spiritual salvation.

Specifically I asked, "What is most important for firefighters?" Immediately, a firefighter named Langley responded, "Safety training."

The truth is, we all need to know the safety plan—from God's point of view.

What Is God's Safety Plan?

God has a plan and purpose for us. He says, "I know the plans I have for you…plans to prosper you and not to harm you, plans to give you hope and a future."[4] Unfortunately, we have all chosen to go against God's perfect plan. This is what the Bible calls *sin.*

Firefighters say: "Our number one enemy is not fire, not heat, but toxic gases!"

Sin is the equivalent of toxic fumes—deadly. The word *sin* refers to anything outside of God's perfect will—both in attitude and action. Interestingly, The letter *i* is the middle letter of the word *sin*—as in, "I am going to do what I want to do when I want to do it." Sin is living independently of God—perhaps still as a "good person," yet independently of God.

Firefighters say: "Don't get separated from your partner."

The problem with sin is this: The Bible says sin *separates* us from God. "Your [sins] have separated you from your God."[5] The Bible also says we've all sinned and fallen short of God's standard of perfection.[6] Most people want to live in heaven, but that's impossible when our sin separates us from God.

Firefighters say: "Our greatest pain is failing to save someone's life."

The firefighters shared this scripture with me: "Be merciful to those who doubt; snatch others from the fire and save them; to others show mercy, mixed with fear—hating even the clothing stained by corrupted flesh" (Jude 22-23).

But here we all have another problem: The Bible says the payment for our sin is "death."[7] Not only physical death but spiritual death, which means eternal separation from God. Now, God doesn't want us separated from Him. He says His desire is that none should perish.[8] He even provided the solution—John 3:16 says, "God so loved the world that he gave his one and only Son, that whoever believes in him shall not perish but have eternal life."

Firefighters say: "Our proudest moment is saving someone's life."

Like a firefighter, Jesus is our Savior, our Rescuer. He can save anyone from the flames...and the fumes. That is the *why* of Jesus Christ. He came literally to die on the cross to pay the penalty you would oth-erwise have to pay for your sins.[9] (By the way, Jesus didn't die a victim...He said, "No one takes it [My life] from me," and "I give [my] life as a ransom for many.")[10]

> You can break free from *any* harmful habit, including a life dominated by inappropriate anger.

Jesus, who is God, came to earth and lived a perfect life. He chose to take our sins—past, present, and future—onto Himself at the cross. If we humble our hearts and ask Him to come into our lives as our Lord and Savior, giving Him control of our lives, He will forgive us of *all* our sins.

Firefighters say: "Don't stop a firefighter from doing his job."

When it comes to tearing down your wall or hacking through your door, the firefighter's way is right.

Realize that Jesus' death is the *only* sacrifice that could open up the way to eternal life. He said, "I am the way and the truth and the life. No one comes to the Father except through me."[11] God created us to spend eternity with Him. This is the eternal benefit that results from our decision to accept Christ's offer of salvation. And the amaz-ing fact is that this salvation is a *free* gift—but it is not cheap, for it cost Christ His life. Salvation is free because He paid for it.

Firefighters say: "Close the door on the fire."

When you are fleeing a room that is on fire, close the door behind you.

Jesus will empower you to close the door on your anger.[12] Simply put, it doesn't matter what negative patterns you've developed from the past. You can break free from *any* harmful habit, including a life dominated by inappropriate anger. And that's not all. When you are in heaven, you will be forever "saved" from the very presence of sin.

Firefighters say: "Put the wet on the red."

"Put the wet on the red" means aim the hose at the hottest part of the fire.

Jesus knows how to put living water on your red-hot anger. He said, "Whoever believes in me, as the Scripture has said, streams of living water will flow from within him."[13]

It is Jesus living through you who enables real and lasting victory over anger.

Firefighters say: "Stop, drop, and roll."

If you are on fire, don't run, because you will fan the flames. You are to stop, drop, and roll. God wants you to cease your self-effort and simply stop and accept His gift of salvation. If you believe Jesus Christ is the risen Son of God and are willing to receive as your personal Lord and Savior...

- *Stop!* Stop running (your own life). The Bible says, "Come back to your senses as you ought, and stop sinning; for there are some who are ignorant of God."[14]

- *Drop!* Bow your head; humble your heart. "Humble yourselves before the Lord, and he will lift you up."[15]

- *Roll!* Roll away the stone guarding your heart and give Jesus control of your life. He said, "I will give them an undivided heart and put a new spirit in them; I will remove from them their heart of stone and give them a heart of flesh."[16]

If you believe God is leading you to enter into a life-changing relationship with Him, you can do that right now by praying...

My Salvation Prayer

"God, I want a real relationship with You.
I admit that many times I've chosen to go my own way instead
of Your way.
Please forgive me for my sins.
Jesus, thank You for dying on the cross to pay the penalty for
my sins and for rising from the grave.
Come into my life to be my Lord and my Savior.

I give You control of my life.
Change me inside out and make me the person
You created me to be.
In Your holy name I pray. Amen."

If you sincerely prayed this prayer, look what Jesus says has happened to you: "Whoever hears my word and believes him who sent me has eternal life and will not be condemned; he has crossed over from death to life."[17]

God never intended for you to be consumed by the punishing flames of anger. Jesus paid the ultimate price so that you can be forever free, saved, healed, and whole. Only a God of love can give us a life of such beauty in exchange for our ashes.[18]

Backdraft: An Explosion in Waiting

Here is a word sure to command a firefighter's attention: *backdraft*.

Of all the conditions faced upon entering a burning building, a backdraft is among the most dangerous. It occurs when fire has consumed most of the oxygen in an enclosed room, depriving the flames of an essential ingredient. But that doesn't mean the heat dissipates.

On the contrary, the space fills with other types of gases that are extremely hot, just waiting for a fresh supply of oxygen to get things moving again. Open a door or break a window, and—*boom!*

Fortunately, there are warning indicators that can signal the possibility of a backdraft: colored smoke, excessive soot on the ground, and windows that appear brown or black from the outside.

Sometimes the dark conditions in the human heart are also just right to ignite explosive anger—painful conditions such as continual injustice with no resolution or blatant betrayal from one you trusted. There are always warning signs along the way.

Learn to read them—and heed them—and take evasive action long before you *blow*.

FUMING AT THE FATHER
How Assumptions About God Result in Bitter Anger

*"People ruin their lives by their own foolishness
and then are angry at the Lord"*
(PROVERBS 19:3 NLT).

THE NEWSPAPER HEADLINE caught my eye: "Man 'Angry at God' Drives Minivan into Church Sanctuary." The article began:

> A man who said he was angry at God drove a minivan through a Catholic church in Rancho Cordova, California, late on Saturday night. Harold David Zequeda, 36, drove a silver Ford Windstar through St. John Vianney Church. Witnesses said the driver pulled onto the church's front lawn and floored the gas pedal.[1]

The van broke through a set of locked steel doors and then a second set of heavy wooden doors. The vehicle then collided with a 100-pound communion table, propelling it across the sanctuary. The car traveled 50 yards across the church, slamming into solid-oak pews and stopping just short of a statue of Jesus.

Amazingly, no one was injured in the incident.

Why would this man do something so extreme? Here's a clue: Police were told that the driver dropped a photograph of several young children and was angry at God.

"It seemed like a cry for help," said the church's priest, Father Martin Moroney. "I just wish he had cried out in some other way."

Zequeda was charged with vandalizing a house of worship—a felony—and driving with a suspended license. He was held on a million dollars bail.

We might shake our heads at this man's behavior, but most of us can relate to his feelings. As I've spoken with thousands of people across the country, I've learned that many have felt anger toward God. Thankfully, most of us do not act on our feelings by smashing vehicles into churches. But our anger, if left unresolved, can be damaging in other ways.

When we feel hurt or victimized or unjustly treated, we naturally feel angry. We want to do something with those fiery feelings—we want to blame someone, we want recompense or revenge, and we want answers as to why this happened. If there is no one else to point fingers at, God serves as a convenient scapegoat, and we blame God for our anger.

God's Anger—a Mystery

Most of us would rather not think about God's wrath. Imagining God as angry can create contradictions in our view of Him that we are hard pressed to resolve. This is especially true when we view anger only as an evil, savage emotion associated with slammed doors, shattered hearts, and splintered relationships. If anger is always a bad thing, how can we comprehend a loving God who gets angry?

Our resistance to the idea is understandable. Anyone who has a truly intimate relationship with God knows the joy of basking in the warm glow of His fatherly affection and the peace of sleeping securely in His fatherly protection.

> The Bible teaches us that anger is every bit as much a part of God's character as mercy and forgiveness.

He invites us, like children, to abandon our cares and climb onto His lap, where we may rest in His reassuring arms. There, by His infinite grace, we are surrounded with love. It's hard to imagine that He is also a thundering, fiery God.

The Lord says to us, "I have loved you with an everlasting love; I have drawn you with loving-kindness" (Jeremiah 31:3).

This is all true, every word. God's love is everlasting; His faithfulness is never ending. The confusion arises when we stop there and believe that's all there is to God's nature. We could simply ignore the whole issue if it weren't for Scripture passages that describe God's anger at His people because of their stubborn and rebellious hearts:

- "Because they have forsaken me...my anger will burn against this place" (2 Kings 22:17).

- "When the LORD heard them, he was very angry...for they did not believe in God or trust in his deliverance" (Psalm 78:21-22).

There's no getting around it: The Bible teaches us that anger is every bit as much a part of God's character as mercy and forgiveness. At times, even Jesus got angry and didn't hesitate to openly—even heatedly—express it. So, what does all this mean?

Is it possible that in trying to eradicate anger entirely we have unintentionally declared war on a natural emotion that can be extremely useful, and even godly? Absolutely—the answer is yes.

Of course our God gets angry—*righteously* angry. Would we really want it any other way? Can you imagine God as One who loves evil, abuse, rape, and incest? We want our God to *hate* evil as a motivation to further the cause of justice. Consider this thought-provoking quote from the Greek philosopher Aristotle:

> It is easy to fly into a passion—anybody can do that. But to be angry with the right person and to the right extent and at the right time and with the right objective and in the right way— that is not easy, and it is not everyone who can do it.[2]

Are You Angry at God?

Problems, pain, and perplexities—you can't escape them. But do you blame God for the pain and heartache in your life? Have you pointed a condemning finger and pronounced judgment on Him because He has not stopped evil or suffering? Or because He has not stopped you from making bad decisions?

Periodically I am asked: "I'm angry at God for allowing bad people to cause so much pain. If God had the power to create the world, why doesn't He stop evil in the world?"

An understandable question! The plain and simple truth is God allows evil because He allows people to exercise free will. He did not create us to be robots with no choice or to do only what the Creator programmed.

God created us to be free-agent human beings who have choice over what we think, say, and do. We can't have it both ways—we can't have God allowing us freedom yet preventing us from doing wrong— that's not freedom.

If you have read the last book of the Bible, Revelation, you know God has appointed a time in the future when He will put an end to evil and suffering. The bad news is, until then, evil will always be in opposition to good and will seek to harm and destroy those who love God.

But the good news is God always turns evil around and uses it to accomplish His purposes. He did so in the life of Joseph, whose evil brothers sold him into slavery. Years later, when the frightened brothers came face-to-face with Joseph—now a prime minister of Egypt who had saved both the Egyptians and Hebrews from famine—he said, "Don't be afraid. Am I in the place of God? You intended to harm me, but God intended it for good to accomplish what is now being done, the saving of many lives" (Genesis 50:19-20).

An Old, Old Lesson

The Old Testament tells the familiar story of Job, one of the greatest tales of suffering ever recorded. The Lord highly honored Job before Satan, saying, "There is no one on earth like him; he is blameless and upright, a man who fears God and shuns evil" (Job 1:8).

Satan's response was to challenge God concerning the faithfulness of His choice servant when under pressure—*intense* pressure. Satan's supposition? If incredibly blessed and righteous Job were thrown into a fiery furnace of affliction, he would rise up and curse God. And so a supernatural showdown ensued.

God allowed Satan to take away Job's wealth, family, and health—everything except his very life (and his wife). Understandably, Job felt unjustly singled out for catastrophe and cried out, "God has turned me over to evil men and thrown me into the clutches of the wicked. All was well with me, but he shattered me; he seized me by the neck and crushed me. He has made me his target" (Job 16:11-12).

How many of us have thought something similar? *Everything was going just fine, but then God caused all these terrible things to happen.*

Job did not understand why God would allow such tragedy in his life. "Even today my complaint is bitter; his hand is heavy in spite of my groaning. If only I knew where to find him; if only I could go to his dwelling! I would state my case before him and fill my mouth with arguments."[3]

Although our pain and suffering probably will never approach what Job endured, we echo his questions and share his feelings. When painful events befall us, we feel confused, abandoned, and aggrieved. Where is God in the midst of our pain? Doesn't He care? Why doesn't He stop this? Hasn't He noticed our deep despair, the tear-stained slips in our anger bowl...*with His name on them?*

Can We Share Our Angry Feelings with God?

You might be wondering if it's okay to have pointed questions for God, or to feel anger toward Him. Many people I speak with preface their comments by saying, "I know I shouldn't feel mad at God, but..." It is my belief that anger toward God can be an understandable response when pain penetrates our lives.

We are in a relationship with the Father, and in every honest, authentic relationship there will be conflicts, tension, and misunderstandings. We may, indeed, find ourselves "fuming at the Father." God can handle our anger. He doesn't turn a deaf ear to our "Why" questions, nor does He distance Himself from our heartache and pain.

Misconceptions and Misplaced Anger

However—and this is a *big* however—I also believe anger toward God is *misplaced anger*. That is true each and every time—no exceptions. The Bible tells us over and over that God is just, holy, loving, perfect, and compassionate. He *always* has our best interests in mind, He *always* wants what is good for us, and He *always* grieves along with us when we hurt. So when we feel anger toward God, it is because we have forgotten or misunderstood His character.

As I've listened to many struggling people tell me about their anger toward God, I've noticed their feelings typically revolve around a cluster of questions:

> Why is God silent?
>
> Why doesn't He answer my prayer?
>
> Why didn't God intervene and help me?
>
> Why do bad people get away with doing evil? Where's the justice?
>
> Why doesn't God protect and bless believers more than unbelievers?

When people ask these questions, it's because they feel neglected, slighted, or even cheated by God. They think He broke His part of the "bargain."

"God, I'll do my part, and You do Yours."

That's the way it works, they think, because the Bible is filled with promises for protection, prosperity, guidance, and deliverance. What happens, then, when God doesn't *seem* to be there or doesn't *appear* to be keeping His promises? They feel disappointed, deflated, disillusioned.

Our heart tells us one thing (God doesn't care about me), while our mind says the opposite (God cares deeply about me). We know intellectually the Lord is faithful and just, but our emotions may lead us to believe He looks the other way when we experience hurt, injustice, fear, and frustration, and He simply leaves us to fend for ourselves.

It's vital to realize that our anger toward God will not bring us any closer to finding peace, overcoming pain, or resolving problems. So, what can we do? Start with the following:

Pour Your Heart Out to Him

Denise called me on *Hope in the Night*, saying she was angry at God for the loss of her beloved 12-year-old daughter, Madeline, who had died of cancer the year before.

Although Denise had enjoyed a close walk with the Lord for years, after her daughter's death she had to force herself, with every ounce of willpower, to attend church, read the Bible, and pray.

I asked if she had told the Lord why she was angry and shared her feelings with Him.

"Oh, no! I couldn't do that! I ask for His strength and pray for the health of my other children, but that's about it."

"Why wouldn't you share your true feelings with Him?"

"I guess I've always been taught to be respectful and reverent when talking with God," she said. "He's perfect and holy...and that's how I'm supposed to be, too."

This sincere woman got part of the equation right—we *are* to approach God with respect. But we are also encouraged to be completely open with Him, even when our sentiments are not all sweet and happy. God is an excellent listener, and He invites us to pour out our hearts to Him.

Like Denise, some people are hesitant, fearing lightning bolts from heaven if they speak openly—much less *angrily*—to God. We can, however, be direct without being disrespectful, blunt without being blasphemous. We can admit we have an anger bowl without hurling it toward heaven.

Above all, God desires a *relationship* with His children, and a genuine relationship is impossible without honest communication.

Get Clear About God's Character

To get to the heart of Denise's heartache, I knew my conversation with her would need to delve directly into the character of God. It is our thoughts about God's character that influence everything we think and do.

June: "Sometimes when we encounter trials, a voice down deep whispers:

'Maybe God isn't as trustworthy as He says. Surely if God loved me, He wouldn't have let this happen.' Have you ever heard that voice?"

Denise: "There hasn't been a day since Madeline died that I *don't* hear that voice. I hate it...I try to ignore it...but it's there."

June: "I understand, Denise. And, more important, God understands, too. In the Garden of Eden, the serpent said to Eve, 'Did God really say, "You must not eat from any tree in the garden?"' [4] Eve responded that God said she and Adam could eat from any tree except for the one in the middle of garden. If they ate of that tree, they would die.

"But the serpent, who is Satan's instrument, scoffed and said, 'You will not surely die...For God knows that when you eat of it your eyes will be opened, and you will be like God, knowing good and evil.' [5] Satan said, in essence, that God was lying; He was trying to trick you; He can't be trusted. And the rest, as they say, is history.

"Could Satan be using this tragedy to drive a wedge between you and your heavenly Father?"

Denise: "I see what you're saying. It's like Satan is whispering lies to harden my heart."

June: "Exactly! He is crafty enough to prey upon us when we're most vulnerable. Even so, we can't pin everything on Satan. Often our own doubts, fragile faith, and wounded emotions can cause us to wonder if Christianity is all it's cracked up to be, or if God is really who He claims to be. That's when we must remind ourselves of what the Bible says about God. We need to solidify what we know about His character. In fact, let's take a moment and do that right now. Tell me, Denise: What are some aspects of God's character that mean the most to you?"

Denise: "Probably the most important thing to me is His love."

June: "Excellent! He is loving! Romans 8:38-39 says, 'I am convinced that neither death nor life, neither angels nor demons, neither the present nor the future, nor any powers, neither height nor depth, nor anything else in all creation, will be able to separate us from the love of God that is in Christ Jesus our Lord.' What else do we know about God's character?"

> When we truly understand who God is…it will be impossible to stay angry at Him for long.

Denise: "I know He doesn't change. The summer before Madeline died, she and I memorized a scripture together: 'Every good and perfect gift is from above, coming down from the Father of the heavenly lights, who does not change like shifting shadows.'" [6]

June: "That's beautiful. Yes! God doesn't change. His character is the same yesterday, today, and forever. What a comfort it is to know that, unlike us, God's perfect character is perfectly constant."

Denise and I continued recounting the virtues of God's character—how, in addition to being loving and unchangeable, the Bible assures us He is also…

> *Eager to forgive*—"If we confess our sins, he is faithful and just and will forgive us our sins and purify us from all unrighteousness." [7]
>
> *Merciful*—"The LORD is gracious and righteous, our God is full of compassion." [8]
>
> *Sovereign*—"He does as he pleases with the powers of heaven and the peoples of the earth. No one can hold back his hand." [9]

As we considered the wonderful attributes of God, I shared my conviction that when we truly understand who God is—and realize His impeccable character can never be compromised—it will be impossible to stay angry at Him for long.

Before hanging up the phone that night, I prayed with Denise, asking God to replace her anger with reassurance of God's perfect love and plan for her life. I also sent her our resource titled *Evil and Suffering...Why?*

I had no reason to believe I'd ever hear from Denise again, but I was wrong. The following year, I received this touching note:

> Dear June,
>
> While figuratively pounding my fists against my heavenly Father's chest and becoming exhausted to the point of surrender, I discovered an incredible aspect of His unfailing love. Standing there emotionally spent and still—before Him—I became aware of His heart...and despite my misdirected anger toward Him, eventually I began to feel His gentle strength... and the security of His tender embrace.
>
> Thank you, June, for helping me see, finally, that God was never to blame for Madeline's death, and that, no matter what happens from here on in my life, His character is my assurance that I can always trust Him.

As for me, it was not hard to imagine the Father gently cleansing every last bit of ashen residue and preparing this special woman to share her newfound faith with other grieving mothers in the months and years to come.

Trust the Judge to Bring Justice

As we've seen, one of the biggest causes of anger can be summed up in a word: injustice. We want to know the wrongdoer will be punished, the criminal will be sent to prison, and the bully will get his comeuppance. So we cry out to God, "You're not going to let him get away with that, are You?" We get mad at the Lord when our offender seems to get off scot-free.

I understand this struggle very well because a desire for justice seems to be hard-wired into my DNA. For many years of my Christian life, I preferred the Old Testament version of justice ("an eye for an eye, a tooth for a tooth") to the New Testament version, in which Jesus seemed to forgive sinners "too easily." Where was the justice?

Then one day it was as if the Spirit spoke to me: "You too are living in the era of Jesus' grace and mercy." It dawned on me that I am the recipient of God's compassion, and He has not dealt with me in the way I deserve. I wouldn't want to incur His wrath and judgment, so was it right to wish that upon others?

But there's more. God *is* just, and He has promised to mete out justice in His time, in His way. Here's what He has told us:

- "It is mine to avenge; I will repay. In due time their foot will slip; their day of disaster is near and their doom rushes upon them" (Deuteronomy 32:35).

- "Will not God bring about justice for his chosen ones, who cry out to him day and night? Will he keep putting them off? I tell you, he will see that they get justice, and quickly" (Luke 18:7-8).

Jesus provides an example that empowers us to trust God with matters of justice: "When they hurled their insults at him, he did not retaliate; when he suffered, he made no threats. Instead, he entrusted himself to him who judges justly" (1 Peter 2:23). It's up to God, the divine Judge, to ensure justice—and He will. It's up to us to trust Him to deliver on His promises.

Recognize Pain Has a Purpose

Anger and pain go hand in hand. Some pain is a mere twinge, some is like a sledgehammer to the skull. Some is short-lived, some seems to last forever.

Over the years, I have counseled many pain-filled people. Most of them have asked the same anguished question: "Why did God let this happen?" We still think pain is random and pointless. We beg God to take it away—*right now.* That's okay. Most people are surprised and encouraged when I remind them Jesus did the very same thing.

Just after the Last Supper, the Lord went with His disciples to pray in the Garden of Gethsemane. Although His followers were still pretty clueless about what was coming, Jesus knew He would soon be arrested and put on trial. It didn't matter that He was entirely blameless; it didn't matter that He had been set up. He foresaw the pain, humiliation, and horrible death that awaited Him, and He was gripped with anguish.

Despite being the Son of God and having all the resources of heaven and earth available to Him, the prospect of His imminent crucifixion was almost more than even He could bear. He told Peter and the others, "'My soul is very sorrowful, even to death. Remain here and watch.' And going a little farther, he fell on the ground and prayed that, if it were possible, the hour might pass from him...'Abba, Father, all things are possible for you. Remove this cup from me.'"[10]

That sounds like something you and I might pray: "Make this problem go away; get rid of this illness; take these struggles off my shoulders." Yet Jesus knew something that escapes most of us when we are crippled by pain and angry because of it: He understood His suffering had a purpose. As much as He wished to be spared, He saw the incomparable good God would bring out of the incomprehensible injustice of His death. So even though His sweat fell to the ground like great drops of blood, He earnestly prayed, "Yet, not my will, but yours be done."[11]

If you are in pain, the right question to ask isn't "Why?" but "How?" "How, Lord? How are You going to use this tough situation to shape my character and deepen my faith? How are You going to accomplish Your will through this ordeal?"

Then, follow in Jesus' steps and pray for God's will to be done, knowing that "in all things God works for the good of those who love him, who have been called according to his purpose."[12] Did you catch that? *All* things.

Every Right to Be Angry

As she lay on an English hillside, Helen Roseveare pledged herself a living sacrifice to the work and call of God. It was 1947 and her spirit had been ignited by the moving testimonies of several missionaries—testimonies that fanned the flame within her to take the gospel to the farthest corners of the world.

For Helen, her heart's desire was, as she put it, "single-eyed for His will and for His glory."[13] Yet even in that monumental moment of surrender, she sensed her resolve might not always be so firm. She knew sacrifice to God's will could be accompanied by great struggle.

"Please go on working in me until I really am transformed into the image of Your Son," she pleaded with God. "Today I mean this, with every ounce of my being, but when You start doing it, and the stirring hurts, and I feel I can't take anymore, maybe I'll cry out to You to stop. Please when that happens, don't listen to my cry to stop."[14]

Mission Field Turned Battlefield

Helen, a physician, heeded God's call and became a medical missionary to the Congo. She and her team established a 250-bed hospital and a training school, with Helen's responsibilities including construction oversight of the school, the development of curriculum, and the training of students. It was not uncommon for her to treat 100 patients a day. She herself contracted several serious illnesses, including malaria. Fatigue was a constant battle—the needs were overwhelming, the conditions so oppressive, and the hours so long.

During the 12-year period Helen served in the Congo, she leaned hard on the solid truth of her mission's motto, claiming it amidst exhaustion, loneliness, divisions within the African church, and rifts among fellow missionaries: "If Jesus Christ be God and died for me, then no sacrifice can be too great for me to make for Him."[15]

But late in 1964, Helen's commitment to those words was put to the ultimate test.

"Fear was in the very air we breathed," Helen recalled, citing a civil uprising by Simba guerillas that reached a climax of tyranny and terror.[16]

Mission: Horror and Humiliation

It began in August when savage violence and ruin decimated the small country. Helen and her fellow missionaries were separated from the Africans they served and placed under guard. "Mama Luka," as she was lovingly addressed, in reference to Luke the doctor in the Bible, was forceably removed from her mission and taken to a place where she witnessed nuns being mercilessly beaten and humiliated. Helen never knew whether she might be next.

During a ten-week siege, thousands of black natives were butchered. As a result, the whites became enemies of the blacks, and 27 missionaries were slaughtered.

Helen was driven to a house in the jungle, which could be likened to a hell on earth. "Food was scarce; water almost unprocurable... Wickedness surrounded us on all sides; it seemed inevitable that we should be killed," Helen said.[17]

Still, her heart sensed an amazing peace because of a divine realization: "I was being highly privileged to be identified with Christ in a new way, in the way of Calvary."[18] And Helen would walk in the path of suffering, a grievous sojourn signified by great sacrifice.

One horrific night, Helen was thrown to the ground and beaten, kicked, and then raped.[19] The horror she saw inflicted on the nuns now finally happened to her—her teeth were broken, her ribs bruised, her mouth bloodied, her nose gashed, and her body violated.

She couldn't understand why all this was happening to her. She literally wanted to die because she knew the brutality that fellow missionaries had experienced. Yet God quietly spoke to her: "Could You thank Me for trusting you with this experience even if I never tell you why?"

"God, I thank You. I haven't a clue why or how, but I'll take it from You that You know what You're doing, that You can never make a mistake. You cannot fail. Your promise must stand true. So, God I'll thank You for trusting me with this even though I haven't any idea how anybody could ever be helped by it."

Soon afterward, Helen was given the death sentence along with the other missionaries. As they were herded away in a group, she had to lean against others to walk because her body had been so brutalized.

When the leader of the rebels spotted her, he asked, "Who made you in that mess?"

She angrily shouted back, "One of your lot!"

The rebel leader shouted, "You're a liar!"

"I'll name him for you," she bravely replied.

So the rebel leader called a people's court. However, before the tribesmen assembled, he instructed them to yell, "She's a liar...she's a liar!" after Helen's testimony.

The time came for Helen's trial. She truthfully told the crowd the details of the assault. Then something miraculous happened. When she finished, 800 men began weeping. They recognized this was their doctor speaking. She had birthed their babies, cared for their cuts, and nursed their wounds. Yet to their deep dismay, one of their own had raped her. Their overpowering repentance triggered a spiritual breakthrough never experienced before among them. Hundreds of hearts were touched and people saved because ultimately, they were so grieved by her suffering.

"Will You Thank Me, Even If I Never Tell You Why?"

Later, back in her native country of England, Helen became a frequent guest speaker. One evening she felt led by the Lord to refer to her rape, which she rarely did. After her talk, everyone left except for two girls. One girl asked, "Can you speak to my sister? Five weeks ago she was raped. For five weeks she has not spoken a word to anyone."

The other girl ran toward Helen, sobbing uncontrollably, and flung her arms around her. For three hours this young victim of rape talked nonstop about the incident. Eventually, the two who had shared the same experience parted ways—both with peace in their hearts. What made the difference? The young girl said, "No one had ever told me that I could thank God even if He didn't tell me why."

Helen was once again reminded that her life—committed to the Lord as a living sacrifice and shaped by extreme hardship—was firmly in the Master's hands. He used her faith, her wounds, and her testimony in powerful service to others and Himself.

But that doesn't mean there weren't moments of weakness, moments of questioning God, especially about that horrific night of assault and pain. Helen has written movingly of how abandoned she felt the night of her rape and beating. Like the Lord Jesus on the cross, she cried out,

> "My God, my God, why have you forsaken me?" His answer to her was a removal of the fear as if it had been rinsed out of her—and a strong sense of his arms around her, holding her, and comforting her. She felt as if God were saying, "When I called you to myself, I called you to the fellowship of my suffering (Philippians 3). They are not attacking you. They are attacking me. I'm just using your body to show myself to the people around you."[20]

Helen could have been angry at God for all she suffered—and who would have blamed her? But she chose to place her life—the highs and the lows—in the context of God's sovereign will and to trust Him in all circumstances.

In fact, Helen even returned to the Congo for another six years of missionary service. Her testimony has inspired thousands of believers to live a life of Christlike service, surrender, and holiness. Her life reflects the heart of 1 Peter 4:19:

> *"Those who suffer according to God's will should commit themselves to their faithful Creator and continue to do good."*

How could Helen have the mind-set to endure a massacre, and still have a godly witness? She shared about her surrendered life and giving God absolute control. "If I will allow God all rights to my life, to stir me until He sees I am ready to be applied, I can trust God then, in His perfect timing, to know where He wants to apply me. God does not need to tell us ahead of time. Until we are stirred, we are not ready for application."[21]

Helen's life serves as a testimony to each of us that even the most agonizing hardship can be used for God's glory. Now, would *you* be willing to trust Him even if He never tells you why?

A poem given to Helen Roseveare as a teenager gave her God's perspective on the unjust trials she would face throughout her life. A part of that poem reads:

> Not till the loom is silent and the shuttles cease to fly
> Shall God unroll the canvas and explain the reason why.
> The dark threads are as needful in the weaver's skillful hand
> As the threads of gold and silver in the pattern He has planned.[22]

Arson: Deliberate Destruction

In every part of the world, arson is considered a very serious crime. To start a dangerous fire on purpose puts people and property in harm's way. If the criminal is arrested, conviction is usually followed by a lengthy prison sentence.

There are many motives for committing arson:

- *Profit*—to collect an insurance payment for the damaged or destroyed property

- *Punishment*—to get even with someone for another offense

- *Pleasure*—to entertain or perversely satisfy

- *Protection*—to cover or destroy evidence of another crime

People who refuse to extinguish their uncontrolled anger are like arsonists in many respects. They kindle fires in relationships without regard for the consequences. Whether you or someone you know is misusing anger, you can stop sabotaging relationships by discovering *why*—why you are misusing fire in the first place.

There are a multitude of sins and painful wounds hidden beneath purposeful, pain-inflicting anger. Uncover the truth...then surrender it to God.

Part Three

FIGHTING FIRE WITH FIRE:

How to Use Anger in Healthy Ways

Smoldering Embers
How to Extinguish the Pain of Unresolved Anger

*"A quarrelsome person starts fights
as easily as hot embers light charcoal or fire lights wood"*
(Proverbs 26:21 NLT).

Last winter, at the end of a long, cold night, I stabbed a metal poker into a pile of ashen coals in my fireplace, only to discover a few briquettes still aglow. Sparkling red shimmers sprayed up from beneath a coat of gray ash, telling me the fire in my hearth was not yet extinguished.

As soft sparks cascaded back toward the ash, my thoughts rewound to the fireworks displays of my youth. As a child, my siblings and I used to spend all our Fourth of July holidays in Idabel, Oklahoma, with my cousins—and an array of bottle rockets, cherry bombs, and other blasting propellants.

When launching a Roman candle, shaped like an eight-inch cylinder, we had been instructed to hold it in the middle and out to the side, angle it upward, light it, and shake it. Yet, after someone lit the fuse on a Roman candle held by my ten-year-old sister Helen, instead of holding it out to the side at a safe distance, she kept it too close to her body, and it backfired! We all ran quickly to help her, but the damage had already been done: Helen was left with a severe burn under her right arm.

Mishandling an exploding firecracker can have dangerous—even disastrous—results. Lingering, unresolved anger can create similar havoc. It can be so deeply submerged in our souls we may no longer feel the heat—but that doesn't mean the fire isn't still smoldering. Just when we think all is well, our anger explodes back on us...and those we love. Unfortunately, that's exactly what happened to Vivian.

Heat Still Bellowing from the Bakery

I first met Vivian one evening after I'd given a seminar on how to resolve persistent anger. She had the panicked look of a woman whose emotional thermostat was set too high.

"I came tonight because I thought I might get some insight into my husband's behavior when he loses his temper," she told me. "But something unexpected happened—I saw *myself* in what you said."

Vivian's "Aha moment" came when I spoke of unresolved anger hanging around for so long we've stopped even being consciously aware of its presence. The fireworks no longer light up the sky, so we think they've burned themselves out. But that's not the case. The emotional pyrotechnics have simply headed underground, boring deep into unguarded areas of our hearts, minds, and emotions, where they continue to simmer and smolder indefinitely.

Such anger still singes us—and others—but in subtle ways that are difficult to trace to the original source.

"I knew you were talking about me," continued Vivian, a look of anguish on her face. "After all these years, my anger suddenly surfaced. Why haven't I seen it before now?"

I began to understand as she told more of her story. As a little girl, Vivian loved to bake breads and pastries. By the time she was in high school, she frequently sent her mother out of the kitchen and prepared desserts for the family by herself. She knew she had found her calling and dreamed of one day running her own bakery.

Vivian's sister, Lorraine, was her polar opposite. While Vivian was creative and spontaneous, Lorraine was serious and sensible. Everyone said she had a head for business.

It was as if God had provided a perfect partnership for success all in one family: Vivian could work the kitchen, and Lorraine could manage the business.

The sisters made a pact to open a neighborhood bakery as soon as Lorraine finished college. But after only two years, Lorraine grew impatient. She told everyone the business courses she took were boring, her professors were fossils stuck in the past, and her classmates were all clueless, bleating sheep.

She felt well-enough equipped to dive into the real world of commerce and get on with it. Lorraine dropped out of school and, through family connections, the sisters found a financial backer for their enterprise. Six months later, they opened a stylish bakery and breakfast bistro in a good location.

"My dream had come true," Vivian recalled. "I pinched myself every time I saw a line of customers stretching all the way to the door."

A Recipe for Financial Disaster

But after a few months, the dream abruptly exploded like the grand finale at a fireworks display. While Vivian held up her end of the bargain—creating delicious food attracting loyal customers—Lorraine was quietly making a mess of hers. She was in way over her head and drowning in the details of the day-to-day financial management of a burgeoning business. Rather than seeking help, she grew even more rash and reckless in her decisions.

"By the time I knew there was a problem," Vivian said, "our operating capital was gone and we were deeply in debt to our suppliers. In the end, we couldn't pay the bills or the staff, and bankruptcy was our only option."

"How awful that must have been for you," I commented.

"I was devastated," Vivian replied. "It was like watching a loved one die."

"And I imagine you were pretty angry at Lorraine for what she had done," I said.

"Absolutely," she responded. "But there wasn't really time to dwell on it or address it."

That's because, as painful as the bankruptcy was for Vivian, it hit Lorraine like a blazing fireball. Realizing it was her fault the business failed, she turned to alcohol and sank into a deep depression lasting several years.

Vivian, alarmed by her sister's emotional frailty, worked almost single-handedly to repay their remaining debts. Even after Lorraine's condition improved, Vivian never mentioned the catastrophe for fear of being "too judgmental" and pushing her sister back into self-destructive behavior.

> The road to forgiveness leads *through* our anger, not around it, as if it had never existed in the first place.

"I felt that's what God wanted of me—to just forgive and forget," she said through her tears. "I was so hurt and so mad, but I did what I had to do to force my anger to go away." Or so she thought. What caused Vivian pain in the present was the dawning realization that her past anger had never really gone away at all. It was as if she had a bowl full of anger that continued to swirl and swirl and swirl.

That affected many of Vivian's subsequent relationships—with her husband, whom she had difficulty trusting; with her children, who often accused her of being hypercritical; and with all the other bosses and business partners.

Vivian had genuinely tried to do the right thing by letting bygones be bygones. But in the process, she forgot an inescapable truth: The road to forgiveness leads *through* our anger, not around it, as if it had never existed in the first place.

Seven Steps to Peace and Freedom

Twenty years had since gone by, and Vivian feared it was too late to overcome her anger and repair the widespread damage it had caused. She worried it had become an inseparable, incurable part of her personality.

Fortunately, she was wrong. I reminded her nothing is beyond God's ability or willingness to heal. I told her God could help her begin anew. Listen to what the Lord says in Isaiah 43:18-19:

"Forget the former things; do not dwell on the past.
See, I am doing a new thing! Now it springs up; do you not perceive it?
I am making a way in the desert and streams in the wasteland."

I told Vivian, "I know it is overwhelming to rummage through past pain. But time is no barrier at all to God's capacity to repair what is broken."

So as long as we are willing to place our trust in God—and do everything we can to help extinguish the smoldering coals—we can resolve our anger, no matter how old it is. Here's how:

1. Realize You Are Still Angry

You can't possibly hope to resolve your anger until you acknowledge it exists. That sounds simple, but for many of us the hardest words we ever say are, "I feel hurt, frustrated, and angry."

It can be difficult enough to express how we feel in the heat of the moment, when there is still an obvious link between cause and effect. So how much more difficult does it become when the original source of our anger is years or even decades old?

Oh, get over it! we say to ourselves accusingly. *Are you still steamed about that? Just put it behind you and move on.*

Contrary to the popular cliché, time does not heal all wounds. It may appear to turn down the temperature, but our anger still burns. The "sleeping dogs" you've been taught to let lie aren't really asleep and are not better left alone. Even the most long-ago unresolved anger will manifest itself in your life—through bitterness, chronic depression, lack of trust, and a defensive, hostile stance in your relationships.

Warning Signs of Hidden Anger

Do you recognize any of these warning signs of hidden anger in your life?

- Do you feel uncomfortable in someone's company, even years later?

- Do you find it difficult to sincerely pray for someone?
- Do you have bitter jealousy of another's successes?
- Do you hope for the worst, instead of the best, for someone?
- Do you secretly find pleasure in someone's defeats?
- Do you take part in critical gossip about someone (or at least do nothing to stop it)?
- Do you become irritable over trifles?
- Do you smile on the outside while you hurt or rage on the inside?
- Do you find your identity and worth in excessive work?
- Do you deny ever being impatient or frustrated?
- Do you have to have the last word?
- Do those close to you say you blame others?
- Do you feel emotionally flat?
- Do you have a loss of interest in life?
- Do you experience physical manifestations—a queasy feeling, clenched stomach muscles, racing heart, and so on—when you think about a particular person or situation?

If any of these describe how you feel, chances are your anger is not as resolved as you had hoped. Don't despair. God knows exactly where you've hidden your pain and rage. Ask Him to pull back the covering of time and show it to you as well—then own up to it. Admit you are still angry so the healing process can finally begin.

2. Reckon with Your Anger Pie

Have you ever systematically considered *how much* anger you are holding inside your heart and *toward whom* you feel angry? If not, I invite you to create your very own Anger Pie. (No baking required!) I've found it to be an amazingly effective tool for surfacing buried anger. Here's how to make it:

- Make a list of people toward whom you have anger (from childhood to present).

- Draw a circle—pie-shaped—that represents all of the anger in your life.

- Divide your pie into different-size wedges. Base the size of each wedge on the size of your anger toward each person on your list.

I've provided a sample Anger Pie for you,[1] using general categories. As you process your anger constructively, you will see the size of your slices shrinking. That's a good indication you are working effectively through your anger issues.

The Anger Pie

3. Revisit Your Reasons for Being Angry

Imagine experiencing two months of terrible stomach pains and severe headaches. Your energy is depleted most of the time, as if your batteries were being drained by an unseen short in your circuitry.

Initially you tell yourself, *That's just life.* But finally, you concede the symptoms are not normal. You're forced to admit something is wrong.

Of course, realizing you are sick is a huge step on the road to wellness. But would you stop there? Most likely, you would want to know the answer to the obvious: Why am I feeling so sick? And you would want to seek a doctor's help because you understand finding a *cure* for your ailment requires knowing the *cause*.

The same is true of anger that is plaguing you. Once you have admitted you're still angry at someone for a past offense, it is necessary to sift through the debris like an arson investigator. Which of the four causes inflames you: hurt, injustice, fear, or frustration...or a combination of two or more of those causes?

What are the triggers that ignite your "smoldering embers"? What were the combustible ingredients? What are the traces of flammable residue? What caused the sparks to fly? In short, why did this thing explode?

This is dangerous work. After all, poking around in hot embers can stoke the flames of fury. Chances are, that's why you've ignored the suppressed heat for so long. It's safer to "stuff it" than expose it to a fresh supply of emotional oxygen and risk a raging inferno that would consume your relationships. But if you hope to put out the fire once and for all, it is a necessary risk.

For one thing, time can act like a magnifying glass by making painful offenses seem larger when we look back at them from a distance. Our wounds can seem more grievous and our enemies can seem more evil. By revisiting "the scene of the crime" with an open mind and a heart bent on healing, we can remove the distortion and see things in proper perspective.

What's more, human conflict is rarely a clear-cut battle between "the good guys" and "the bad guys." Nearly every time I look back on an angry skirmish with someone in my life, I see things *I* did to fan the flames or at least keep things boiling longer than necessary.

Vivian discovered that very thing in herself when she examined her anger toward her sister. She had to admit there were plenty of warning signs showing Lorraine was in trouble, if only she'd been willing to notice them.

"Every day she grew more sullen and withdrawn," Vivian recalled. "But I was happier than I'd ever been and didn't want to be pulled down by her gloominess. I never once asked if she was okay or needed help."

Gaining an honest and accurate perspective of what really happened—and taking responsibility for the part we may have played—begins to douse the smoldering coals and prepares us for the next step toward resolving our anger.

4. Release Those Who Have Wronged You

If we wish to be free of past anger, there is a key question we must ask ourselves: What have I not yet forgiven?

Anger doesn't materialize out of thin air. This strong emotion naturally arises when someone's actions cause us to feel hurt, afraid, frustrated, or offended at an injustice. Anger can be a constructive response to anything that threatens us. But it quickly becomes *destructive* when we hang on to our fears and wounds and refuse to forgive those who cause them.

Why should I forgive? we think. *I'm the one who was wronged!*

Yet as hard as it is, God has commanded us to forgive each other and even made it a condition for our own forgiveness. We can't expect to receive a benefit from Him that we have stubbornly withheld from another. As Jesus told His disciples: "When you stand praying, if you hold anything against anyone, forgive him, so that your Father in heaven may forgive you your sins" (Mark 11:25).

> If we refuse to forgive, we are taking on the role of being a higher judge than God Himself!

Here are a number of helpful thoughts concerning forgiveness: First, *forgiving* someone is not the same as *condoning* offensive behavior.

It is unfortunate many of us have the habit of saying, "It's okay" when what we mean is, "I forgive you." Saying that an offense is okay mistakenly implies it is no big deal. But it's never okay when you've been unjustly hurt by someone.

Some people sincerely but mistakenly assume that if they forgive an offender, they must re-establish the relationship. Unfortunately, this mistaken assumption has kept countless victims from forgiving their victimizers. Very simply, forgiveness is not the same as reconciliation.

- Forgiveness can take place with only one person; reconciliation requires at least two people.

- Forgiveness is a free gift to the one who has broken trust; reconciliation is a restored relationship based on restored trust.

- Forgiveness is extended even if it is never, ever earned; reconciliation is offered to the offender because it has been earned.

- Forgiveness is unconditional, regardless of a lack of repentance; reconciliation is conditional based on repentance.

Many other misconceptions abound about forgiveness. Often people won't forgive because they don't "feel like it." But forgiveness is not a feeling, it is a choice—an act of the will. Also:

- *Forgiveness is not* based on what is fair. It was not fair for Jesus to hang on the cross, but He did so that we could be forgiven.

- *Forgiveness is not* being a weak martyr. It is being strong enough to be Christlike.

- *Forgiveness is not* letting the guilty off the hook. It is moving the guilty from your hook to God's hook.

Why Should We Forgive?

We are called to forgive others because that is precisely what Jesus came on earth to do for us. He died on the cross so that our sins would be forgiven. Likewise, He tells us to forgive our offenders. Therefore, if we refuse to forgive, we are taking on the role of being a higher judge than God Himself!

Second, as author William Walton vividly described it, "To carry a grudge is like being stung to death by one bee."[2] What a picture! In other words, just one grudge can eventually debilitate us.

Angry unforgiveness harms you just as much, if not more, than the one who hurt you. It binds you to your pain and perpetuates your anger. To forgive by releasing your resentment is to free *yourself* as well.

How Do You Actually Forgive Someone?

Make a list of all your offender's offenses—they are your "rocks" of resentment. Imagine a meat hook around your neck. Then imagine a burlap bag filled with your heavy rocks of resentment hanging from the hook. Everywhere you go, this heavy burden weighs you down. Ask yourself: *Do I really want to carry all this pain the rest of my life?* (Obviously not!)

Are you willing to take your offender and the offenses off your emotional hook and put this person and all the pain onto God's hook? The Lord knows how to handle it all, in His time and in His way. Deuteronomy 32:35 says, "It is mine to avenge; I will repay."

You can release your resentment right now by sincerely praying this prayer:

Forgiveness Prayer

"Heavenly Father, thank You for caring about how much my heart has been hurt. You know the pain I have felt because of (list every offense). Right now I release all that pain into Your hands. Thank You, for Jesus' dying on the cross for me and extending Your forgiveness to me. As an act of my will, I choose to forgive (name). Right now, I move (name) off my emotional hook to Your hook. I refuse all thoughts of revenge. I trust that in Your time and in Your way You will deal with my offender as You see fit. And Lord, thank You for giving me Jesus' power to forgive so that I can be set free. In Jesus' holy name I pray. Amen."

5. Replace Your Anger with Trust in God's Love

Anger is a defense mechanism. It is designed to help you avoid further pain when you've experienced something traumatic. When you stay mad for a long period of time, you can become attached—and accustomed—to your habitual anger.

That's why, when you begin to let go, it's important to fill the emotional void with a new source of comfort and security: the assurance of God's unfailing protection in your life. Whereas you once defended yourself behind a firewall of hostility, you must learn to take shelter in the invincible fortress of God's love. Not that you won't still experience attacks—fireballs will still be hurled. But never forget that God's shielding grace surrounds you.

The only fireballs that will land in your life are those God allows to get through. In that case, they are used for *your good* and *His purposes.*

Does this sound familiar? Do you have the feeling you are not the first to walk this path? If you've read the Psalms, the answer is surely yes. On page after page, David and other psalmists poured out their heart-wrenching feelings of hurt, fear, frustration, and injustice—only to return time and time again to the familiar touchstone of God's infinite goodness and might. As David wrote:

> *"My salvation and my honor depend on God;*
> *He is my mighty rock, my refuge...*
> *One thing God has spoken, two things have I heard;*
> *that you, O God, are strong,*
> *and that you, O Lord, are loving.*
> *Surely you will reward each person*
> *according to what he has done"*
> (PSALM 62:7,11-12).

Here's a powerful path to freedom: As you learn to let go of unresolved anger, let God's Word speak to you. Read at least five psalms a day for a month. Read them out loud, and soon peace will permeate your mind and spirit instead of painful angst.

When I made the conscious choice to forgive my father and release all my grievances to God, it was not because my father *asked* forgiveness or showed any signs of remorse or repentance. It was not because I thought he deserved it or because I knew I "should." It was because God said, "Do it," which meant it was in my best interest.

Convinced of God's love for me and persuaded of His trustworthiness, I wholeheartedly trusted His instructions to me. So for me the choice was clear and the decision definite—it was a no-brainer. I would do whatever God asked of me, just as Jesus did whatever the Father asked of Him—even if it meant forgiving the guilty and trusting God with the "little" matter of justice.

Just as Jesus entrusted Himself to the Father, He asks us to entrust ourselves to Him. And when you know you are loved unconditionally and sacrificially, it is more than doable! So as an act of my will, I chose to forgive my father.

From all outward appearances, nothing changed. My father was the same. Our relationship was still the same. But God knew my heart was not the same. It had been deeply—and forever—changed.

6. Restore the Relationship When Possible

Once you have *realized* and *revisited* your ancient anger, as well as *released* the ones who hurt you from their debt, be ready to seize the opportunity to *rebuild* the trust needed for a healthy relationship. Naturally, God's purpose is for us to live peacefully with each other whenever possible.

The apostle Paul wrote in Romans 12:17-18, "Do not repay anyone evil for evil. Be careful to do what is right in the eyes of everybody. If it is possible, as far as it depends on you, live at peace with everyone."

That is a recipe for harmony in all our relationships. But notice a key phrase in this verse: "If it is possible, as far as it depends on you…" When it comes to restoring a broken relationship, this is the crux of the matter. Reconciliation isn't always possible or even desirable.

God doesn't expect us to "get along" no matter what.

Our protection from further harm always comes first. If the person who wronged you refuses to take responsibility for hurtful actions and shows no signs of genuine contrition, then it probably wouldn't be wise to pursue restoration of the relationship.

Again, forgiveness is a commandment. It is a volitional act of obedience to God's will. Healing from unresolved anger requires genuine determination on your part alone to cancel the debt owed you.

But reconciling a broken relationship takes two people—both need to reassemble the pieces of shattered confidence. It takes genuine repentance—a change of mind, heart, and behavior and the completion of verifiable steps to prevent a recurrence of a breakdown in trust. Both people must work toward restoring the relationship.

> The ultimate purpose of our fiery trials is to clear away everything holding us back from a more mature, more empowered walk with Christ.

Here's the bottom line: If the one who made you angry is willing to take responsibility for wrongs done and to start over, don't hesitate to do your part as well. Reconciliation pleases the heart of God.

7. Rejoice in God's Purpose

Few things on earth are more desolate than a forest after a ravaging fire has reduced it to ashes. It *is* easy to look at the charred stumps and think life will never recover.

But oh, how appearances can deceive! Return to the scorched area the following spring, and you'll see a vivid illustration of God's ability to turn any tribulation into triumph. In relatively little time, "dead" hillsides come alive with colorful wildflowers and green grasses. Old growth previously choking out the new is gone, clearing the way for an explosion of fresh life.

Our hearts, once laid waste by pain and anger, are no different. The ultimate purpose of our fiery trials is to clear away everything holding us back from a more mature, more empowered walk with Christ.

As the inspired apostle Paul wrote:

*"In all these things we are more than conquerors through
him who loved us. For I am convinced that neither death nor life,
neither angels nor demons, neither the present nor the future,
nor any powers, neither height nor depth, nor anything else
in all creation, will be able to separate us from the love of God
that is in Christ Jesus our Lord"*
(ROMANS 8:37-38).

So the final step in dousing the smoldering anger inside you is to rejoice in the *good* God promises to produce out of all you've been through as you commit your trials to Him. As forgiveness douses those burning embers, begin to look for signs of new life in your own heart and soul. Look for the beauty God will bring from the ashes.

You Can Find Serenity After Surfacing Your Anger

Vivian called me months later to report she was making steady progress toward shedding the unnecessary burden of her unresolved anger. She and Lorraine finally talked through their past and forgave each other.

"It's like all those years I've been dragging around a one-hundred-pound sack of potatoes," she told me. "Now with the weight lifted, I feel like a whole new person without it."

Hidden anger may be difficult to recognize, but it's definitely *felt*— by you, and by those around you. While Vivian's anger had stayed on a slow simmer, her emotional stove had kept cooking. But when Vivian learned a new recipe for success—admit it, forgive it, release it—then her anger was taken off her emotional burner altogether, and finally cooled.

Fireworks: A Short Fuse Is Bad News

It's hard to say which is scarier: watching a bomb explode and witnessing fiery debris fly in every direction, or being near a bomb that should have exploded, but didn't.

It happens every Fourth of July in the United States. Someone lights the fuse on a firecracker and runs a safe distance away. Covering their ears, a watching crowd excitedly waits for the blast. The sparks sizzle and crackle all the way down to the end of the fuse—then *boom*—the black powder ignites!

Unfortunately, not all firecrackers detonate as they should. Yes, the fuse burns—same as before. And everyone waits: *three, two, one...* but nothing happens—no flash, no boom. No longer is the air filled with excitement, but it is thick with anxiety...caution...hesitation. Is it really a dud, or just slow to blow? Who will go near to investigate? Do you dare pick it up? Maybe the fuse didn't stay lit. Or maybe the embers are still smoldering on the inside, unseen—call it destruction in slow motion.

Without a doubt, anger and fireworks have a lot in common. If not handled properly, both can explode on you and on those around you. Like a cantankerous Roman candle, red-hot anger can appear to fizzle and disappear inside. Although out of sight and mind, this inner anger is just as damaging as a powerful explosion—simply because the pent-up force will eventually explode on the inside harms your emotional stability. This can happen anytime we attempt to ignore smoldering embers of anger rather than permanently extinguishing them in a healthy way.

Let Cooler Heads Prevail
How to Put Out the Flames of Present Anger

"Good sense makes one slow to anger"
(Proverbs 19:11 esv).

NOT LONG AGO, I read an article about a man named Steve Tran of Westminster, California, who discovered his apartment had been infested by cockroaches. He decided to take action by fumigating with "bug bombs"—25 of them!

After activating all the bombs, he closed the door behind him and assumed he would no longer be bugged by bugs. But when the toxic spray reached the pilot light of his stove, a fiery explosion blasted Steve's screen door across the street, shattered all his windows, and set his furniture ablaze.

"I wanted to kill all of them," he said. "I thought if I used a lot more, it would last longer."

According to the instructions on the label, just two canisters of the fumigant would have solved Steve's pest predicament. The blast caused more than $10,000 of damage to the apartment building. But looking on the bright side of the situation, at least it ended the cockroach problem, right? Wrong.

According to Steve, "By Sunday, I saw them walking around."[1]

How Do We Prevent an Eruption?

You could certainly say this was a clear case of overkill, an over-the-top response to irritating circumstances. Sounds like the way some people handle their anger, doesn't it? The goal is to express feelings appropriately rather than inappropriately, and proportionate rather than disproportionate to the situation. We want to resolve the issue without making it worse. Moreover, we want to *alleviate our anger* in a way that is honoring to God, ourselves, and others.

But that can sometimes be a tall order. After all, the potential for anger remains ever present. A spark of irritation can be ignited intentionally by hurtful people or unintentionally by those who love you. Regardless, God wants you to seek His answer for anger quickly before it singes your heart and burns the bridges of your relationships.

What to Do When Your Fuse Is Lit

In the late 1700s, President Thomas Jefferson presented a preventative solution for anger out of control, which is applicable for us all in today's world: "When angry, count ten, before you speak; if very angry, an [*sic*] hundred."[2]

When you prepare ahead of time for any angry eruption, you are putting up "fire walls" that will halt the growing flames of anger.

We all need strategies for dealing with anger in the heat of the moment. When an incendiary incident occurs—when you feel the fuse lit in your heart—what will you do? The aim is to heed the words of Peter: "Be self-controlled...be compassionate and humble...Do not repay evil with evil or insult with insult, but with blessing, because to this you were called so that you may inherit a blessing."[3]

Imagine yourself suddenly thrust into one of these situations:

- At an important work meeting, someone takes credit for a big idea you've spent weeks preparing. He gets all the credit; you get none. *Grrrr!*

- Your kids have a raucous pillow fight in the living room—which they've been told not to do—and they break your most cherished sentimental gift (the old clock passed down from your grandparents). *No!*

- Your accountant calls with bad news about an error on your tax return. With fees, penalties, and so on, you'll need to come up with an extra $7,500. *What?!*

- The one you love the most snaps at you, "I'm leaving! I hate you—I never want to see you again!" *Ouch!*

I'm sure you could describe your own blood-boiling, anger-inducing scenario from real life. It's only natural you would feel upset and angry. No one could blame you. But now, the question becomes this: What are you going to do with those red-hot emotions?

Nine Anger Alleviators

What follows are nine strategies, each starting with the letter *A* for easy recall.

1. Acknowledge Your Anger

The first thing to do is *recognize* and *admit* to yourself when your internal temperature is rising. Become aware of your feelings of anger, and be alert to the temptation to suppress your emotions because of fear. It takes only a moment to stop and ask, "Okay, what's *really* going on inside of me?"

Be willing to take responsibility for any inappropriate anger. As Proverbs 28:13 states, "He who conceals his sins does not prosper, but whoever confesses and renounces them finds mercy."

If you find yourself getting mad, just admit it. Accept it for what it is. Once you identify your feelings, you can deal with them. But if you deny or suppress them, they're bound to leak out—or explode—in unhealthy ways.

2. Assess the Source

We've talked about the four reasons we get angry: hurt, injustice, fear, and frustration. If we look closely, we'll realize our heated feelings stem from one or more of these sources. So when you start to get mad, it's helpful to identify what exactly is stirring up your emotions. Identify if your anger comes from...

- *hurt* feelings from the words or actions of others
- *unjust* actions of someone toward you or another person
- *fear* of some kind of loss
- *frustration* because something didn't go as you planned

Knowing precisely what is causing your flared-up feelings will enable you to respond wisely. If you know *what* you're dealing with, you'll know better *how* to deal with it. The Bible says, "Surely you desire truth in the inner parts; you teach me wisdom in the inmost place" (Psalm 51:6).

3. Analyze Your Style

Ask yourself the following questions:

- How often do I feel angry? (Often? Sometimes? Seldom? Never?)
- How do I know when I am angry?
- How do others know when I am angry?
- How do I release my anger?

Do you explode? Do you become teary-eyed? Do you joke or tease? Do you become sarcastic? Do you criticize? Do you become defensive?

As you seek to understand your style, pray...

"Test me, O LORD, and try me, examine my heart and my mind."[4]

4. Appraise Your Thinking

Those who call me on *Hope in the Night* almost always are experiencing some sort of problem or pain. I don't often encounter, nor do I expect, levity or humor from people pouring out their hearts to me late at night. So I was surprised by the fun call from Terri. But even lighthearted banter couldn't disguise her out-of-control thought life.

Terri: "I want you to tell me exactly what is wrong with me."

June: "Uh-oh! What's the matter?"

Terri: "I used to have a bad temper. I decided I needed either a shrink or a church…so I tried church. I trusted Jesus, but my temper didn't go away…it just went underground. Now I get mad in my mind. But there's an upside: I have a great time visualizing the things I want to do to people."

June: "Ahhh…like what? May I have an example?"

Terri: (laughing) "Well, the other day—right in front of my employees—my manager snatched a folder out of my hands. She just turned on her heel and walked away. Ever since then, in my mind, she's been suspended—head-first—outside my office window…which happens to be on the fifth floor of a downtown bank."

June: (laughing) "So you're telling me I should be grateful I have managed, so far, to stay on your good side!"

Terri: "Exactly! There was a time in my life I didn't know these thoughts were wrong. But since giving my life to Christ, I know they are."

June: "Terri, I'm hearing you say, now that you're a Christian, you don't act out on your anger as you used to—you don't blow your top—but you're finding yourself struggling with your thought life. What's good is that you have a grasp of the danger of letting your thoughts go uncontrollably wild. Tell me, are you familiar with the concept of a spiritual stronghold?"

Terri: "It's an area of our lives that we can't seem to get the victory over. That's what this feels like to me."

June: "That's right. Strong emotions can distort your thinking. When your mind is under siege, it's helpful to intentionally pause and recognize what is going through your head. Paul tells us, 'Take captive every thought to make it obedient.'[5] We can grab hold of our thoughts to assess if they're accurate and truthful and if they pass the test of Philippians 4:8—true, noble, right, pure, lovely, admirable, excellent, and praiseworthy. This is the litmus test for taking our thoughts captive and making them obedient to Christ. If a thought flunks the test, it's to be thrown out—rejected and ejected from your mind."

As our call progressed, Terri and I talked about other ways to guard our minds from out-of-control anger. I explained that too often our anger is fueled by our own misinterpretations or misconceptions. When offended by someone, we can easily:

- *Exaggerate* the situation: "He said my presentation could be more polished. What he really means is that I *bombed*."
- *Assume* the worst: "She didn't show up for the party even though she promised to. *I think she probably hates me.*"
- *Mislabel* someone based on misconstrued actions: "I don't care if she insists she just 'misunderstood' or 'got her facts wrong'—*she's nothing but a liar.*"
- *Generalize*: "He is *always* rude. He *never* says anything positive."

As we talked more, Terri began to grasp the importance of guarding her thought life so she could control her anger.

June: "Terri, our thoughts are filtered through our fears, our personal interpretations, and our past experiences. We would be wise to ask God to help us, because 'the Lord searches every heart and understands every motive behind the thoughts.'"[6]

Terri: "I'm beginning to understand. I need to look into my own heart, examine the issues that are making me angry, and ask God to help me see truth. If I can learn to evaluate my thinking accurately—compare it to what God says is true—my life will change...and so will my anger problem."

June: "Exactly!"

Terri seemed well on her way to getting her thought life under control—and with it, her runaway anger.

Now back to our nine anger alleviators.

5. Admit Your Needs

God creates each of us with three basic emotional needs—love, significance, and security—and there is nothing wrong with seeking to fulfill them.[7] The trouble comes when we inappropriately express anger as a means to getting these inner needs met.

Do you use anger as a manipulative ploy, demanding certain "musts" in an attempt to *feel loved*? Do you use anger as a tool for intimidation, always posturing to get your way in an attempt to *feel significant*? Do you use anger as a grasp for control, insisting on certain conditions in order to *feel secure*?

Ultimately, only Christ can meet all our inner needs for love, significance, and security. As Paul assures us, "My God will meet all your needs according to his glorious riches in Christ Jesus."[8]

6. Abandon Your Demands

Instead of demanding that others meet our inner need for *love*, we must allow the Lord to meet that need. We can pray, "Lord, though I would like to feel more love from others, I know You love me unconditionally." Listen to His response: "I have loved you with an everlasting love; I have drawn you with loving-kindness" (Jeremiah 31:3).

When it comes to our need for *significance*, we can pray, "Lord, though I would like to feel more significant to those around me, I know I am significant in Your eyes." Indeed, you are already significant to Him. He says, "I know the plans I have for you...plans to prosper you and not to harm you, plans to give you hope and a future" (Jeremiah 29:11).

And concerning our need for *security*, we can pray, "Lord, though I wish I felt more secure in my relationships, I know I am secure in my relationship with You." Be assured—God promises to meet that need. He says, "The LORD himself goes before you and will be with you; he will never leave you nor forsake you. Do not be afraid; do not be discouraged" (Deuteronomy 31:8).

Listen to the psalmist's reassurance: "The LORD is with me; I will not be afraid. What can man do to me?"[9]

It's true that God sometimes uses people and circumstances to meet our needs, but when a need arises, we should choose to look first to our ultimate source of fulfillment, the Lord Himself.

7. Alter Your Attitudes

It's likely the process of introspection—looking deep within—will bring to light the need for some attitude adjustments. No surprise there. Anger has a way of turning positive thoughts into negative ones and generous intentions into vindictive ones. Our goal is always to be more like Christ, putting others first, looking out for the interests of others, not pushing our own rights.

Our minds produce a steady stream of thoughts, observations, and perceptions. These combine to shape the attitudes we have toward people and situations. When we're in a tense situation, the stream of thoughts speeds up and can become like a raging river. Suppose you could reach down into that current and pull out a thought. What would it be?

- *I am so mad! That guy is going to pay big time!*
- *She drives me crazy. I'm crossing her name off the list!*
- *What a jerk! How could he say such a thing?*
- *Who does she think she is? I'm going to put her in her place!*

If your flow of thoughts is headed in a negative direction, the outcome of your conflict will be negative as well. Conversely, if your stream is stocked with mostly positive thoughts, the outcome will probably be positive.

The Bible says, "Do nothing out of selfish ambition or vain conceit, but in humility consider others better than yourselves. Each of you should look not only to your own interests, but also to the interests of others."[10]

Through our own willpower and determination, we'll get only so far. We may be able to stamp out a few small grass fires here and there, but a raging inferno always threatens. Nevertheless, it is only through the power of God that we can achieve real, lasting change, which leads to our next point.

8. Access the Spirit's Power

It's amazing, and unfortunate, how often we fail to dip our ladle into the well of God's wisdom when we are thirsting for answers. Angry situations can confuse us and prompt us to make unwise choices. In reality, a bowl full of anger can quickly become a cauldron of chaos.

To prevent us from falling into a pattern of ungodly reactions, we need guidance that comes from heaven. Jesus gave us this promise: "When he, the Spirit of truth, comes, he will guide you into all truth."[11] Scripture tells us this kind of guidance is available to all believers who truly seek it.

> When emotions are running high, ask God for help to accomplish His will, not yours.

It may strike some as unrealistic to pause and pray right in the middle of an emotion-filled episode. But I submit to you this is precisely the time to seek God's wisdom, power, and the "peace...which transcends all understanding."[12] There is no need for a long, drawn-out prayer—a quick SOS sent heavenward is all that's needed to invite the Spirit of God to take control of your temper and tame your tongue.

The Lord knows what is in your heart. He knows if you desire to be humble and gracious in the most trying of times, and He will provide strength to carry you through—the ability to "let cooler heads prevail." God can use your anger to produce honorable results—correcting injustice, revealing deceit, or protecting victims. When emotions are running high, ask God for help to accomplish His will, not yours.

9. Address Your Anger

Now comes the tricky part: acting on all the information you've gathered. This is the moment when you ask, What am I going to do about it? What's the best response? Here are some answers, and each begins with the letter *D*:

- *Determine* whether your anger is really justified. "A wicked man puts up a bold front, but an upright man gives thought to his ways."[13]

- *Decide* on the appropriate response. As Solomon tells us, "There is...a time to be silent and a time to speak."[14] How important is the issue? Would a good purpose be served if you mention it? Should you acknowledge your anger only to the Lord, or should you express it to the person involved?

- *Depend* on the Holy Spirit for guidance. Pour out your heart to God and seek His wisdom. Be sure to search the Scriptures for insight and take time to patiently wait upon the Lord (John 16:13).

- *Develop* constructive dialogue when you confront. Paul wrote, "Let your conversation be always full of grace, seasoned with salt, so that you may know how to answer everyone."[15] Keep these guidelines in mind:

  —*Don't* speak from a heart of unforgiveness.

  —*Do* think before you speak.

  —*Don't* use phrases such as "How could you?" or "Why can't you?"

  —*Do* use personal statements such as "I feel..."

  —*Don't* bring up past grievances.

  —*Do* stay focused on the present issue.

  —*Don't* assume the other person is wrong.

  —*Do* listen for feedback from another point of view.

- *Demonstrate* the grace of God by saying to yourself, "I placed my anger on the cross with Christ. I am no longer controlled by anger; I am alive with Christ living inside me." As the apostle Paul said, "I have been crucified with Christ and I no longer live, but Christ lives in me. The life I live in the body, I live by faith in the Son of God, who loved me and gave himself for me" (Galatians 2:20).

And when I live this way then...

- I will let Christ forgive through me.
- I will let Christ speak through me.
- I will let Christ love through me.

Putting the A's into Action

A colleague of mine who knew I was writing a book about anger recently asked, "So, June, when was the last time you got mad about something?"

I had to stop and think about it. Since I have a pretty easygoing, laid-back temperament, I am not easily provoked to anger. I get bothered by traffic jams and canceled airline flights, of course, but those kinds of irritants are in a different category than the ones that make me *mad*.

Finally, I answered, "I honestly can't remember. So it must have been quite a while ago." I wasn't trying to sound pious, and I wasn't in denial—that was the truth.

But my time to get angry came just four hours later. I probably shouldn't have been surprised because it seems the Lord likes to make sure I "practice what I preach"—and here was an opportunity to "road test" my beliefs about releasing anger.

It was late at night, after I'd finished airing *Hope in the Night*, when I sat down in my home office to review new printed material produced by our ministry. I was excited to see the new booklet—hot off the press—that would be distributed through Hope for the Heart.

But a moment later, my excitement turned to dismay...and then my stomach started churning.

Before the booklet had gone to the printer, I'd read it over, spotted a few errors, flagged the mistakes, and mentioned them to the staff member in charge of the project. I followed up with an e-mail to ensure I had communicated clearly. But now, as I looked at the printed piece, the errors were still there. The inattention kindled a flame that spread like a wildfire within me.

"How did this happen?" I sputtered. "I know I pointed out these problems. Why won't they listen to me?"

It was then I had a choice to make: I could do something hurtful (such as fire off a rash note) or I could immediately work through the "A-list" of anger alleviators described on pages 201-09. Thankfully, I chose the latter (especially because I'm telling you to do the same thing!). In just a matter of seconds, my internal thought process moved forward like this:

Acknowledge my anger: I am definitely angry!

Assess the source: Why am I feeling this way? Is my sense of indignation, rooted in hurt, fear, injustice, or frustration? I'm frustrated that what I'd asked to get done didn't happen.

Ascertain my style: Although I seldom get angry, I know I'm angry when my heart starts beating faster and my stomach feels tied in knots. Others know I'm angry when I get unusually quiet. I try to release my anger by speaking slowly, quietly, and distinctly—that's my way of trying to keep a cap on my anger!

Appraise my thinking: All right, slow down. Am I exaggerating the problem? Well, it's not the end of the world, but the booklets are already printed. We'll either have to live with the problem or eat the cost to reprint. *Am I assuming the worst?* No, the person responsible is a conscientious worker. This one just slipped by in the hustle and bustle. *Am I labeling?* It was a mistake—nothing more than that. *Am I generalizing?* Yes, I'm generalizing. My thought, *Why won't they listen to me?* isn't accurate. Thankfully, this is not an everyday occurrence.

Admit my needs: I have a need to be heard and taken seriously. I suppose being heard not only makes me feel loved, but significant and secure. When something like this happens, a little doubt and mistrust creeps in.

Also, when something doesn't meet the high standards I have set for the ministry, I begin to question the significance of my work and how we will be viewed. Although these needs are perfectly legitimate, in my mind and heart I know my inner need for love, security, and significance comes from the Lord, not anything I do.

Abandon my demands: I must not demand that people do everything "perfectly" just to help me feel significant. The Lord is the source of my significance. Before I was born, He established His plan and purpose.

Alter attitudes: When things don't get done or are done poorly, I'm tempted to think other people don't share my commitment to high standards and top-notch service. But that kind of attitude puts me in a one-up position. Besides, it's probably flat-out wrong. I know every one of my staff members works diligently and serves the Lord wholeheartedly. I choose this attitude: Mistakes happen because humans aren't perfect. We'll learn from this and do better next time.

Access the Holy Spirit's power: "Dear Lord, though I'm worked up about this, I want Your peace and guidance. Help me to respond wisely and lovingly, to act rather than react."

Address my anger: I decided to do nothing until the following afternoon, when I would be able to communicate in a calm and clearheaded way.

The next day, I phoned the person responsible for overseeing the project (using the "sandwich method" from pages 82-83):

> *Bread of Praise:* "I want to tell you how much I value you and your work. You've made a wonderful contribution to our ministry."

> *Meat of the Matter:* "I also want to mention an issue that came to my attention last night..." I then explained that I'd spotted the errors.

> *Bread of Encouragement:* "This is definitely a solvable problem.

Let's work together to devise a plan ensuring it doesn't happen again. I'm confident you'll get the changes in the next printing. I know you have the perseverance to help our process to be the best it can be. Thank you for being a team player."

Personally, I'm so glad I didn't resort to a knee-jerk reaction when I got angry, and I'm also glad I didn't turn a blind eye. I'm grateful this one incident didn't evolve into an anger bowl "slip," with me making a deposit into my bowl and nursing a grudge. I don't always handle my anger wisely, but in this case, my effort to clearly think through my response helped greatly.

How the A-List Spells Relief

The next time you find yourself feeling the heat, take a moment to work through the list of anger alleviators. Doing so can save you from acting in ways you might regret later and spare yourself and others around you much heartache. The A-list serves as a guide to navigate you through fiery scenarios with emotional and spiritual maturity. The more you utilize it, the more you'll be able to extinguish the most powerful blaze.

Rapid Intervention Crew: Ready for Action

Trained firefighters know it is foolish—and dangerous—to send an entire team into a burning building at the same time. That's why it is standard protocol to have a Rapid Intervention Crew (RIC) ready for action. This is a standby team prepared to quickly move in to rescue or to help should any firefighting comrades face peril.

Most crews follow a procedure called "Two In/Two Out," which is a safety measure whereby two firefighters enter a hazardous zone while at least two others stand by outside in case the first two need rescuing. Thus, a minimum of four firefighters must be on the scene before any can enter a burning building.

Talk to any experienced firefighter, and you'll find there are dozens of safety procedures in place and practiced long before they encounter a real emergency. Once called into action, all personnel know precisely how to proceed. They have spent many hours preparing mentally and physically for nearly every possible scenario.

When it comes to anger, we too should prepare with the same diligence. We know our emotions are going to threaten to rage out of control sooner or later, and we can have safety measures in place to address the blaze the moment it erupts. Learn to fight volatile anger like a Rapid Intervention Crew—use precaution and the safest preventative measures!

CREATIVE COMBUSTION
How to Fight for Right with Justifiable Anger

"In your anger do not sin:
Do not let the sun go down while you are still angry"
(EPHESIANS 4:26).

CONSIDER: WHAT IS THE DIFFERENCE between a rocket capable of carrying astronauts to the moon and a lethal bomb that can lay waste to whole cities? Both are loaded with dangerous and volatile fuel. Both explode with violent force. Both can serve humanity, and both can be used to commit crimes against humanity. What sets them apart?

Conclusion: *The intentions of the people who use them determines the difference.*

Contemplate: Two men are standing before you, guns in hand. Their weapons contain an explosive mixture of sulfur, charcoal, and potassium nitrate, a trio of chemical agents that burn rapidly and emit hot solids and gases that act as a propellant. Gunpowder, it would seem, in the possession of these two men, serves two very distinct purposes.

Cross purposes: One man with a menacing demeanor waves his gun threateningly, intent on harming anyone who doesn't comply with his demands for money, drugs, sexual submission. The other man is steadily composed and clothed in a police uniform, intent on defending anyone who could be violated or victimized. One uses gunpowder constructively, the other, destructively.

Anger is a lot like gunpowder, rockets, and bombs: It can be evil and dangerous, but not always. Not everything that is ignited is destructive and deplorable. Sometimes a spark and a flame are exactly what we need to address critical issues or get important work done.

It's true that intense heat can hurt people, but under the right conditions, it can also become the catalyst for constructive transformation. I'm sure you would agree pancake batter isn't particularly appetizing until it's been on a sizzling-hot griddle. And what good is a 5,000-pound car without an internal combustion engine to release the explosive potential of gasoline and propel it down the road? The same is also true of fiery anger: It can reduce a relationship to ashes, or spark a flame for positive change.

Contrary to what we may have been taught, anger is not always an emotional dead end, with no way out and no hope for change. It is more like a fork in the road. The destination you reach is up to you. Turn one direction—the way most commonly taken—and you enter a demolition derby of revenge and retribution. That road leads only to more pain, broken relationships, unforgiveness, and words and actions you will come to regret.

Channeling Anger into Positive Change

But like every fork in the road, there is an alternate path. To choose it, you must change your deeply ingrained thinking about anger. The philosophy you learn from the world fits neatly on a bumper sticker: Don't get mad, get even!

On the road less traveled, you will learn a new way: to neither run from your anger nor give in to it, but to face it and direct its explosive power toward a beneficial purpose—the purpose God intends.

Every step you take in that direction harmonizes your life with the will of God. As Paul wrote, "Do not be conformed to this world, but be transformed by the renewal of your mind, that by testing you may discern what is the will of God, what is good and acceptable and perfect."[1]

And what begins as a personal commitment to transform your

thinking and harness your anger might end up being used by God to bless countless lives. That's His specialty, you know—taking one person's commitment to transformation and causing it to spread like wildfire throughout a family, a community, a city, a country…and sometimes even the world.

The Scenario that Ignited Anger[2]

As a young man, César Chávez had more reason than most people to be angry. He already knew a lot about racial prejudice, social and economic injustice, and the personal pain they can cause. What he knew wasn't learned from books in history class at school; he lived it and experienced it every day.

César was born in 1927 on his family's small farm near Yuma, Arizona. In addition to working the land, his father, Librado, ran a local grocery store that did enough business for the family to get by. Poor by modern standards, they didn't think of themselves that way.

César's mother, Juana, a devout Christian, was known for sharing what little they had with vagrants and others down on their luck. From her, César learned the importance of giving, and he developed an ironclad commitment to Christlike nonviolence that would define him later in life.

But the boy's world was far from perfect. He had been born into a society that considered people with his skin color and heritage to be inferior. Many in the community thought nothing of creating rules that made it more difficult for people like the Chávez family to prosper, even in the best of times. But the 1930s were not the best of times for anyone in America.

Through the early years of the Great Depression, Librado and Juana managed to stay on their land and feed their children. The kids spent half the day in school and the remaining hours working, either in the family store or in the fields.

However, by 1938, the economic stress became too much to handle, and the Chávez family could no longer afford to pay property taxes on the farm. They were eligible for an emergency loan from the federal government for people in their circumstance, but the application was blocked numerous times by an unscrupulous local banker who wanted to buy the land himself for pennies on the dollar.

When the Chávez homestead was auctioned later that year, the only bidder was the bullying banker. César and his brother watched as he took possession of their home and tore down many of the structures their father had built.

César later recalled, "We were pushed off the land...When we left the farm our whole life was upset, turned upside down. We had been part of a very stable community, and we were about to become migrant workers. We had been uprooted."[3]

This was just one more event in a long history of unfair treatment at the hands of prejudiced neighbors and community leaders. And it burned in César's heart like a brush fire, spreading flames of indignation. For years, he and his family moved from place to place in California, picking crops in a harsh new life of never-ending, back-breaking labor.

Firsthand, César witnessed the deplorable conditions and unfair—often brutal—treatment the workers endured. He quit school after eighth grade. In 1944, he lied about his age and joined the navy at 17, serving two years.

Yet even wearing a serviceman's uniform was not enough to break down the cultural barriers of segregation and discrimination when he returned home. He remembers a typical incident in a local diner:

> There was a sign on the door that said "white trade only" but we went in anyway. We heard they had these big hamburgers and we wanted one. There was a blonde, blue-eyed girl behind the counter. She said, "We don't serve Mexicans," and she laughed when she said it. She enjoyed doing that, laughing at us. We went out but I was real mad. Enraged. It had to do with my manhood.[4]

Who can blame him? Wouldn't you be angry if you'd been treated so disrespectfully? Especially after years of watching the people you cared for being cheated, oppressed, exploited, and exposed to dangerous and degrading working conditions? It is the kind of anger that has sparked ruinous riots and even bloody revolutions.

The Pitchfork for Positive Change

Soon César had a family of his own and was working the fields of California beside his father and mother to put food on the table. His anger smoldered deep within his heart. He had arrived at a crossroad. Would he go down the path of hostility and destruction, or would he channel his anger and let it work for good?

> With God's help, you truly can rule anger instead of letting anger rule you.

To the benefit of millions of people, César chose the latter. True to his Christian upbringing, he refused to create more hatred in the world. Until his death in 1993, César Chávez devoted himself to bringing dignity and prosperity to poor, powerless farm workers all over America.

César's tireless and courageous work as founder of the United Farm Workers eventually won for farm laborers wage increases, health benefits, improved working conditions, and the right to bring grievances to their employers. As César's biographer pointed out:

> He taught [the people] to demand not just a better life, but an altogether different society. Taking literally Jesus' words in the Sermon on the Mount that "the last shall be first," Chávez gathered the farm workers and made them a peaceful force for social change.[5]

César Chávez could have become just another violent, angry young man. He could have started a gang instead of a social movement. But he didn't. The deciding factor lay in his determination to use his anger, and not to be ruled by it.

Ways to Harness Your Heat

That same choice presents itself every time any of us gets angry. The issues at stake needn't be world-changing for your anger to become a positive force in your life. Sometimes the benefit can be as simple as an infusion of courage as you stand up to someone who mistreats you—a boss who unfairly takes credit for your work, a teenager who repeatedly shows disrespect for you and your rules, or a neighbor who spreads nasty rumors about your friend.

In any situation, no matter how seemingly small and mundane or massive and monumental, you are the one who decides what to do with your anger. Inward transformation resulting in outward change is always possible. With God's help, you truly can rule anger instead of letting anger rule you.

The challenge is making the right choice when your anger is at its hottest. It takes both discipline and determination to refrain from lashing out and, instead, redirecting your "creative combustion" down positive pathways. Here are four strategies to help you do just that:

Identify Your Objective

As we've already discussed, most of the time the purpose of your anger is pretty straightforward. You get angry as a way to...

- alleviate your hurt
- express outrage at an injustice
- confront your fear
- vent your frustration

And your goal in each case is simple: Make it stop.

But in order to redirect the explosive energy of your anger into a constructive pursuit, you've got to move beyond protective reflexes and ask yourself, *What do I want to accomplish? If my anger is a rocket I can steer, where do I want it to go?*

Think of it as creating a personal mission statement. Businesses and other organizations often put their philosophy and purpose in writing at their inception to let clients and the community know what to expect from them. This written document also becomes a navigational beacon for the company or organization. Being intentional about what they set out to do makes it easier for them to notice if they have wandered off course.

For the same reasons, when your mission is to make positive use of your anger, you will find it helpful to clearly state your intentions.

A Meddling Mother-in-Law

When Anita called me at *Hope in the Night,* she began by saying, "I know this will sound cliché, but my mother-in-law is driving me completely insane."

I assured her clichés exist for a reason. Just because an experience is common doesn't make it less real or painful.

For the first few years of marriage, Tom and Anita lived hundreds of miles from either of their parents. At times, they regretted the limited contact the kids had with their grandparents. But on the whole, Tom and Anita were grateful for the freedom to establish their household as they saw fit.

All that changed when Tom's father died suddenly and his mother, Patricia, came to live nearby.

"She was in mourning—we all were—so for the first few months I let things slide that otherwise would have made me mad," Anita told me. "Now I'm just mad all the time, but after two years, it's hard to know what to do about it."

The problem was Patricia took on more responsibility and authority with her grandchildren than Anita wanted to relinquish. Patricia elbowed her way into Anita's parenting territory. She frequently reversed decisions her daughter-in-law made about important issues such as bedtime and how many treats the kids could have during the day.

Tom backed up Anita as best he could, but his job required him to travel and he was often unavailable. *Meddling* was the word most often written on the slips of paper blanketing the bottom of Anita's anger bowl.

"I've reached a breaking point," Anita said. "If I don't figure out how to get rid of my anger, it could get really ugly."

"It could get even uglier if you try to force your anger to just go away," I said. "That never works. How about this: If you could make your anger work toward a positive outcome, what would it be?"

She thought for a moment, then laughed as she said, "I was going to say I'd like Patricia to leave town again and never come back! But I realize that's not true. What I really want is to be treated with respect in my own home."

Bull's-eye! Although the way forward might still involve painful and even angry confrontation, the goal Anita identified was a worthy one. By targeting her anger on creating respect, Anita set a course that made it possible for everyone to win.

By stating her objective aloud, her blurred perception about what to do came into sharper focus. Don't let the destination of your anger remain vague or undefined. Set yourself a course for constructive resolution.

We can deceive ourselves by creating a smoke screen that makes us feel like we can change others. But we don't have the ability to change others. In fact, we don't even have the ability to truly change ourselves through our own will, strength, or desire. Change comes through our dependence on God's grace to transform lives—both ours and others.

This dependence upon God is extremely important. For example, what if Anita's goal had been to force her mother-in-law to show her more respect? Her chances of success would have been next to zero. Why? It wasn't within Anita's power to make Patricia do things differently. Attempting to bring change in our own power generally results in the opposite of what we intend.

Resist or Respect

"Most of the time, the harder you push someone in a direction they don't want to go, the more they resist," I told Anita. "It is human nature. The best you can do is to make sure you respect yourself enough to draw firm boundaries and to enforce them, no matter who steps across the line."

At the time, that person was Patricia. The next time, it could be a neighbor or a church leader. If Anita did the work to alter her own inner landscape, she would be empowered and prepared to prevent another encroachment, whatever its source.

When you identify a positive goal for your anger, make sure it is achievable by concentrating on the only thing you can control: you.

Employ the Power of Prayer

After years of counseling hurting people on *Hope in the Night,* I am still surprised at how many attempt to struggle through life's hardships without taking advantage of one of God's greatest gifts: the privilege of prayer. Prayer is like making an SOS call to the Creator and Master of all things—yet this vital communication link and source of divine power too often goes unused. The Bible says, "You do not have because you do not ask" (James 4:2). It's like we're trying to control our anger with our hearts and minds disconnected from their power source. And it's both frustrating and futile, for the result is certain failure.

Unfortunately, too many people perceive prayer more as a dreary duty than a precious privilege. To pray is not to beg or to engage in wishful thinking. It is to stand before God as sons and daughters in the full confidence of our salvation and to trust Him to answer our prayers according to His perfect will.

God's eagerness to answer prayer is reflected in the words of the apostle John: "This is the confidence we have in approaching God: that if we ask

> True empathy, found in prayer, will open pathways to peace you hadn't seen before or believed possible.

anything according to his will, he hears us. And if we know that he hears us—whatever we ask—we know that we have what we asked of him" (1 John 5:14-15).

If you struggle with anger and want to make a commitment to channel your churning, often volatile feelings into a positive force, there is no better way to start than by having a candid conversation with God.

First, pray for discernment. As theologian Reinhold Niebuhr wrote in his famous *Serenity Prayer:* "God grant me the serenity to accept the things I cannot change, the courage to change the things I can, and the wisdom to know the difference." When our hearts and minds are open to His leading, the Spirit will guide us into all truth.

Second, pray for those with whom you are in conflict. Ask God to give you insight and understanding into why they think and behave as they do. You will certainly discover your "enemies" are only human— misguided, perhaps—but just as vulnerable to pain and fear as you are.

True empathy, found in prayer, will open pathways to peace you hadn't seen before or believed possible.

Finally, pray for God's will, not yours, to be done. We've all prayed for things and later thanked God for not answering our prayers with a yes. And we've all heard accounts of people attending high school reunions, seeing their former sweethearts, and thanking God for not answering the prayers voiced by their foolish young hearts years before.

Truth is, the human eye is not well adapted to see the big picture. We have trouble perceiving the value of paradox and mystery. When it comes to harnessing anger for good, what looks like a setback is sometimes the key to victory. It is important to surrender to God's purpose no matter what.

As Proverbs 3:5-6 says, "Trust in the LORD with all your heart and lean not on your own understanding; in all your ways acknowledge him, and he will make your paths straight." That's good advice. To "acknowledge him" refers to seeking God in prayer, seeking His perfect will in all situations, including your battle with blazing anger. God *wants* to be involved; He is eager to help and strengthen you.

How do you release your anger? First, delve deeply into your heart and honestly reflect on the pain you are holding onto. Then go to God in all humility, refusing to demand your rights and rejecting any thought of revenge, and surrender the situation and yourself—past, present, and future—to the Lord. Although you, like Anita, may feel completely powerless, in reality you have the power to release your pain and anger to Him.

The "Releasing Your Anger" Prayer

"Lord Jesus, thank You for loving me;
thank You for caring about me.
Because You know everything,
You know the strong sense of (hurt, injustice, fear, frustration)
I have felt about (name or situation).
Thank You for understanding my anger.
Right now, I release all my anger to You.
I trust You with my future and with me.
In Christ's name I pray. Amen."

Tangible Action: Using Anger for Good

What good would it have done for César Chávez, or Martin Luther King, Jr., or William Wilberforce (the English abolitionist who fought against slavery) to channel their anger at injustice into positive change if they had never set foot out of their houses? Not much, I'd say. Only because they stepped into society and turned angry passion into viable action do millions of us enjoy a more egalitarian world.

The same is required of you if you hope to translate your anger into positive change, if you hope to turn wishful thinking into progress you can measure. Once you know what you want to accomplish, decide what you must *do* to make it happen...and then do it.

For Anita that meant finally sharing her feelings with her mother-in-law, a conversation she had avoided for years. She kept her goal in mind as she planned how and when to broach the subject, making sure the two of them would not be interrupted. She carefully scripted her initial comments to avoid making inflammatory accusations.

"I realized I could succeed in reaching my goal no matter how Patricia reacted," Anita told me later. "Once I defined my boundaries, she was free to honor them, or not. And I was free to continue accepting old patterns of behavior, or not.

"It was so liberating! Why should I stuff my anger down and watch it turn to bitterness when I could draw strength from it instead?"

The key to Anita's "liberation" was respecting herself enough to establish firm boundaries and enforce them, plus a willingness to act on her anger so she could reach her goal. At first, Patricia reacted as Anita feared she might. She was defensive and resistant. But Anita was undeterred, like Chávez and his farm workers on a picket line. Eventually Anita's firm yet gentle determination paid off as Patricia admitted to being too intrusive, and apologized.

"It was like the relationship was reborn," Anita said. "From that time on, she treated me more as an equal. She even confided for the first time how much she still grieved for her husband, and I was able to help her through it. None of that would have happened if I hadn't trusted my anger and used it to set things right."

As Anita surrendered her bowl of anger to God, He melted each "meddling" slip—forever.

Anger can be frightening. It can thunder and roar. It can erupt and blow, and bury your life in smoldering ash. But if you'll resist the temptation to run from your anger—if you'll heed it and harness its energy for good—like the engine of a Boeing 747, it can deliver the thrust you need to rise above hurt, injustice, fear, and frustration so you can soar to new heights—and even change the world!

Blacksmithing: Pyrotechnics with a Purpose

When you wield the cold steel of a wrench or a hammer, it's easy to forget the element without which they would not exist: heat. Today, much of our technology is dependent upon precise tools and parts that were forged in a fiery inferno.

For centuries, the village iron forger, called the *blacksmith*—a name derived from the Old English word *smite* which means "to strike"— was one of the most esteemed members of any rural community. That's because he possessed the know-how for creating tools necessary for survival: plows, weapons, armor, and more. Like an artist who masterfully swirls paint or a sculptor who molds and shapes clay, the blacksmith skillfully manages and manipulates the most feared element of all—fire—to produce a bevy of beneficial tools.

Before hard metals become malleable, they must be heated to a red-hot temperature roughly half their melting point. Traditionally, the blacksmith then formed the metal mass into a specified shape by striking it with a hammer as he held the mass against an anvil. When the blacksmith was satisfied with his creation, he would thrust it into cool water to solidify its shape.

Anger too can provide just the right amount of emotional heat to create something constructive and useful, a positive force capable of changing attitudes, correcting injustices, and channeling opportunities for Christ-like growth. Like the blacksmith, who shapes metal objects, learn how to manage your fiery anger, and watch something positive and promising emerge off the anvil.

BOMB SQUAD BASICS
How to Handle Hotheaded People

*"Do not make friends with a hot-tempered man,
do not associate with one easily angered"*
(PROVERBS 22:24).

"I'M NOT A VERY GOOD PERSON," Sylvia said when I prompted her to share why she had called me at *Hope in the Night.* Most people who phone in—especially those in great pain—have a determined, demonstrative quality to their voice. They are calling because they've finally had enough of some difficult circumstance in their life. I listen for this last-hope resignation in their voice because it's evidence of a readiness on their part to let God intervene in their lives and circumstances and lead them toward emotional and spiritual health and healing.

I'm *Supposed* to Take It

Sylvia sounded lifeless, flat, and utterly defeated. Her voice had the telltale emptiness of someone who has given up on herself. Later I learned it wasn't Sylvia's idea to phone in. A concerned friend dialed the studio number and put the phone in Sylvia's hand.

"What makes you think that about yourself?" I gently asked when she referred to herself as a substandard person.

After a lengthy pause, she said, "My husband, Gene, has a terrible temper. I don't blame him for that. He came from a very angry family, so it's pretty much all he knows. I've tried to love him unconditionally, to lay down my life, and turn the other cheek—all those things God expects me to do. But I always fail miserably, and things just get worse."

At that point, I suspected Sylvia's ideas about how to handle an angry person—and what it takes to be a good wife—were significantly different from God's. Something had indeed gone wrong in her life, but probably not in the way she imagined. I asked her to describe her relationship with Gene. What did she mean when she said that, despite her efforts, things "get worse"?

"I always know I've pushed him too far when he gets in a rage and starts swearing uncontrollably or throwing things," she said.

"That sounds extreme," I told her.

"Well, he doesn't throw things *at me*," she explained. "He's not really abusive, just angry. Usually he gets that way after I've become angry myself."

Right away it seemed to me Sylvia excused her husband's rage because she thought that's what God expects of her, as if it was His will for her to suffocate beneath Gene's pile of paper slips in his colossal anger bowl. And she blamed herself for provoking him, as if she was the detonator for his explosive temper.

As a result, Sylvia couldn't see Gene's unresolved anger as abusive. But, to the objective observer, throwing things, slamming doors, and yelling without restraint are all very threatening behaviors. Their presence day after day creates a climate of fear that is severely damaging to any relationship.

Although Gene's anger could apparently be ignited by any number of things Sylvia said or did, the most incendiary issue in their relationship was money. He kept tight control over what she was allowed to spend, yet he would often bring home expensive electronic gadgets or power tools he seldom used. If Sylvia questioned a purchase, Gene would start shouting and defend his right to spend his hard-earned money as he pleased. She also suspected he gambled a good deal with his co-workers and on occasion lost considerable amounts of money.

"I used to believe if I could just love him well enough, he'd see there was no need to be so angry at me or the world," Sylvia said. "Now I think it must be God's will for me to just love him unconditionally in spite of how he treats me. The only problem is, I just can't seem to do it…not for long, anyway." Again, there was defeat and heartbreaking heaviness in her voice.

"I certainly agree with that last part," I said. "You *can't* do it."

> God sets clear limits on what behavior He will accept.

There was silence as she thought about that.

"You can't do it because you shouldn't do it," I continued.

"I shouldn't love my husband?" she asked, as if she hadn't heard me correctly.

"No—what I mean is, you shouldn't assume it's ever God's perfect will for you to suffer abusive mistreatment from anyone for any reason, and especially not from your husband," I replied.

Misconceptions About Turning the Other Cheek

Over the years, I've learned how startling that statement can be to many people—both men and women. Somewhere along the way, we have mistaken God's exhortation to love our enemies and to turn the other cheek as commandments to become doormats in His name.

Even Jesus did not subject Himself to abuse by those who wanted to harm Him. On several occasions, He escaped an angry crowd. The only time He submitted to abuse was when it was time for Him to die for us. And His instruction to turn the other cheek was said in the context of not retaliating or taking revenge, not returning evil for evil. Inexplicably, we equate standing up for ourselves with aggression, selfishness, and sinful pride.

Even though God sets clear limits on what behavior He will accept, we somehow believe He has prohibited us from doing the same for ourselves. We allow abuse on the assumption that holding an offender accountable is less godly than quietly accepting the mistreatment and hoping the person will eventually see God's love in it. Surely the Lord wants better for His children.

When it comes to dealing with angry people, this flaw in our thinking is the first and most formidable obstacle we have to overcome. In truth, offering no resistance to angry people can actually work *against* helping them resolve the issues that make them angry in the first place.

In Sylvia's case, what incentive did Gene have for confronting his own pain and consequent anger when he was free to dish it out day after day with no repercussions and no consequences? Indeed, God's will for Sylvia was to require dignity and respect in *all* of her relationships, including her marriage with Gene.

Self-defense or Going on the Offensive

It is true there is often a fine line between self-defense and going on the offensive. You cross that line the moment you set out to cause reciprocal pain toward someone who has wounded you, rather than simply preventing further harm to yourself. That's a trap Christians are right to painstakingly avoid. As the apostle Paul wrote, "Do not grieve the Holy Spirit of God, with whom you were sealed for the day of redemption. Get rid of all bitterness, rage and anger, brawling and slander, along with every form of malice."[1]

But many people operate on the other end of the spectrum, avoiding conflict at all costs. In the name of what they mistakenly think is Christlike love, they don't set healthy boundaries for themselves.

There is a big difference between the "brawling and slander" and "malice" Paul warned us about, and justifiable self-preservation. Misunderstanding this distinction renders us powerless to protect ourselves from mistreatment and abuse—primarily because of this one reason: *We don't believe we even have a right to defend ourselves.*

Private Property, No Trespassing

Look around. Society is full of signs sending messages about personal rights and the boundaries that protect them, such as "Private property. Keep out." We know to cross those boundaries by invitation only—or face the consequences of violating another's right to protect their property. Our legal system provides backup, making it a punishable crime to steal, destroy, or vandalize someone else's possessions, or to trespass where we don't belong. These judicial laws help form the foundation of civilized society.

All abusive husbands—Christian or not—seem to know this one scripture; "Wives, submit to your husbands."[2] The all-too-prevalent mind-set is that a wife must submit to all mistreatment at the hands of her husband. There is no recourse, for that is God's will.

However, anyone who decidedly wants to be in God's will *must* know what God says in His Word in context of the *whole* Bible. We must correct the confusion that is too prevalent worldwide.

Correcting the Confusion

The woman who sincerely wants to please God but is not grounded in the Word of God can become captive to an incorrect understanding of biblical submission. All too easily she will *accept* abuse, thinking it is right when God says it is wrong.

Likewise, the man who sincerely wants to please God but who is not grounded in the Word can become captive to an incorrect understanding of sacrificial love. All too easily he will *accept* abuse, thinking it is right when God says it is wrong. One key to correcting the confusion is to read Scripture passages in light of their context. So when we read, "Wives, submit to your husbands" or "Husbands, love your wives, just as Christ loved the church," we need to...

- look at the surrounding verses
- look at the purpose of the passage or book in which the verse is found
- look at the whole counsel of God's Word on submission and love and how we are to relate to one another: "Do your best to present yourself to God as one approved, a workman who

does not need to be ashamed and who correctly handles the word of truth" (2 Timothy 2:15).

When I was teaching in Russia, Ukraine, and Romania, I remember the sincere attitudes of many pastors and spiritual leaders who assumed that wives had to submit to abuse. I said, "Show me the scriptures you are using to substantiate this position"—and indeed they did. The next day I addressed each one of their scriptural misconceptions. At the conclusion they said, "We've never heard teaching on this. We've known that somehow violence was wrong, but never knew what to say."

I want to give you this assurance: You are going to be the knight in shining armor—the desperately needed "Good Samaritan"—when you know how to help a woman suffering the devastating pain and the demoralizing shame of domestic violence. (The statistics are one out of every three women *worldwide*.)

Here are the arguments and answers regarding this matter:

Argument: When Jesus said, "Turn the other cheek," He meant that marriage partners should submit to abuse.[3]

Answer: When you look at the words of Jesus, the context is the issue of retaliation: Refuse to retaliate evil for evil. Jesus was not saying we should willingly accept abuse.

> *"You have heard that it was said, 'Eye for eye, and tooth for tooth.'*
> *But I tell you, Do not resist an evil person. If someone strikes you*
> *on the right cheek, turn to him the other also"*
> (MATTHEW 5:38-39).

The backdrop of "turning the other cheek" was refusing to take personal revenge rather than promoting or accepting abuse.

Argument: Because Jesus submitted Himself to abuse, people who want to be Christlike must also submit to abuse.

Answer: It is important to notice that on numerous occasions when the enemies of Jesus sought to harm Him, He eluded them and escaped. However, when the time came for Him to take away the sins of the world, Jesus allowed His blood to be the payment to purchase our forgiveness. Clearly, Jesus did not submit to abuse, except when it was time for Him to go to the cross.

> *"Jesus went around in Galilee, purposely staying away from Judea because the Jews there were waiting to take his life...
> Again they tried to seize him, but he escaped their grasp"*
> (JOHN 7:1; 10:39).

Argument: In 1 Peter 2 we are called to endure "unjust suffering." Therefore, abused mates should take such suffering as commendable before God.

> *"It is commendable if a man bears up under the pain of unjust suffering because he is conscious of God"*
> (1 PETER 2:19).

Answer: The context of this passage in 1 Peter refers to suffering "because [you] are conscious of God," which means suffering ridicule, criticism, and rejection because of your faith, not because you are someone's mate.

God does not call anyone to accept abuse from their mates. To the contrary, spouses who abuse their mates do so because of their own ungodliness. In fact, God specifically calls husbands and wives to sacrificially love their mates and treat them with respect.

> *"Wives, in the same way be submissive to your husband...
> so that they may be won over without words by [your] behavior...
> Husbands, in the same way be considerate as you live with your wives,
> and treat them with respect as the weaker partner and as heirs with you of
> the gracious gift of life, so that nothing will hinder your prayers"*
> (1 PETER 3:1-2,7).

Argument: An abused mate should view suffering as a legitimate "cross" to be taken up and carried for the sake of Christ.

> *"If anyone would come after me [Jesus],*
> *he must deny himself and take up his cross and follow me"*
> (Matthew 16:24).

Answer: Nowhere does the Bible indicate that the cross is an instrument of physical and emotional pain to be inflicted upon a mate. In context, Jesus was saying the cross is a symbol of death—death to self-centered living, death to self-rule so that the Lord can rule our hearts and lives. The very next verse confirms that the cross stands for yielding our lives to the Lord, not yielding our lives to abuse.

> *"Whoever wants to save his life will lose it,*
> *but whoever loses his life for me will find it"*
> (Matthew 16:25).

Argument: God made men superior/inferior to women.

Answer: God made women and men different from one another, with different roles and functions. The Bible does not say that God regards one gender as superior and the other as inferior; rather, He regards them as equal.

> *"There is neither Jew nor Greek, slave nor free,*
> *male nor female, for you are all one in Christ Jesus"*
> (Galatians 3:28).

Argument: Because Ephesians 5:21 says, "Submit to one another," a mate must submit unconditionally—even to abuse.[4]

Answer: This conclusion contradicts other scriptures. A hierarchy of submission is demonstrated when the apostles refuse to obey the high priest and instead obey the Great Commission by continuing to teach in the name of Jesus (Matthew 28:19-20). They committed a severely punishable offense by directly disobeying the high priest in order to submit to God.

Similarly, if a mate expects a marriage partner to do something that God says is wrong, the partner is to disobey the erring mate in order to submit to God. Our Lord clearly states His opposition to violence, as well as His position that spouses are to treat their mates with respect.

> *"Peter and the other apostles replied:*
> *'We must obey God rather than men!'"*
> (Acts 5:29).

Argument: Because the Bible says, "The husband is the head of the wife," a wife must not resist being abused by her husband.[5]

Answer: A wife is to submit to the *headship* of her husband, but the Bible nowhere implies she is to submit to the abuse of her husband. She is to respect his position, not be victimized by his power.

In Ephesians 5:23, the husband-wife relationship is compared to the relationship between Christ and the church. Christ is "the head of the church, his body." Although the husband is the head of his wife, no head abuses its own body. A husband never chooses to beat his body—unless, of course, he is "out of his head" (mentally ill)! Instead, he does whatever he can to protect and provide for his own body. A godly man will treat his wife in the same way.

> *"The husband is the head of the wife as Christ is the head*
> *of the church, his body, of which he is the Savior...*
> *husbands ought to love their wives as their own bodies.*
> *He who loves his wife loves himself. After all, no one ever hated*
> *his own body, but he feeds and cares for it,*
> *just as Christ does the church"*
> (Ephesians 5:23,28-29).

How Could She Tell Anyone?

Intelligent, competent, assured—these words painted the picture of my friend Gail, an attractive, energetic young woman whom I had known casually for over ten years. But when I received word that, at the hands of her husband, she had been a victim of repeated violence, my first thought was, *How could this be?*

After all, Gail had worked several years at a Christian ministry training people how to study the Bible. Then she attended a respected seminary, where she met her future husband, Andy. However, after they married, her confidence decreased and her fear increased. Unbeknownst to family and friends, Gail was being abused.

But how could she tell anyone? She wanted to protect the image of her little family. Surely if she "tried hard enough" he would stop—that's what all abused women typically think.

> We have a heavenly Father who wants us to be safe and secure—physically, emotionally, and spiritually.

But not so. Now Andy was divorcing her for another woman, and they were in the midst of a custody battle over their two young sons. The judge ruled that until a decision was made as to which parent would have custodial care, this arrangement was to be followed: The children were to stay in the home, and each parent would rotate in and out every other week. So every other week for about a year and a half, Gail stayed in my home.

We had many late-night talks. The one that stands out most in my memory is the evening I asked if she had any pictures to prove to the judge that Andy was an untrustworthy, violent man. Immediately she went to the guest bedroom and returned with pictures of herself—police photographs—that showed her head severely bruised and swollen.

I was stunned. I hadn't expected such graphic pictures. (Andy had denied the abuse, claiming instead that she had inflicted the injuries on herself—a common "blame game" tactic!)

When I gave Gail our Biblical Counseling Keys on wife abuse, she quickly affirmed what it said about many wife batterers being adept at manipulating their wives with scriptures such as, "Wives, submit to your husbands," yet are careless about heeding all the Bible's verses against violence. (And sadly, as of yet, I have never talked with a wife who has heard scriptures presented from the pulpit that encourage her to seek the protection she so desperately needs if she is being abused.) Rather, after an incident of wife abuse, too many women hear foolish statements like, "What did you do to cause it?" as though the husband's violent sin is her fault. This doubly victimizes the woman.

No wonder many women who suffer abuse are disheartened, confused, and distressed. They wonder, *Must I really suffer at the hands of someone who has sworn to protect and cherish me? And where is God when I am hurting so much?*

Not only is God with those who suffer, He also has provided a way of deliverance through His Word. The joy of victory and healing is available to any who seek it. My prayer is that the biblical truths shared within the pages of this book will be used by God to free you or someone you know from the shackles of unjust suffering.

> *"Then you will know the truth,*
> *and the truth will set you free"*
> (John 8:32).

Now, for the rest of the story: First, after two years, my friend was awarded custody of her children. Second, the judge admitted that, in retrospect, his better judgment would have been to assign only one parent custodial care until a permanent decision was made. And last, tragically, Andy served no time in jail and received no sentence for his abuse.

We All Have God-given Rights

Consider the following "bomb squad basics"—ground rules for relating to the angry people in your life:

1. You have the right to be safe from physical and emotional harm

It is staggering to realize how many people suffer needlessly at the hands of angry, abusive people because they think God is calling them to stick it out in unsafe situations. I've talked with far too many wounded women—women who are precious to God—who remained in abusive marriages in the name of submission. I've heard from employee after employee who endured crass conduct and cruel behavior from their bosses because they felt God wanted them to put up with such treatment. And I've spoken with countless people who, assuming it was God's will, remained in friendships in which they were continually used and manipulated.

Situations like these are complex, and there is no one-size-fits-all solution. But be assured of this: We have a heavenly Father who wants us to be safe and secure—physically, emotionally, and spiritually.

In most societies, a parent who deliberately puts a child in danger is scorned and punished. Yet some people mistakenly believe our heavenly Father puts us in perilous situations with no concern for our safety and leaves us to fend for ourselves. To the contrary, we have a God who is a loving protector. Jesus assured,

> *"Which of you, if his son asks for bread, will give him a stone? Or if he asks for a fish, will give him a snake? If you, then, though you are evil, know how to give good gifts to your children, how much more will your Father in heaven give good gifts to those who ask him!"*[6]

Here's the bottom-line truth: Of course, you have a right to be safe. God is never pleased or honored when His people are mistreated in abusive relationships. When He encouraged us to rejoice when we encounter various trials,[7] He was *not* saying pain and trauma are always part of His will for us. Rather, He was saying trials are inevitable in a sinful world filled with sinful people who do sinful things.

But the good news is those very trials can provide a valuable opportunity to grow and mature as Christians. And if we love God, He promises to use our every experience for our good. Living with an angry person has the challenging potential to teach us how to protect ourselves in firm, loving, godly ways and to stop ignoring our wounds by suffering in silence.

2. You have the right to set your own boundaries

Only you know what behavior hurts your heart or makes you feel threatened and uncomfortable. And only you can decide what behavior you will accept and what you won't. That right belongs to you alone. For example, because Gene grew up in a home where aggressive actions and attitudes among family members were commonplace, he often chided Sylvia for being oversensitive if she objected to his angry outbursts. Unconcealed hostility that Gene called "normal" made Sylvia feel frightened and insecure.

"Come on! I was only joking!"

"Everybody gets mad and flies off the handle sometimes. Don't make a federal case out of it."

"Lighten up, will you?"

"So what if I get mad? You're the one making a big deal out of it."

Comments like these are clues that the angry person wants to control you by having the final say in where your boundaries are drawn. Anger bowls can also operate as tools of manipulation. Don't fall into that fire pit.

As I told Sylvia, your boundaries are just that—*yours*. In fact, setting standards for yourself is more than a right. Proverbs 4:23 tells us it is an important responsibility: "Above all else, guard your heart, for it is the wellspring of life."

3. You have the right to enforce your boundaries with consequences for encroachment

Hopefully, you have claimed your right to be safe and to stay safe by setting boundaries. Wonderful! Your next step in successfully dealing with angry people is affirming your right to insist on repercussions when a boundary has been crossed and when trespassers refuse to retreat—even if they are spouses. They too must know there are consequences for angrily screaming, smashing, and slamming their way into your territory.

4. You have the right to defend your cause

Most believers fear being too quick to defend their borders and impose repercussions. In taking to heart Paul's admonition to live up to our calling as Christians "bearing with one another in love, eager to maintain the unity of the Spirit in the bond of peace,"[8] too often we wind up taking no action at all. Naturally, that communicates to those whose anger spews into our territory that our boundaries are not real, but only imaginary and not to be taken seriously.

However, the phrase "Bearing with one another" in Ephesians 4:2 doesn't mean we are to ignore sinful behavior. Rather, it means we are to accept our differences.

Jesus affirmed our right, our obligation to impose consequences on someone who has wronged us:

> *"If your brother sins against you, go and show him his fault,*
> *just between the two of you. If he listens to you, you have won*
> *your brother over. But if he will not listen, take one or two others*
> *along, so that 'every matter may be established by the testimony*
> *of two or three witnesses.' If he refuses to listen to them,*
> *tell it to the church; and if he refuses to listen even to the church,*
> *treat him as you would a pagan or a tax collector"*
> (MATTHEW 18:15-17).

It's simple: If someone sins against you, your God-given right and responsibility is to confront—with a stinging rebuke, if necessary. If the person is clearly in the wrong but fails to take responsibility for the misbehavior, consequences should be enacted.

Three Keys to Peace (or at Least a Cease-Fire)

Now that you know God has empowered you with the right to live in safety and peace, you are ready to learn the art of "de-escalation" in any conflict with an angry person.

Fair warning: This isn't always easy. It requires a challenging blend of toughness and compassion, determination and patience, humility and self-respect. But the payoff is there for anyone willing to do the work. As an old German proverb says, "God makes the nuts, but He doesn't crack them."[9] You've got to do that yourself. Here's how:

1. Don't Pour Gasoline on the Fire

If there is one thing that acts like gasoline doused on someone's fiery anger, it is *more* anger, coming from someone else and aimed at the angry person. Yes, you have the right to be safe, to set boundaries, and to stand firm when those boundaries are broken. But using fiery anger to retaliate against fiery anger is the path least likely to lead to peace and most likely to lead to war. In fact, it can just as easily change you from an innocent victim to a guilty accomplice—something Brianna learned the hard way.

> *"There is...a time to be silent and a time to speak"*
> (Ecclesiastes 3:1,7).

Brianna was a chef at a prestigious fine-dining restaurant. She'd worked hard to get the job and was proud to be part of such an elite team. She enjoyed and respected the people with whom she created beautiful meals every night—except one. Tracy took an instant—and inexplicable—dislike to Brianna. Every attempt Brianna made to break the ice between them was returned with raw sarcasm and rudeness. Because the two women worked elbow to elbow in the kitchen, the situation quickly became a recipe for misery.

"I had never been around someone so determined to be angry," Brianna told me. "Every night she lost her cool over something new I had allegedly done to make her life more difficult. I got fed up pretty quick."

Soon, in spite of herself, Brianna began hurling insults back at Tracy...tit for tat. Their mutual anger escalated until one evening it ended in a physical scuffle resulting in overturned simmering saucepans and a painful burn on Brianna's hand. It was a colossal confrontation that brought serious consequences: Both women were suspended from work for a week.

"It seemed so unfair," Brianna said. "I hadn't realized that by letting her make me angry too, I had become part of the problem. That's certainly how my boss saw me. He didn't care who started it."

It is important to stay calm when dealing with an angry person. Remember, anger is an extremely powerful emotion that God's Spirit— who lives in you—can both tame and temper. It has no power to force you to respond one way or another.

We can choose to see that anger is contagious only if we let it be. Above all, don't allow sparks from someone else's anger to ignite your own.

In other words, fighting fire with fire can quickly kindle a raging inferno. Proverbs 15:1 tells us, "A gentle answer turns away wrath, but a harsh word stirs up anger." If you habitually respond to anger with a "gentle answer," you'll see the other person's wrath diminish, *as well as your own.*

2. Don't Hesitate to Evacuate

If you were to suddenly realize you were holding a live grenade, I'm pretty sure what you would do—toss it, or drop it and run! Yet when it comes to dealing with an explosive person, many of us ignore the best defense: safe distance. We remain engaged in battle, on the angry person's terms, long past when it is productive or prudent to do so. Perhaps we feel withdrawal is the same as surrender. But every good general knows retreating and regrouping today is sometimes the only way to advance tomorrow.

Here's the bottom line: Protecting yourself is paramount. In extreme cases, where physical violence is a possibility, it is vital you leave immediately. Don't wait until after a blow is struck. If you feel threatened, go! *Now.*

But even when you aren't subject to bodily harm, there is no need to submit to an angry emotional beating either. It is important to learn how to recognize when the heat of rage has burned away any possibility of reason or compromise. When that happens, it is time to retreat to avoid further emotional abuse. The "time-out" can last minutes, hours, days, or longer.

The point is, you are entitled to maintain a safe distance as long as you continue to feel threatened by the flames of someone's unresolved anger. The writer of Proverbs tells us, "A prudent mans sees danger and takes refuge, but the simple keep going and suffer for it" (22:3).

3. Call for Reinforcements

Sylvia's friend, the one who dialed the number the night Sylvia spoke to me on *Hope in the Night,* understood we are seldom called to face a giant one-on-one like David did Goliath. More often, we're able to face our angry enemies in the strength and safety of supportive company—friends, family members, fellow believers, a trusted pastor, or a professional counselor. When physical violence is present, help can also come in the form of court orders and police protection.

The truth is, an angry person's chief weapon against you is psychological and emotional control—something that's all too easy to achieve when you are isolated and alone. You need others to remind you of your rights and to stand with you in securing the boundaries you set for yourself.

Sylvia eventually saw the wisdom in that. With the help of a support group for abused women at her church, she began to change her mistaken beliefs about what God expected of her and claim her right to be safe. As a result, she moved out of the house for a period of separation to let Gene know she was serious about being free from his angry, threatening behavior.

"I could never have done that without backup," she told me later. "Others helped me see it wasn't about changing Gene. Only God can do that, and I still pray He will. But now, it was about changing me and protecting myself and making the most of the life God gave *me.*"

The biblical call and necessity of giving tangible support is undeniably clear:

*"Rescue those being led away to death; hold back those
staggering toward slaughter. If you say, 'But we knew nothing
about this,' does not he who weighs the heart perceive it?
Does not he who guards your life know it? Will he not repay
each person according to what he has done?"*
(PROVERBS 24:11-12).

Don't battle the blazing fires of anger alone. Even firefighters know
not to send one of their own alone into a burning building. Engage
reinforcements, and be better prepared to face anger flare-ups.

Out of Harm's Way

Your heavenly Father wants you to be safe and free from the effects
of living with an angry person. But He never intends for you to take
harmful risks in securing a safe and peaceful environment.

God expects you to love angry people, to forgive them, to treat them
as you would wish to be treated—but at a safe distance. He does not
expect you to helplessly endure and continue to facilitate their fiery
incursions into your territory.

Know your rights.

Draw your boundaries.

Guard them firmly.

Fire Extinguishers: Beating the Heat

A fire cannot flare up to full force unless it has three things in abundance: heat, oxygen, and fuel.

A fire extinguisher will live up to its name only if it succeeds in taking away one or more of these elements. However, not all extinguishing materials are right for every fire. Water is great for robbing a blaze of heat, but it can scatter liquid fuels and make matters worse. It can also conduct a dangerous current in an electrical fire. Extinguishers filled with carbon dioxide or baking soda may cut off a fire's supply of oxygen, but do little to cool things down when the heat is extreme.

In the same way, a one-size-fits-all approach to disarming anger won't work well, and could even make matters worse. (Confront exploding anger with a similar explosion, for instance, and you could detonate a blast of devastating proportions.) Instead, you want a variety of "fire extinguishers" in your emotional arsenal, each filled with specialized anti-inflammatory agents. Acquire firm and fair boundaries—compassion, prayer, and faith in God's healing love—and practice using them to extinguish flare-ups. They'll help you manage even the fiercest blazes... and keep you from getting burned in the process.

QUENCHING THE COALS
How to Plan Ahead for Anger Flare-Ups

"The wise turn away wrath"
(PROVERBS 29:8 ESV).

"I DON'T MEAN to be so mad."

"I feel guilty about getting so angry."

"I fly off the handle...then hate myself!"

Each weeknight, during our live two-hour call-in counseling program *Hope in the Night,* people call to share their life struggles and receive real solutions. Regularly, I hear callers say things like:

"My temper comes out of nowhere—like a monster in my closet!"

"I live with a rage-aholic, and we all walk on eggshells."

"She makes me furious, but now my own anger frightens me!"

Many people feel miffed for even experiencing anger in the first place. They don't know where it comes from, and don't know what to do with it. What they do know is it causes pain, and they want to get rid of it.

Anger by Another Name

During the first year our small Hope for the Heart staff in Dallas met for a weekly devotional, I asked everyone around the circle to share about what made them the most angry. After I and several other members of our team had shared, I turned to the person to my right and asked, "What makes you the most angry?" Looking at me with the sweetest smile, Nancy batted her beautiful brown eyes and said, "I don't get angry."

"You don't ever get angry?" I probed. "No," she answered confidently. "Really?" I questioned. Again, she responded ever so sweetly, "No, really."

So we went on to the next person, who explained that her anger arose when, as a pastor's wife, she and her children had been criticized for not being "perfect." Then the next person said, "Well, I begin to feel angry when I want to communicate but I get no response. I get put off, then I feel rejected. That really hurts!"

We were more than halfway around the circle when Nancy—who has to be one of the dearest people in the world—interrupted, "June, excuse me: I just realized I *do* get angry. I really do; I just always called it *frustration*!" It turns out Nancy did have an anger bowl—by another name.

Sadly, the sum total of what most of us think or know about anger is this: We have it, but we don't like it—not in ourselves, and certainly not in others. Anger is usually as welcome as a broken toe or a bad toothache.

Who can blame us? Anger can be dangerous, destructive, and dysfunctional. It can make us feel embarrassed and ashamed, or wounded and victimized, depending on whether we're dishing it out or receiving it. We've all seen the devastating damage anger can do to relationships, physical and mental health, and spiritual well-being.

After I taught on anger at our Hope Biblical Counseling Institute, one of our staff members, Jennifer, shared a story from her past. Her father's anger threatened to leave her awash in grief, resentment, and anger. Would she lash back?

Buried Anger

Jennifer's father called to say that her grandmother (his mother) had been admitted to the hospital. Although Jennifer's "Gammy" was expected to be in the hospital only a short time, Jennifer promised to visit the following evening.

However, the next day this young mother of small children came down with the flu. Not wanting to expose her sick grandmother to the flu, Jennifer stayed home and suffered through her own illness. She was bedridden for four days.

After Jennifer recovered, she phoned her dad to ask how Gammy was doing. His curt reply was, "We buried her yesterday."

"Wh-what?" Jennifer stammered.

He robotically repeated, "We buried her yesterday."

Jennifer was stunned. She couldn't process her father's words. Suddenly, she was overcome with sorrow, regret, and anger.

"Why didn't somebody call me?"

"Apparently you were too busy to come see her, so why bother to call?"

Jennifer tried to explain she had been sick and that she wanted to avoid spreading a viral infection. At a loss for words, she stuttered and stammered—then became silent. She doesn't remember how the call ended or who ended it. She just knows she was horribly hurt and unbelievably angry!

Reeling from the shock of the news, with sorrowful sobs, Jennifer vowed *never, never, never* to speak to her father again. How could he be so heartless...so unfeeling...so vengeful? How could he so nonchalantly throw out such callous, uncaring words about her beloved grandmother—"We buried her yesterday"? Beneath the blaze of her anger, she suffered through the anguish of deep sorrow.

As she vowed never to subject herself to her father's cruelty again, she also determined to shield her children from his flaming arrows. She felt this injustice gave her the "right" to sever the relationship.

Seeking comfort, Jennifer returned to a collection of cherished letters from Gammy. Letters filled with encouraging words helped Jennifer survive the turmoil of living with an alcoholic father. Gammy's example of Christlike love, despite the faults and failures of others, was a legacy Jennifer could treasure.

Fanning the Flames

Over time, when Jennifer's fury at her father seemed to be lessening to a glowing ember, she would begin to fan her anger back into a roaring blaze by replaying her father's vengeful words over and over again.

As Jennifer recounted her story, I couldn't believe what I was hearing, and my heart broke for her.

Jennifer admitted her struggle with the famous fifth commandment in the Bible: "Honor your father..." How could she possibly honor her father when he had been so cold, so callous, so cruel? If she ever let go of what was certainly *justified* anger, she would be left with piercing pain.

Jennifer then shared how she began sifting through the ashes and slowly examining the situation from her father's point of view—his grief over the loss of his precious mother, his hurt and disappointment in Jennifer, and probably his disappointment in himself.

Of course, none of these things justified what Jennifer's father had done or how coldly he had said it. But Jennifer could remember seeing her father lash out many times, striking the first blow before someone else could hurt him. She knew that was how he defended his heart.

"Regardless of how he acted, I knew I was responsible for my own actions, and I knew I needed to forgive my dad—for my own sake as much as his. Only by releasing my dad and relinquishing my anger could I *realize* freedom from the festering wound... the tension and the tears."

> God gives us the power to be assertive without being aggressive, resolute without seeking revenge.

Slowly, God's grace began to soften Jennifer until she was able to forgive her dad, and herself. By doing so, she was able to re-establish a relationship with her father, honoring him because she chose to obey her heavenly Father.

They never discussed the time surrounding Gammy's death, but when he died ten years later, Jennifer felt genuine grief, sorrow, and pain—without remorse, recriminations, or regrets.

Jennifer's story encourages us that we can work through our anger. It's a process whereby we can find true freedom when we relinquish our hurts and release those who hurt us.

When we are drawn into anger-inducing situations, we need not be at the mercy of our emotions. There is no need for impulsive, knee-jerk responses. God gives us the power to be assertive without being aggressive, resolute without seeking revenge.

When you are angry, does reason rule, or do tense emotions take charge? Do you allow the mind of Christ within you to determine how you should act, making a choice that leads to *appropriate action*, or do you give a hasty response that leads to an *inappropriate reaction*?

If you have never evaluated what happens when you feel angry, or if you lack insight as to how others perceive you when you are angry, seek God's wisdom and understanding. The writer of Proverbs tells us:

> *"If you call out for insight and cry aloud for understanding,*
> *and if you look for it as for silver and search for it as for hidden treasure,*
> *then you will understand the fear of the LORD and find the*
> *knowledge of God. For the LORD gives wisdom, and from his mouth*
> *come knowledge and understanding"*
> (PROVERBS 2:3-6).

How can we learn to act (with conviction, clarity, and confidence) rather than react (out of compulsion, confusion, and callousness)? The first step is to simply recognize that reacting is not likely to produce a helpful outcome. In fact, it will probably make matters worse. Acting, on the other hand, helps us achieve positive, godly results. Consider Darren, a man quite transparent about his anger and eager for transformation.

The Proverbs Project

On a Friday years ago, I traveled to Orlando, Florida, for a week of speaking and media engagements. I felt blessed to stay in the home of an exceptional couple, Darren and Diana, along with their teenage daughter, Tina. I've never felt more warmly welcomed and included.

On Monday morning, I sat at the kitchen table with Diana, sharing how much I admired Darren.

"He's wonderful—a totally trustworthy husband," she said. Then she confided, "But for as long as I've known him—26 years—he's had an anger problem. It really concerns me."

I listened empathetically and nodded. Then Diana quickly moved on to other topics.

On Tuesday afternoon, I chatted with Tina about her senior year, her high school graduation, and her plans for college. Then the conversation came around to her parents. She shared how supportive they were. But then she leaned in close and whispered, "I love my dad so much. I just wish he didn't have such a bad temper."

I was surprised she brought this up—unprompted. I had not mentioned anything her mom had shared.

Then on Wednesday night, Darren said, "I know you've got a television appearance in West Palm Beach on Friday. I have some business I could do in West Palm, if you'd like for me to drive you."

"That's wonderful!" I exclaimed.

So Friday morning, during our three-hour trek, Darren and I discussed his business, his heart for God, and bits and pieces about his background.

After a couple hours of conversation, he apparently felt comfortable enough to interject, "June, there's a problem I've struggled with for a long time. I've never figured out how to control my anger. No matter how hard I try, I just keep failing. Do you have any ideas?"

Impressed at his authenticity and humility, I offered, "Would you be willing to do a project for a month? Just read the thirty-one chapters of Proverbs, one chapter a day for a month. Begin with the first chapter, reading slowly so the words will sink into your mind and heart. Each day, write down any verses about anger or speech or attitude. When you're finished," I explained, "review the verses you've written and ask the Lord what He wants you to learn from them."

Darren agreed to undertake the Proverbs Project, as we called it.

The next day, I returned to Dallas.

Eight weeks later I received a note from Darren stating, "Every morning after breakfast, Diana and I read a chapter in Proverbs. At first I thought, *Why did you give me this project? Nothing I've read has anything to do with anger.* But later, I saw what I needed to see. I needed a *new me.* I did what you suggested—I completed the Proverbs Project.

"When I read all the verses that show what an angry man looks like, I was overwhelmed by the image of the person I *did not* want to become—someone who stirs up strife and dissension, someone people should avoid. I knew I needed to change. Well, now the Lord is changing me!"

A short time later, I had dinner with Darren and Diana, who had come to Dallas on business. What a joy! Diana quickly confirmed, "It's made all the difference in the world!"

I was so grateful to God.

Since that time, I have "prescribed" the Proverbs Project to many a struggler. This exercise is usually not a cure-all—not a quick fix—but it provides the motivation to cooperate with God, the motivation to let Him change anyone who is willing. The Bible says, "The one who calls you is faithful and he will do it" (1 Thessalonians 5:24).

How to Head Off Anger at the Pass

If you ever watched those old black-and-white Westerns on television, you probably remember the phrase uttered frequently by the good guys: "Let's head 'em off at the pass." That meant they were determined to arrive at a strategic point before the bad guys so they could thwart any villainous plans.

Well, determining to act rather than react is the same thing: We *anticipate* what might happen when we get angry, and we *plan ahead* to keep things from getting out of hand. We prepare ahead of time for "quenching the coals" of heated episodes and therefore limit the potential destruction.

Let me offer four ways we can head off our anger at the pass:

1. Identify Your Triggers

All of us have certain situations that trigger our anger. Although a lot of things in life can make us mad, each of us has certain "recurring themes" when it comes to being provoked. That is, our anger episodes are usually caused by the same triggers over and over. Analyzing your anger patterns can help move you from subjectivity to objectivity, from being controlled by anger to benefiting from it.

To identify your triggers, ask yourself the following questions:

- We learned earlier that there are four sources of anger (hurt, injustice, fear, frustration). Is there one that tends to provoke your anger more than the others?

- When you review your recent anger episodes, does a pattern emerge?

- What painful issues from your past, especially from childhood, stir up present-day emotions? What experiences from back *then* inflame anger here and *now*?

- Are there certain environments that seem to "conduct" your anger energy more than others (the workplace, family get-togethers, competitive events, neighborhood gatherings)?

- Is there a certain type of personality that tends to push your buttons (loud and bossy, quiet and conniving, syrupy sweet)? Why do you think this is so?

- If you could label the kinds of things that make you mad, what would they be? Think of at least three or four of the most prominent ones for you (such as disrespect, manipulation, dishonesty, sarcasm, irresponsibility).

By thinking through these questions, you can gain insight into what activates your anger. By identifying the triggers, you can be proactive in dealing with them.

As for me, two situations in particular tend to accelerate my adrenaline and agitate my anger.

First, I have difficulty with arrogant people who put others down through belittling comments. A haughty attitude smacks of a prideful spirit and heats up my temper! I tend to think puffed-up people need deflating, and I have to be careful not to be the nail that lets the air out of them. When I'm around men and women like this, I remain vigilant to keep my emotions in check. I purposely pray that God would change their hearts and ways, and meet the needs they are seeking to meet in their own strength.

Second, I become incensed when people are taken advantage of— particularly when it's done in the name of God or Christianity.

Recently I got a call from Alice, a young woman who is a new believer and susceptible to misguided teaching. Unfortunately, she had been attending a church that promotes what I call the prosperity gospel, or name-it-claim-it theology.

Though Alice earns only a modest income and is struggling to get out of debt, her pastor and his wife had been urging everyone in the congregation to "demonstrate their faith" by digging deeper and giving more to support "the Lord's work. Just give all your money, and God is sure to bless you materially tenfold."

Imagine my outrage at learning that Alice's pastor had embarrassed her in front of the entire congregation by announcing that her reluctance to donate her retirement account constituted sinful selfishness. Alice reluctantly handed over the funds. But she remained confused about why the pastor and his wife both drove Jaguars, dressed ostentatiously, and owned several vacation homes.

While I didn't know what was in the hearts of this pastor and his wife, I did know Alice's faith was fragile and that her growth could be stunted by her exposure to unscrupulous leaders and unscriptural teaching. It made me mad to even think this dear person might have been swindled. I think I probably felt much like Jesus must have felt when He drove the thieves and swindlers out of the temple. Even Jesus had a strong reaction at times, a righteous indignation in response to hypocrisy and dishonesty.

2. Train Your Brain

A key point in this book so far has been that denying or suppressing angry feelings is counterproductive. We must acknowledge and accept our emotions so we can deal with them in a healthy way.

This doesn't mean our feelings should trump logical thinking. We all know people who are ruled by their unhealthy emotions, and it isn't a pretty picture. It's all about first acknowledging our emotions, then learning how to control them and use them for their intended purpose.

I am fascinated by how much God's Word has to say about both our hearts and minds, and how they are interrelated. Jesus told His followers to "love the Lord your God with all your heart and with all your soul and with all your mind."[1] And the psalmist wrote, "Test me, O Lord, and try me, examine my heart and my mind."[2]

I'm so grateful that God created us with the capacity to fulfill His desires and comply with His truth. Clearly, the Lord intends for both our thoughts and emotions to be used in conjunction with one another. Our hearts can be reshaped and our brains rewired so our behaviors will become more and more Christlike.

That's why Paul said, "Do not conform any longer to the pattern of this world, but be transformed by the renewing of your mind. Then you will be able to test and approve what God's will is—his good, pleasing, and perfect will."[3] Peter said to "prepare your minds for action; be self-controlled."[4]

Understanding these and other scriptures is essential for those of us who want to change the way we handle anger. When we *train our brain*, we *change our behavior*.

One of the best ways to do this is by consistently studying and memorizing God's Word. Some people today question the value and necessity of Scripture memorization. After all, anyone with an Internet connection can look up Bible passages in a matter of seconds.

But gathering information about the Bible is just a small part of what God had in mind when He said, "How can a young person stay pure? By obeying your Word...I have hidden your word in my heart that I might not sin against you."[5]

Jesus put the matter in straightforward terms: "The good man brings good things out of the good stored up in him, and the evil man brings evil things out of the evil stored up in him."[6] If we want to change our responses to anger, one of the best ways is by saturating our thoughts…with the life-changing truths of God's Word.

3. Prepare an Anger Action Plan

All too frequently we read about another shooting at a school, a mall, or even a church. Because of this, many institutions have drawn up emergency action plans so they'll know how to respond should a crisis occur.

> You will find it helpful to think through *in advance* the appropriate, productive response when your emotions get hot.

Let's take that idea and apply it to our anger. You will find it helpful to think through *in advance* the appropriate, productive response when your emotions get hot. Consider:

An appropriate action is to cautiously express your thoughts and feelings with understanding and concern for the other person's welfare. Proverbs 17:27 says, "A man of knowledge uses words with restraint, and a man of understanding is even-tempered."

An inappropriate reaction is to express your thoughts and feelings in such a way they stir up anger in others and produce strife. Proverbs 30:33 paints this graphic picture: "As churning the milk produces butter, and as twisting the nose produces blood, so stirring up anger produces strife."

While you're calm and unhurried, envision how you would like to respond the next time you get angry. You can start devising your individualized "anger action plan" by thinking carefully about how you want to respond in heated situations:

Appropriate Actions	Inappropriate Reactions
Ask Yourself...	
Will I use tactful, compassionate words?	Will I use tactless, condemning words?
Will I try to see the other person's point of view?	Will I see only my point of view?
Will I want to help the one who angers me?	Will I want to punish the one who angers me?
Will I focus first on my own faults?	Will I focus only on the faults of others?
Will I have realistic expectations?	Will I have unrealistic expectations?
Will I have a flexible and cooperative attitude?	Will I have a rigid and uncooperative attitude?
Will I forgive personal injustices?	Will I avenge personal injustices?

4. Communicate Your Anger to Another

Learning how to convey anger appropriately will better help you put out the fires that could scorch your relationships.

Before communicating your anger toward someone, take time to evaluate whether expressing your anger is needful, appropriate, and will prove beneficial.

Some people simply do not know how to handle anger directed toward them. They become hostile and defensive, or weak and placating, resolving nothing.

If you simply want to vent your feelings, to release some pent-up steam, then pour out your heart to God and maybe to another person, but not to the person with whom you are angry. Should you decide to arrange a meeting and comfort the one who has angered you, here are some things you will need to do in preparation:

Choose to be proactive

- Examine your motivation.
- Be realistic in your expectations.
- Know what you want to accomplish.
- Assess the legitimacy of your request.
- Rehearse how you will approach the subject.
- Anticipate possible reactions from the other person.
- Think through how you might respond to those reactions.
- Decide if you are willing to live with any negative repercussions.
- Talk with a wise and trusted person if you are uncertain what to do.

Choose a time and place to talk

- Select a time and place convenient for both of you; find an atmosphere conducive for listening and sharing.
- Meet on "neutral turf" so both of you are likely to feel equal in power and importance.
- Allot sufficient time to address both of your concerns.
- Commit the time to God and seek His wisdom and understanding.
- Communicate your desires for open and honest communication and resolution.
- Express your pain and anger in a loving, nonaccusatory way without criticizing the person's character, utilizing the "sandwich technique" (see pages 82-83).
- Evaluate the willingness of the other person to receive your rebuke without becoming angry or defensive and to understand your hurt, fear, frustration, or indignation over an injustice.

- Give opportunity for a response without interruption or defensiveness on your part.

- Affirm what is being said by repeating and clarifying spoken statements.

- Request any desired changes in behavior you believe will resolve the present problem and prevent future problems.

- Agree to change any problematic behavior on your part.

- Promote fairness and objectivity, openness and optimism.

- Extend total forgiveness unreservedly and willingly.

- Value differences in goals, desires, and priorities.

- Applaud the person's willingness to listen to you, to resolve the problem, and to work toward improving your relationship.

Always keep this in mind: "A word aptly spoken is like apples of gold in settings of silver."[7]

I also recommend creating written outline of the way you want to think and act when hurt, injustice, fear, or frustration come your way—a series of steps to deal with the inevitable sources of anger that each of us struggle with from time to time.

So...how exactly can you respond in a godly way? What will you avoid doing? How can you remain calm and clearheaded? What is the optimal outcome for a conflict? (If you have trouble developing a plan, remember that chapter 13 outlines a process for alleviating present anger. These steps will provide a framework you can apply to your individual situation and anger style.)

Jesus encouraged us to plan ahead. He said,

> *"Suppose one of you wants to build a tower.*
> *Will he not first sit down and estimate the cost to see*
> *if he has enough money to complete it?...*
> *Or suppose a king is about to go to war against another king.*

Will he not first sit down and consider whether
he is able with ten thousand men to oppose the one coming
against him with twenty thousand?"
(LUKE 14:28,31).

Don't wait until you're in the heat of battle to figure out how to respond. Sit down now, and create an "anger action plan" before the moment of need arrives.

Surrender Yourself to God's Healing

In the mid-1800s, a woman named Frances Ridley Havergal authored more than 70 beloved hymns, including "Take My Life and Let It Be" and "Like a River Glorious," as well as numerous volumes of poetry and devotional works. During her lifetime, Frances was widely popular and greatly admired. She was one of the most creative and devout Christians of her era. Even today her hymns are sung in churches throughout the world.

Here's something else, though, about Frances: She had a very bad temper—the kind characterized as *explosive*. After her anger eruptions, she would be mortified and confess her wrongdoing to the Lord. But then she would lose her temper again…and again.

One day after a particularly bad explosion, she threw herself down by her bed and wept. She prayed, "Lord, must it always be so? Will I always have this temper to keep me humble before You?"

While she was on her knees, the Lord planted a verse in her mind: "The Egyptians whom you have seen today you will see no more forever." Initially mystified as to the meaning of God's message, Frances then remembered God speaking these words to Moses when the Egyptians pursued the Israelites to take them back into bondage.

She applied the verse to her own situation by equating the Egyptians to her temper and the way in which Satan wanted to use it to pull her into bondage. She had never doubted God's ability to free her, but now she realized God not only *could* free her, but *would* free her. He was going to take her temper away.

Brimming over with joy, Frances boldly asked, "Lord, could it be forever?"

It seemed to her the words came back from the Lord, "Yes. 'No more...forever.'"

Frances's sister said from that day on, Frances never again lost her temper. She believed God, and God did a miracle.[8] Anger was never a problem for Frances again.

If we want to change the way we deal with anger, let's first go to God with humble and contrite hearts, asking Him to heal us, change our hurtful behavior, and conform us to the character of Christ. The Bible says, "The righteous cry out, and the LORD hears them; he delivers them from all their troubles. The LORD is close to the brokenhearted and saves those who are crushed in spirit" (Psalm 34:17-18).

God may choose to bring instant change, as He did with Frances. Or He may cause growth and transformation over a period of time, which more often seems to be the case. Either way, when we surrender our lives to the Lord, we can be assured He'll work powerfully *within* us to make us like Christ and *through* us to show Christ to others.

Firebreak: Preparing a Line of Defense

When you drive through forested areas, you may notice what appear to be lines or dirt-strewn scars stretching up a mountainside. These are likely firebreaks, man-made swaths of terrain where trees and vegetation have been cleared to help with fire containment.

Especially in hilly or mountainous areas, wide paths are cut through brush with a tractor, bulldozer, or other ground-moving equipment. These bare strips of land create an area with no brush and thus no "fuel" for a fire. If a wildfire were to rage through the area, hopefully it would burn out at the firebreak rather than move forward. Firebreaks also allow firefighting equipment and vehicles easier access to the fire itself.

Sometimes when I see these breaks snaking up a mountainside, I think, *What tremendous effort that must have taken!* I imagine heavy machinery and crews with chainsaws plodding through the forest. But surely, when a forest fire roars to life, everyone in the area is grateful beyond words for the firebreaks. Such foresight and planning was very wise!

So it is with our anger. By choosing ahead of time to act rather than react, we are establishing a firebreak—a cooling-off space—that ensures our heated emotions don't spread too far, too fast. Determine to do the hard work in advance so you have a line of defense ready when a blaze erupts.

THE REFINER'S FIRE

How to Respond to Blowups by Setting Boundaries

> *"You, O God, tested us;*
> *you refined us like silver"*
> (PSALM 66:10).

THE SETTING: JERUSALEM. The time: 1000 B.C.

Silas the silversmith closely examines the rough ore before him—silver tainted with zinc, copper, and tin. He anticipates the amazing change soon to take place—taking a chunk of rock with little or no value and transforming it into the purest silver. Silas is a superb craftsman, skilled at separating the impurities from the silver, skilled at surfacing dross and removing it.

Silas knows it will take heat—varying degrees of intense heat—to purge the dross from the silver. This purification process will forever change the composition of the rough rock. But first he must hammer it, break it, and grind it so that he can place it in a crucible.

His clay crucible—the impenetrable pot that withstands the highest degrees of heat—is placed over a fire. The ore melts, and a layer of dross forms on the surface. Patiently, Silas waits and watches...then skims off the impurities. Eventually, he looks down into the pot and gazes upon a dim image—his own image—yet still a dull reflection. The liquefied mass still lacks purity. So after raising the heat even higher, the refiner carefully places the crucible back into the blistering furnace.

It's a process the expert silversmith will repeat as he doggedly determines to remove all the dross. Silas knows the refining is completely finished when he sees a clear image, a perfect reflection of himself, in the molten ore. This will signify the silver has attained the highest degree of purity possible.

Like the silversmiths of old, God is a Master Refiner. In Jeremiah 9:7 we read, "The LORD Almighty says: 'See, I will refine and test them.'" But it's His children, not chunks of ore, that He seeks to purify. And there is a distinct image He too is yearning to see. Only after spending considerable time *in the crucible*—only after the Refiner continues to remove our dross—can we be purified. He loves to look upon us and see a clearer reflection—a shining reflection of Christ.

My personal experiences in the crucible have been hot and hard—but also helpful, and even more so, healing.

Finding Faulty Thinking

When it comes to getting angry—red-hot angry—it takes a *whole lot* to "light my fire." I attribute that to spending so many years fearfully sidestepping anger—both mine and everyone else's. People who know me say I have a long, long fuse.

Yet on one occasion some years back, my five-mile-long fuse was snipped off to five millimeters—and quickly lit. My emotions exploded. In my mind's eye I saw bright red—crimson red, fiery red! Let me further paint the picture for you...

We can all look back and identify a few people who, in one way or another, made huge contributions to our lives. God brought them into our lives to teach us profound lessons and to refine us. They were key players He then moved from center stage into the wings, or out the exit doors of our lives.

"Meg" was one such significant person in my life. I never suspected our relationship would enter the Refiner's fire.

Thrown together at a Christian music conference, we clicked almost immediately. Smart, talented, and superb with lyrics, Meg quickly gained my admiration and almost as quickly became a trusted confidant.

She offered immense encouragement, something I sorely needed, especially at that tender time in my growth.

God had me on a fast track back then. After graduating from college with a degree in music and serving for five years as a youth director, I was unexpectedly thrust into the public spotlight. Within a two-year time frame, I had appeared on NBC's *Today Show*, been a guest soloist for televised Billy Graham crusades, and performed with the USO on multiple overseas military bases.

Naturally, as a result of all that public exposure, I was flooded with hundreds of invitations to sing and to speak for all kinds of gatherings. Meg instantly became essential to my life—at least that's how I felt at the time.

My friend encouraged me musically. Occasionally I would say, "I wish I could find a song with just the right words for this situation." I'll never forget the day she said, "If you can't find it, why not write it?" I responded, "Well…at least I can try."

So, with classical guitar in hand and favorite chord progressions, I did just that. I wrote certain songs for certain purposes, and was surprised with the outcome. Meg simply smiled as if to say, "I knew you could do it."

As a side note, two of the songs I wrote at that time later became the theme songs for our ministry's two radio programs, *Hope for the Heart* and *Hope in the Night*.

The Lord especially used Meg to help me recognize some of the faulty thinking I developed during my early years of emotional pain. Naturally, I thought "my normal" was everyone's "normal"—I knew nothing else. Over time, she persistently pointed out the problems "my normal" was producing in various relationships and helped me replace some of my wrong beliefs with healthier ways of living life. Needless to say, I was developing a greater and greater appreciation for Meg… and dependence upon her.

As the months went by, we spent more and more time together brainstorming and planning. We talked openly, sharing our struggles, experiences, and aspirations. We often prayed together, asking God for

His blessing. We were riding a wave of enthusiasm, clinging to high hopes and close-knit hearts.

Or so it seemed...

Poisoning the Well

One day Meg suggested we employ "Paula," who was young, bright, and gifted—a woman whose talents I truly admired. The pair had worked together on several projects with excellent results. However, I was surprised at the suggestion and somewhat skeptical. Paula so resented my friendship with Meg that she had given me the silent treatment for the previous two years.

During that time, I was respectful, friendly, and thoughtful toward Paula—but nothing helped. So I decided to try a more direct approach. I told Paula I sensed a barrier between us and asked if I'd done something to offend her. "No," she replied. Then she paused and abruptly added, "June, you need to realize not everyone likes you." Her cold words cut into my heart like a laser beam.

So now, fast forward a few years. Here was Paula showering assurances of loyalty to both of us. In truth, I knew Paula could do a great job—plus Meg really wanted her on board. So hesitantly I agreed to the arrangement, and for well over a year everything ran smoothly.

Then I began to sense Meg distancing herself from me. Several times I asked about it, but each time she brushed my concern aside. I struggled to put the pieces together.

On numerous occasions, Meg would become uncharacteristically abrupt, curt, angry. I couldn't understand it. She had been so supportive. I felt I was helplessly watching the warm fire of friendship fade to a glimmer. I was heartbroken.

At the same time, I knew I hadn't been a perfect friend. And for the sake of fairness, I must admit I, too, had made many mistakes. How deeply I regretted my failures—failing to be the friend I *could* have been, the friend I *should* have been.

Nevertheless, I was mystified; I couldn't understand. *What had happened? What had changed her?* I was confused. I didn't realize the

Master Refiner had placed me in the crucible and suspended me over a fire.

One day as Paula was talking with me, a startling realization hit me. Finally, I saw what had been happening to my heart-connection with Meg. All the negative phrases I'd been hearing—uncharacteristically—from her, I now heard coming from Paula's lips. Suddenly I thought, "So *that's* where Meg's getting it."

To my way of thinking, there had obviously been a "poisoning of the well." I believe my unsuspecting friend had been drinking Paula's poison, which was now threatening to destroy my friendship with Meg.

Two months later, Paula came to me and said, very directly, "I want you to know I'm really supportive of your friendship with Meg. I want what is best for both of you. I know there has been a strain between the two of you, but I want your relationship healed."

At that moment, I felt so grateful, so relieved. Her words of affirmation—so meaningful—were spoken at Meg's home after the three of us had completed one of our marathon work sessions.

The Card that Caused a Kaboom

Meg and Paula then left to pick up a late dinner. I stayed behind to finish writing the promotional copy for an upcoming retreat. After making a few copies, I walked back to the large shared office area. Rather than going to my desk for paper clips, I stopped at Meg's, which was closer to the copier.

When I opened Meg's desk drawer I noticed Paula's handwriting on a card she had given to Meg. Like a magnet, my eyes fell upon *my name*, then fixated on one line: "We don't need any more June Hunts in this world." This was the match that lit my fuse—and ignited a powder keg of emotion.

I was stunned...hurt...and *very, very angry*. Just an hour earlier—*just one hour*—Paula had looked straight into my eyes and declared, "June, I'm really *for* you. I want to *help* you. I want to *support* you and your relationship with Meg."

To this day, the words on that card have remained seared into my mind as if impressed upon it with a hot branding iron. I felt utterly manipulated and deceived, maligned and betrayed.

Fury coursed through my body, my anger pulsated, adrenaline pumped through my veins. My cheeks were hot, my heart inflamed. I knew if I didn't find a way to bring down the temperature of my boiling anger, I would explode at my "friend."

To prevent saying what I would later regret, I needed to leave— *immediately!*

I have to get out of here! I thought, *Jogging will release all this steam and cool me down.* Abruptly gathering my things, I scribbled a note to Meg that something had come up and I had to leave. Then I bolted out the door.

> To prevent saying what I would later regret, I needed to leave—*immediately!*

As soon as I returned to my home, I laced up my running shoes—tighter than normal—and hurried outside. I was ready to "run off" my rage. (At that time, I customarily did a two-mile trek—a run-walk-run routine.)

A few minutes into my run, I noticed my arms swinging higher than normal—intensely, vigorously, aggressively. I remember thinking, *How unusual!*

However, even after 20 minutes of running, *I felt no relief.* I had expected the physical exertion to be my anger-reducer—like the valve that releases the steam inside a pressure cooker. But it didn't work. My valve seemed to be stuck! In fact, the longer I jogged, the more pressure I felt.

From Rehearsal to Reversal

Soon I realized *why* there was no relief. The Bible makes it clear, "Love...keeps no record of wrongs."[1] Keeps no record! That's the very thing—the *only* thing I had been doing! Over and over, I had been rehearsing how much I had been wronged, how much I had been betrayed.

And the more I did it, the more difficult it became *not* to do it.

This much was certain: All that "rehearsing" wasn't helping! The fire roaring inside me continued to rage. And no wonder—you can't put out a fire by continuing to fuel it!

I remember thinking, *I've got to do something else! Lord, teach me to act rather than react.* I repeated those words again and again. Soon I was rhythmically praying, right in sync with my running stride, over and over: "Teach me to act rather than react…teach me to act rather than react."

By the end of my hour-long jog, my pounding heart was finally at peace. I was no longer controlled by the debilitating sense of betrayal. Of course, the initial problem had yet to be confronted, but that night I successfully released all my anger to the Lord.

The next day, when I confronted Meg about the note from Paula, I have to admit my anger was sparked again. But this time I was able to control the fire, rather than let the fire control me. I was not consumed by its explosive heat as I had been the night before.

At the time, the intensity of my initial anger shocked me—it was unusual for me to get *so* angry *so* fast. In retrospect, I realize I had experienced the four sources of anger (hurt, injustice, fear, frustration)—not just one at a time, but all four at once! Although it was Paula

> When you find yourself becoming angry, pray, "Lord, teach me to act rather than react."

who undermined me on that card, I had to face the fact that it was my close friend, Meg, who chose to keep Paula's card rather than discard it. As I think back on it:

- I felt *hurt* that someone so dear to me was becoming distant from me.
- I felt *injustice* over the betrayal of one who promised loyalty.
- I felt *fearful* of losing such a significant person in my life.
- I felt *frustrated* knowing I could do nothing about it.

Although the Lord eventually moved Meg out of my life, He used this experience in His refining fire to remove more of my dross. He intended to purify me, and this wouldn't be the last time I would be found in the Refiner's fire.

Yet ever since that day, when I feel a strong surge of anger, *if*—and I do mean *if*—I sincerely pray, "Lord, teach me to act rather than react," God gives me the wisdom to carefully weigh my words and to speak with self-control.

And my heart is soon at peace.

Lessons Learned in the Furnace

God taught me four practical points concerning the need to *act* rather than *react* since my experiences with Meg and Paula:

1. Anger is *not* a sin. What you do in response to anger determines whether you are sinning or not.

2. There are four causes of anger: hurt, injustice, fear, and frustration. Or, you can experience a combination of two, three, or all four causes simultaneously.

3. There are healthy ways to deal with anger. Ask, "Can I change it?" If so, change it. If not, release it to the Lord.

4. When you find yourself becoming angry, pray, "Lord, teach me to act rather than react."

When I've been hurt, frustrated, or angry, I've asked questions like, "Why has this happened? It makes no sense! How on earth did I get here?!" These questions are understandable; we *want* life to make sense. And usually after a period of time we can see some genuine benefit from being in the furnace of affliction. The Lord says, "See, I have refined you, though not as silver; I have tested you in the furnace of affliction" (Isaiah 48:10).

Of course, there are also those times when we feel the heat rising, and then—as the old saying goes—we jump from the frying pan into the fire! Obviously, such a jump only makes matters worse. Remember, God will use heat to be helpful and pain to be purposeful.

Years ago, I found a picture in both the Old and New Testaments that helped me—more than anything else—to make sense of my personal pain.

The Bible says of God, "He will sit as a refiner and purifier of silver,"[2] and He sees us as unrefined silver. As our Refiner, He first places us into a crucible, then puts the crucible into the furnace—the furnace of affliction—not to punish us, but to purify us.

In a parallel way, God saw me as rough ore that needed much refining. By putting pressure on me through my experiences with Meg and Paula, I became finely ground so that He could fit me into His crucible. Of course, I was totally unaware of all the impurities within me—impurities that took a long time for me to see.

Not long after this "visit" in the furnace when Meg distanced herself from me, the Refiner reheated the furnace to His desired temperature and put me back in the crucible. I was in the sweltering furnace and I definitely wanted out, but instead, the Refiner wanted the dross out.

After the impure silver (the impure me) took on a liquid form, the Refiner removed the crucible from the furnace and skimmed off the dross (the impurities I really did want removed!). Then the Refiner slipped the crucible back in the furnace and raised the temperature. Why? Because certain impurities are released only at certain temperatures, and it took that card—with its caustic message—to bring to the surface the dross deeply embedded in me.

Every silversmith in ancient times knew that purity was never achieved after just one firing in the furnace. The refining of the silver could be repeated up to seven times. Interestingly, the Bible even says, "The words of the LORD are flawless, like silver refined in a furnace of clay, purified seven times" (Psalm 12:6). The silversmith is never satisfied until he sees his image clearly reflected in the molten metal before him.

The dross I didn't see was my being too dependent on Meg—assuming she was "essential" to my life—and my deep fear of being abandoned. With the dross removed, I saw that my deepest dependence needed to always be on Jesus, and that He would never abandon me.

The Bible promises, "The LORD himself goes before you and will be with you; he will never leave you nor forsake you. Do not be afraid; do not be discouraged."[3] What assurance, what comfort!

Anger Hits Home, Relatively Speaking

There would be more for me to learn about how to deal with anger, especially anger directed *toward me*. The image the Master Refiner saw in my crucible must have still been muddy. So, exit Meg and enter "Peg" for another bout in the blazing heat.

Peg is an endearing relative I didn't know well while I was growing up because she was raised in another state. But when she moved to Dallas, we became instant friends. The bond between us was especially close because we are related—plus, we loved being together as "friends." Through Peg, God showed me how He could bring both healing and wholeness...but only after anger in a relationship is recognized and resolved.

When Peg and I began spending time together, we got involved in numerous projects, played games, and "problem-solved"—anything and everything.

Growing Concerns

However, despite Peg's many wonderful qualities, she was, at times, controlling. Given my tendency to be an *anger avoider* and my "need" to be a *peace-at-all-costs person*, I often allowed her to control *me*. Periodically she would accuse me of having motives that I had never even considered.

> Don't let another person's problem become your problem.

Sometimes Peg would call me on the phone and start yelling at me. On one occasion, I was a guest speaker at a conference in Kansas. I was summoned from the hotel ballroom to a kitchen phone. After I said "Hello," Peg began yelling accusations. No matter what my explanation, she refused to accept the truth. I was left stymied and stunned. And that was just one of many calls.

Increasingly, Peg became disrespectful. Several people revealed negative comments she had made about me. A few people asked, "June, why do you take it? Why don't you stand up for yourself? You shouldn't let her control you." Hard as it was for me to admit, they were right (but, I thought I had no choice).

For the sake of preserving the relationship, and thereby practicing peace at any price, I was really *caretaking.* I shielded Peg from the truth about her behavior; I also fooled myself into thinking I wasn't really angry. Then, believe it or not, the studying, writing, and teaching I was doing on verbal and emotional abuse helped me see I was simply perpetuating unhealthy patterns learned from my past.

Building Boundaries

When Peg acted angrily toward me, I knew I needed to get my brain in gear by guarding my thoughts and emotions. I developed the following three-step process:

1. *I prayed for God's protection.* Psalm 141:3 says, "Set a guard over my mouth, O LORD; keep watch over the door of my lips." I submitted my mouth to the Refiner.

2. *I corrected my thinking* by saying to myself, not her, "She has a problem. I'm not going to let her problem be my problem." I submitted my mind to the Refiner.

3. *I set boundaries* with a *repercussion* and a *reward.* I submitted my will to the Refiner.

I had always been intimidated by anger, afraid of being abandoned, and distrusting of God's promise to meet my emotional needs (deeply embedded impurities only the Refiner could see). These were difficult truths to swallow, but I was committed to being a person of integrity and to becoming the person God created me to be. How well I remember establishing my first boundary with Peg. I laid down the groundwork with these words (and I've included her basic responses):

- "Do you want us to have the best relationship possible?" *("Yes.")*
- "Do you believe that we are truly encouraging one another?" *("No.")*
- "In a close relationship both people should be better because of each other. Do you agree?" *("Yes, I do.")*
- "Peg, I value our friendship and want us to encourage one another. But when anger explodes, it hurts both of us." *("I agree.")*
- "I don't want to fear you; I want to enjoy you. So, in the future, if either one of us has destructive anger, we need to step back and part from one another for a while so that the anger doesn't damage our relationship further."

Peg said she understood, but of course, the boundary hadn't yet been tested. I knew that the next time we related negatively, it would be best for us to distance ourselves for awhile. And that day came within a week.

On that day, I arrived at Peg's home—30 minutes later than planned because of an important phone call—and as soon as she saw me she began yelling, "Where have you been?!"

When Peg's temper flared, I followed my previously prepared plan of action. (I had repeatedly rehearsed each point until I could confidently and calmly communicate each one.) I reminded her of our previous agreement, but she kept up her angry criticism.

Instead of *talking* with me, Peg exploded onto me, *telling* me what I was thinking, which wasn't even close to the truth. She continued for several minutes, and I thought, *No more.*

Holding up my hand (palm toward her), I said, "Stop!" To my astonishment, she did—she stopped!

Speaking slowly in a low voice I said, "Obviously now is not a good time for us to be together." Again, slow and low, I said, "I'm going to leave."

Surprised, Peg said, "You can't leave."

I responded, "This conversation isn't encouraging either of us, so I need to leave. Later on we can try again." When I returned home, I used my time productively. (Actually, I was amazed that I had set a boundary and kept it!)

Disengage from Rage

Now, whenever I sense self-control giving way to irrational anger—whether in me or in others—I know it's time to put on the brakes, call a truce, and take a time-out. Heated conversations will only escalate unless we do something to intervene in the process. Here's what I do:

- *I hold up my hands to indicate I am "surrendering"* for the time being by calling a halt to what is taking place.
  —"Stop! Time-out!"
  —"Wait! We need to start over!"

- *I state slowly in a low tone of voice* (remember, "sloooow and loooow"):
  —"Our conversation isn't going in a positive direction."
  —"We won't be able to resolve anything this way."

- *I explain my need to disengage from the person who is angry* by taking a walk around the block, retreating to a quiet place, listening to music, taking a shower, or doing whatever I think will help me and/or the other person cool down and regain composure.
  —"I'm going to leave for a while."
  —"I will be back later"...(if that's wise).

- *I agree on a time to resume the conversation* when we can both talk calmly.
  —"When is a good time for us to discuss this?"

—"Where can we meet with no distractions?"

If we reach an impasse where agreement is not possible, we can:

• *Agree to disagree by allowing different opinions* but not letting that become a problem.

—*Decide to engage in stimulating conversations* where varied opinions are expressed (consider them opportunities to develop listening skills, glean insights, process opinions, and express those opinions clearly and concisely in a nonoffensive way).

—*Commit to valuing and respecting* each other and growing in understanding of one another. Proverbs 18:2 says, "A fool finds no pleasure in understanding but delights in airing his own opinions."

Different Dynamics, Different Tactics

My newfound dedication to constructively expressing my anger through boundaries shifted the dynamics of my relationship with Peg. It's true there were other times Peg would get angry at me. But once I learned to hold the line—*and not have to have her approval*—a major change occurred. Over a span of many months, our relationship moved from negative to positive.

When I felt fear welling up in me concerning my relationship with Peg, I claimed God's promises to meet my deepest inner needs for love, significance, and security. The Bible says, "My God will meet all your needs according to his glorious riches in Christ Jesus."[4]

Have you ever noticed that many people were angry at Jesus, but He wasn't controlled by their anger? He knew they had a problem, but He didn't let their problem become His problem. When I thought about Him, that helped me.

In a relatively short time, I was amazed at the change within me. (I learned that *not* being controlled by someone's anger is truly life-changing.) And much of what I learned came from forays in the fire.

By expressing my feelings—even anger—in a caring and productive way and challenging Peg to do the same, I gained new courage and confidence which, in turn, resulted in unmistakable improvements in us both. Over time, Peg softened and learned to communicate without harsh words. Today our friendship has become more and more refined and we recognize how the Refiner has brought healing—not only to us individually, but also to our relationship. What a joy!

> The Refiner has but one goal in mind: to turn you into a masterpiece, something that shines with lasting beauty.

As I applied my newly honed skills to situations at work and in other relationships, God repeatedly proved His faithfulness to me, and now my security truly rests in Him alone! Although I'm still a work in progress, a lot of dross has been drawn away for good.

Although we will all experience fiery trials, not everyone is willing to learn from their trials. The book of Jeremiah refers to certain people—"they are called rejected silver."[5] They have hardened their hearts, rejecting the purifying work of God in their lives. What sad words from the Master Refiner: "The bellows blow fiercely to burn away the lead with fire, but the refining goes on in vain" (Jeremiah 6:29).

As you feel the heat of refining fires in your own life, don't allow yourself to be characterized as "rejected silver" because you are clamoring to climb out of the crucible and refusing to submit to the purifying flames. Remember, the Refiner has but one goal in mind: to turn you into a masterpiece, something that shines with lasting beauty.

When I was preparing to teach on the topic of anger, I came upon an impressive quote by Henry Ward Beecher: "Speak when you are angry and you will make the best speech you will ever regret."[6]

Now, read it again, and slowly: "Speak when you are angry...and you will make the best speech...you will ever...regret."

What a thought! When you become angry, will your actions end in a way that results in relief, or regret? Will your choice make the situation better, or worse? Will you choose to act, or react? We all have a choice.

Atop my desk is a rectangular block of silver—a reminder of how God purifies me in His refining fire. This small bar has been designed, shaped, and cooled, having completed its rigorous purification process.

Process...oh yes, it is most definitely a process! I look at my silver bar and remember my frequent stays in the furnace of affliction, of being confined to the crucible and desperately wanting out. Yet today I'm grateful and say, "Thank You, Father, for all that I've learned through these trials...through Your purifying fire." My silver bar is a reminder that as long as I live on this earth, I will experience times of pain.

You also have a choice of how to respond. You can either become *rejected* silver or *refined* silver. And instead of staying angry about your pain, realize that the pathway to your purification *is* pain.

Because being purified like silver is a *process,* you are a work in *progress*—you are God's work. His fire of purification will never result in harm *to* you, but will merely clear away what is worthless *in* you...so that the countenance of Christ can shine *through* you.

Are you in the crucible right now? Take comfort—the Refiner knows you. He cares for you; He loves you. The Bible says, "He will sit as a refiner and purifier of silver."[7]

Just as the silversmith waits ever present during the entire refining process, so our Lord is ever present with you. Intently, He sits with you and watches over you. His eyes are locked upon what is happening to you. His tender love will not allow Him to look away—not even for an instant.

The Refiner's Fire: Gold in the Making

It is a sweltering inferno, a bastion of blazing heat purposefully designed to purify precious metals. At specific melting points, a curious substance forms on the surface of gold, silver, and other molten metals—a liquid layer of impurities considered worthless, waste, *scum*. Heat is necessary for doing away with the dross.

In 1874, Emil Wohlwill invented a refining process for gold that today produces the highest degree of purity possible—99.999 percent. But when it comes to the Master Refiner, God Himself, He never fails to achieve perfection.

God's handiwork doesn't center on precious metals, but *precious people*. He is committed to refining us like silver and gold. And it's through the fiery trials of life that the impurities buried deep within our character surface like dross and are scooped away by the hand of God. It's a lifelong process that ever moves us toward our standard for perfection, Jesus Christ. The Refiner's fire makes us ever more resemble our Redeemer.

But where there is fire, there is also pain, and the apostle Peter was keenly aware of the connection: "Now for a little while you may have had to suffer grief in all kinds of trials. These have come so that your faith—of greater worth than gold, which perishes even though refined by fire—may be proved genuine."[8]

So when God turns up the heat, will you *act* rather than *react*? And when He detects more dross inside your heart and turns up the heat even higher, will you allow Him to forge within you a faith "of greater worth than gold"?

In Zechariah 13:9, God says, "I will refine them like silver and test them like gold." When you come under the care of the Master Refiner and consent to be in His crucible, you will more and more reflect the character of Christ. You will shine like silver...you will glitter like gold.

Epilogue: The Fire Extinguisher
How to "Act Rather Than React"

"Don't sin by letting anger control you.
Think about it overnight and remain silent"
(PSALM 4:4 NLT).

SO OFTEN I'VE THOUGHT about the time of my short-fuse emotional explosion...my futile effort to run off my rage...and the simple prayer that brought me peace: "Lord, teach me to act rather than react." I remember that volatile evening when I walked into my bedroom with those words reverberating in my mind—in rhythm—and thinking, *That could make a memorable song.*

Within three days, I had written the words and music. Even though it was born out of trials and tears, every time I sing it before an audience, it seems to cause a smile, lighten a load, lift a heart. *And my sincere prayer is that it will do the same for you...*that God will use it to help you keep your cool when your anger is hot.

Isn't it interesting that nothing is wasted when released into the care of the Refiner—released as a sacrificial offering, released to reflect the character of Christ?

Lord, Teach Me to Act Rather Than React

(Rhythmic, country flavor)

Chorus

Lord, teach me to act rather than react,
　with Your Spirit in control of me.
Lord, teach me to help rather than hinder,
　with the Lord being Lord of me.
Lord, teach me to trust rather than mistrust,
　with Your Spirit inside my soul.
Lord, teach me to act rather than react,
　I give You complete control.

Verse 1

It was stop-and-go traffic, the scene was so graphic,
　When headin' back home from town.
A car was behind me, and then pulled beside me,
　The driver had a serious frown.
He looked straight at me, it was plain to see,
　He was forcin' his way around.
I said, "No, you won't! Oh, no you don't!"
　Then pushed my foot to the ground. Oh...

Chorus

Verse 2

It was quarter to 3:00 for the luncheon with Lee—
　But the meetin' was planned at 1:00!
This had happened before, so my feelin's were sore,
　Now this was not my picture of fun.
Lee came in with a grin—no repentance within—
　Civil war had just begun.
I was feelin' rejection, and voiced my objection,
　"You selfish son of a gun!" Oh...

Chorus

Verse 3 (Slow, half time)
>
> When I feel disappointment, with no soothing ointment,
>> And nothin' is goin' my way.
>
> When my heart has been breaking, and my soul is aching,
>> And I have no more words to say.
>
> I'm not under illusion, the only solution,
>> Is to die to my rights each day.
>
> Because Christ is inside me to comfort and guide me,
>> And His life has taught me to pray...

Chorus (slow, half time)
>
> Lord, teach me to act rather than react,
>> with Your Spirit in control of me.
>
> Lord, teach me to help rather than hinder,
>> with the Lord being Lord of me.
>
> Lord, teach me to trust rather than mistrust,
>> with Your Spirit inside my soul.
>
> Lord, teach me to act rather than react,
>> I give You complete...
>>
>>> I won't take defeat...I give You complete control.*

---

* To hear June sing "Lord, Teach Me to Act Rather Than React,"
  visit http:www.hopefortheheart.org/Anger.

Notes

Introduction—A View Behind the Interview
1. Proverbs 29:22; 22:24.
2. Ephesians 4:26 NKJV.

Chapter 1—The Anger Bowl
1. Frank Minirth et al., *Love Hunger* (Nashville: Thomas Nelson, 1990), p. 13.
2. American Psychiatric Association, *Diagnostic and Statistical Manual of Mental Disorders: DSM-III-R*, 3d ed. (Washington, DC: American Psychiatric Association, 1987), pp. 65-67.
3. 2 Samuel 24:24.
4. 1 Peter 5:7.
5. Revelation 8:4.

Chapter 2—Turning Up the Heat
1. Proverbs 20:2.
2. Ray Burwick, *The Menace Within: Hurt or Anger?* (Birmingham, AL: Ray Burwick, 1985), 18; Gary D. Chapman, *The Other Side of Love: Handling Anger in a Godly Way* (Chicago: Moody, 1999), pp. 17-18.
3. W.E. Vine, *Vine's Complete Expository Dictionary of Biblical Words*, electronic ed. (Nashville: Thomas Nelson, 1996).
4. Proverbs 22:24.
5. Matthew 26:4.
6. Mark 10:14.
7. Romans 1:18.
8. A.W. Tozer, from the *Alliance Weekly*, July 1946.
9. Acts 5:33.
10. Proverbs 27:4.
11. Proverbs 19:3.
12. Romans 8:28 NKJV.
13. Ecclesiastes 7:9.
14. Proverbs 29:8.
15. With special thanks to my cousin, Swann Waterhouse, for sharing information learned from working for several years in the burn unit at Parkland Memorial Hospital in Dallas, Texas.

Chapter 3—Fuel for the Fire

1. Proverbs 23:7.

2. Deuteronomy 34:10.

3. Deuteronomy 34:12.

4. See Exodus chapter 2.

5. Charles Dickens, *Great Expectations* (Whitefish, MT: Kessinger Publishing, 2004), p. 60.

6. 1 John 4:18.

7. Numbers 20:3-5.

8. See Exodus 17:1-6.

9. See Numbers 20:1-12.

Chapter 4—Ashes to Ashes

1. Proverbs 6:27.

2. Matthew 6:34.

3. Lisa Erickson and S. Alicia Williams-Evans, "Attitudes of Emergency Nurses Regarding Patient Assaults," *Journal of Emergency Nursing*, vol. 26, issue 3 (June 2000), pp. 210-15.

4. John T. Slania, "Putting Violence Policies to Work; System Can Help Prevent Tragedies," *Crain's Chicago Business*, February 19, 2001.

5. Psalm 37:8-9.

6. Gary Bousman, "Anger: It Can Be Like Slow-acting Poison, Robbing You of Mental and Physical Health," *Vibrant Life*, July 1, 1995.

7. Rachel Lampert, M.D., et al., "Anger Induced T-Wave Alternans Predicts Future Ventricular Arrythmias in Patients with Implantable Cardioverter-Defibrillators," *Journal of the American College Cardiology*, March 3, 2009, pp. 774-78.

8. Renee C. Lee, "Anger in Men Has Link to Strokes," *Charleston Gazette*, March 2, 2004.

9. Daniel Goleman, "Study Documents How Anger Can Impair Heart Function," *The New York Times*, September 2, 1992.

10. Goleman, "Study," *The New York Times*.

11. Troy Goodman, "Study: Anger Triggers Heart Attacks," *The Cincinnati Post*, May 2, 2000.

12. Alan Sherzagier, "Hospital Research Discovers Anger Raises Risk of Injury," *Deseret News* (Salt Lake City), February 2, 2006 (emphasis added).

13. Nicole Walker, "Why Anger Is Bad for Your Health," *Jet*, May 1, 2000.

14. James 1:19-20.

15. Joseph Carey, *Brain Facts: A Primer on the Brain and Nervous System*, 5th ed. (Wash-

ington, DC: Society for Neuroscience, 2006), pp. 29-30. Retrieved June 2, 2008 from http://www.sfn.org/skins/main/pdf/brainfacts/brainfacts.pdf.

16. Philippians 4:6.

17. Philippians 4:7.

18. Matthew 11:28-29.

19. Ephesians 4:26-27.

20. Matthew 5:44.

21. 1 John 5:3.

22. 2 Corinthians 5:17.

23. Romans 12:18.

Chapter 5—The Fire Eaters

1. Ephesians 4:26-27.

2. Marcia L. Conner, James G. Clawson, *Creating a Learning Culture* (Cambridge University Press, 2004), p. 328.

3. Albert Einstein, as quoted in Ronald J. Comer, *Abnormal Psychology,* 5th ed. (New York: Macmillan, 2003), p. 5.

4. Deuteronomy 32:35.

5. Romans 12:17.

6. Proverbs 15:1.

7. Romans 8:33-34.

Chapter 6—The Flamethrowers

1. Much of this story is adapted from Mike Barber, "Crotchety Harry Truman Remains an Icon of the Eruption," *Seattle Post-Intelligencer Reporter,* May 11, 2000. Accessed at http://seattlepi.nwsource.com/mountsthelens/hary11.shtml.

2. William Safire, *Safire's Political Dictionary* (New York: Oxford University Press, 2008), p. 348.

3. Donna duBeth, "Give 'em Hell, Harry," *The Daily News,* March 26, 1980. Accessed at http://www.tdn.com/helens/flash/mainpage.php?p=1113365891&w=D.

4. For information on the Mount St. Helen's eruption, see "Mt. St. Helen's Eruption, 1980," http://www.geology.sdsu.edu/how_volcanoes_work/Sthelens.html.

5. Proverbs 22:24.

6. esv.

7. Frederick Buechner, *Beyond Words* (San Francisco: HarperSanFrancisco, 2004), p. 18.

8. Hebrews 12:15.

9. Matthew 5:25.

10. Ephesians 4:26-27.

11. 1 John 1:8-10 tlb.

12. John 8:32.

13. L. Heise, M. Ellsberg, and M. Gottemoeller, "Ending Violence Against Women," *Population Reports*, Series L, no. 11 (Baltimore, MD: Johns Hopkins University School of Public Health, December 1999), p. 1.

14. The Commonwealth Fund, *Health Concerns Across a Woman's Lifespan* (Rochester, NY: Louis Harris and Associates, May 1999), p. 27.

15. E. Cohen and J. Knitzer, "Children Living with Domestic Violence," a report prepared for "Early Childhood, Domestic Violence, and Poverty: Taking the Next Steps to Help Young Children and Their Families," May 2002, as cited in *National Task Force to End Sexual and Domestic Violence Against Women,* "Violence Against Women Act 2005, Title IV-Prevention."

16. 2 Corinthians 7:10-11.

17. James 5:16.

Chapter 7—Blast from the Past

1. Gary Chapman, *Anger: Handling a Powerful Emotion in a Healthy Way* (Chicago, IL: Northfield Publishing, 2007), p. 99.

2. 2 Corinthians 5:17.

3. For the hierarchy of needs, see Abraham Maslow, "A Theory of Human Motivation," *Psychological Review,* vol. 50 (Washington, DC: American Psychological Association, July 1943), pp. 370-96.

Chapter 8—Too Hot to Handle

1. Matthew 7:12.

2. William Shakespeare, *Romeo and Juliet*, Act 5, Scene 3.

3. Martin Luther King and Coretta Scott King, *The Martin Luther King, Jr. Companion: Quotations from the Speeches, Essays, and Books of Martin Luther King, Jr.* (New York: Macmillan, 1993), p. 56.

Chapter 9—Fire and Ice

1. 1 Samuel 20:34.

2. Jonah 1:9.

3. Jonah 1:17.

4. Jonah 4:1.

5. Luke 10:40.

6. Luke 10:41-42.

7. Matthew 6:25.

8. Matthew 6:27.

9. Matthew 11:28-30.

10. Proverbs 15:1.

11. Louis Lalleman, Jean-Pierre de Caussade, and Claude De La Colombiere, *For God's Greater Glory: Gems of Jesuit Spirituality*, Jean-Pierre Lafouge, ed. (Bloomington, IN: World Wisdom, 2006), p. 71.

Chapter 10—Self-Inflicted Flames

1. 1 John 1:9.

2. William Joseph Federer, *America's God and Country: Encyclopedia of Quotations* (St. Louis, MO: Amerisearch, 1994), p. 294.

3. James 1:12.

4. Jeremiah 29:11.

5. Isaiah 59:2.

6. Romans 3:23.

7. Romans 6:23.

8. See 2 Peter 3:9.

9. Romans 5:8.

10. See John 10:18 and Matthew 20:28.

11. John 14:6.

12. Philippians 4:13.

13. John 7:38.

14. 1 Corinthians 15:34.

15. James 4:10.

16. Ezekiel 11:19.

17. John 5:24.

18. See Isaiah 61:3.

Chapter 11—Fuming at the Father

1. "Man 'Angry at God' Drives Minivan into Church Sanctuary," Catholic News Agency, February 21, 2008. Additional background information: Hudson Sangree, "Minivan Plows into Church," *Sacramento Bee,* February 21, 2008.

2. Aristotle, *The Nicomachean Ethics*, 2.9, translated by J.A.K. Thomson, revised by Hugh Tredennick (New York: Penguin Classics, 2004), p. 48.

3. Job 23:2-4.

4. Genesis 3:1.

5. Genesis 3:4-5.

6. James 1:17.

7. 1 John 1:9.

8. Psalm 116:5.

9. Daniel 4:35.

10. Mark 14:34-36 ESV.

11. Luke 22:42.

12. Romans 8:28.

13. Helen Roseveare, *Living Faith* (Minneapolis: Bethany House, 1980), p. 27.

14. Roseveare, *Living Faith,* p. 27.

15. Helen Roseveare, *Give Me This Mountain* (London: InterVarsity Fellowship, 1966), p. 144.

16. Roseveare, *Give Me This Mountain*, p. 148.

17. Roseveare, *Give Me This Mountain*.

18. Roseveare, *Give Me This Mountain*.

19. The following narrative is adapted from Helen Roseveare, "Why Does a God of Love Allow Suffering?" (Barrie, Ontario: Woman Alive, n.d.), audiocassette.

20. Quote taken from Noel Piper "Helen Roseveare: Faithful in Loss," *Faithful Women and Their Extraordinary God* (Wheaton, IL: Crossway Books, 2005), p. 166. For a concise retelling of Helen's story, this book is a helpful and inspiring resource.

21. Roseveare, *Living Faith*, p. 69.

22. Excerpted from Dr. Helen Roseveare, "Why Does a God of Love Allow Suffering?" audiocassette.

Chapter 12—Smoldering Embers

1. See also Ronald T. Potter-Efron, *Angry All the Time: An Emergency Guide to Anger Control*, 2d ed. (Oakland, CA: New Harbinger, 2005).

2. William H. Walton as quoted in Charles Gerber, *Healing for a Bitter Heart* (Joplin, MO: College Press, 1996), p. 74.

Chapter 13—Cooler Heads Prevail

1. *Arizona Republic*, April 25, 1995.

2. Thomas Jefferson, as quoted in *Respectfully Quoted: A Dictionary of Quotations*, Suzy Platt, ed. (New York: Barnes & Noble, 1989), p. 213.

3. 1 Peter 1:13; 3:8-9.

4. Psalm 26:2.

5. 2 Corinthians 10:5.

6. 1 Chronicles 28:9.

7. On the three God-given inner needs, see Lawrence J. Crabb, Jr., *Understanding*

People: Deep Longings for Relationship (Grand Rapids: Zondervan, 1987), pp. 15-16; Robert S. McGee, *The Search for Significance*, 2d ed. (Houston, TX: Rapha, 1990), pp. 27-30.

8. Philippians 4:19.

9. Psalm 118:6.

10. Philippians 2:3-4.

11. John 16:13.

12. Philippians 4:7.

13. Proverbs 21:29.

14. Ecclesiastes 3:1,7.

15. Colossians 4:6.

Chapter 14—Creative Combustion

1. Romans 12:2 ESV.

2. See Richard W. Etulain, *César Chávez* (New York: Macmillan, 2002), p. 117.

3. Dan La Botz, *César Chávez and La Causa* (London: Longman, 2005), p. 7.

4. Peter Matthiessen, *Sal si puedes (Escape if you can): César Chávez and the New American Revolution* (Berkeley, CA: University of California Press, 2000), p. x.

5. La Botz, *César Chávez and La Causa*, p. 175.

Chapter 15—Bomb Squad Basics

1. Ephesians 4:30-31.

2. Ephesians 5:22.

3. Marie M. Fortune, *Keeping the Faith: Questions and Answers for the Abused Woman* (San Francisco: Harper & Row, 1991), pp. 28-29.

4. See Kay Marshall Strom, *In the Name of Submission* (Portland, OR: Multnomah Publishers, 1985), p. 56.

5. See Strom, *In the Name of Submission,* pp. 56-58.

6. Matthew 7:9-11.

7. See 1 Peter 1:6-7.

8. Ephesians 4:2-3 ESV.

9. John Cook, as cited in *The Book of Positive Quotations*, Steve Deger and Leslie Ann Gibson, eds. (Minneapolis: Fairview Press, 2007), p. 261.

Chapter 16—Quenching the Coals

1. Matthew 22:37.

2. Psalm 26:2.

3. Romans 12:2.

4. 1 Peter 1:13.

5. Psalm 119:9,11 TLB.

6. Matthew 12:35.

7. Proverbs 25:11.

8. This story was adapted from J. Oswald Sanders, "How Do You Love?" *Discipleship Journal*, March/April 1981. To learn more about the life of the great hymn writer and poet, see *Frances Ridley Havergal: A Full Sketch of Her Life* by Edward Davies and *Memorials of Frances Ridley Havergal* by Maria Vernon Graham Havergal (her sister).

Chapter 17—The Refiner's Fire

1. 1 Corinthians 13:4-5.

2. Malachi 3:3.

3. Deuteronomy 31:8.

4. Philippians 4:19.

5. Jeremiah 6:30.

6. Henry Ward Beecher as quoted in Roy B. Zuck, *The Speaker's Quote Book: Over 4,500 Illustrations and Quotations for All Occasions* (Grand Rapids: Kregel Publications, 1997), p. 13.

7. Malachi 3:3.

8. 1 Peter 1:6-7.

MORE HARVEST HOUSE BOOKS
BY JUNE HUNT

SEEING YOURSELF THROUGH GOD'S EYES

How well do you know your "identity" as a true Christian? Discover the great riches of your identity in the 31 devotions in this book. For example:

- I am adopted by God.
- I am a child of God.
- I am precious to God.

Experience the exciting transformation that comes from seeing yourself through God's eyes. Great for personal or group Bible study (Leader's Guide included).

COUNSELING THROUGH YOUR BIBLE HANDBOOK

No matter what the problem, God doesn't leave us without hope or help. The Bible is richly relevant when it comes to the difficult dilemmas we all face. Here you will find 50 chapters of spiritual wisdom and compassionate counsel on even the hardest issues, such as...

- anger & adultery
- alcohol & drug abuse
- codependency & cults
- depression & dating
- fear & phobias
- guilt & grief
- rejection & rape
- self-worth & suicide

The guidance in this handbook is grounded in Scripture which—when used properly—has the power to pull us out of life's ditches and put us on the road to inner freedom and fulfillment. (Also to become available in hardback only from Hope for the Heart.)

HOW TO FORGIVE...
WHEN YOU DON'T FEEL LIKE IT

When someone hurts us, our natural response is to strike back. Rather than forgive, we want to return the pain and suffering. Rather than let go, we cling to our rocks of resentment, our boulders of bitterness. The result? We struggle under the weight of our grievances—all because we find it too hard to forgive.

Though we know God has called us to forgive, we find ourselves asking hard questions:

- What if it hurts too much to forgive?
- What if the other person isn't sorry?
- How can I let someone off the hook for doing something *so wrong*?

Biblical counselor June Hunt has been there herself, enabling her to speak from experience as she offers biblical help and hope with heartfelt compassion. If you've been pinned down under a landslide of pain, here's how to find true freedom through forgiveness.

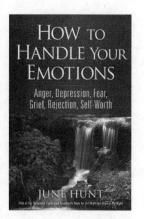

HOW TO HANDLE YOUR EMOTIONS

God created us with the ability to experience emotions. But all too often it's easy for our emotions to get the best of us. Discover how you can bring your emotions under control, and allow God to use them to strengthen you and build up others.

About the Author

June Hunt is an author, singer, speaker, and founder of Hope for the Heart, a worldwide biblical counseling ministry featuring the award-winning radio broadcast by the same name heard daily across America. In addition, *Hope in the Night* is June's live two-hour call-in counseling program that helps people untie their tangled problems with biblical hope and practical help. Hope for the Heart radio broadcasts currently air in more than 25 countries.

Early family pain was the catalyst that shaped June's compassionate heart. Later, as youth director for more than 600 teenagers, she became aware of the need for sound biblical counseling. Her work with young people and their parents led June to a life commitment of *providing God's truth for today's problems.*

After years of teaching and research, June began developing scripturally based counseling tools called *Biblical Counseling Keys,* which address definitions, characteristics, causes, and solutions for 100 topics (such as marriage and parenting, anger and abuse, guilt and grief). Recently these individual topics were compiled to create the landmark *Biblical Counseling Library.*

The *Counseling Keys* have become the foundation for the Hope Biblical Counseling Institute initiated by The Criswell College. Each monthly conference in the Dallas-based institute provides training to help spiritual leaders, counselors, and other caring Christians meet the very real needs of others.

June has served as a guest professor at colleges and seminaries, both nationally and internationally, teaching on topics such as crisis counseling, child abuse, wife abuse, homosexuality, forgiveness, singleness, and self-worth. Her works are currently available in 60 countries and more than 20 languages, including Russian, Romanian, Ukrainian, Spanish, Portuguese, German, Mandarin, Korean, Japanese, and Arabic.

She is the author of *How to Forgive...When You Don't Feel Like It, Seeing Yourself Through God's Eyes, Counseling Through Your Bible Handbook, How to Handle Your Emotions, Caring for a Loved One with Cancer,* and more than 40 topical HopeBooks. June is also a contributor to the *Soul Care Bible* and the *Women's Devotional Bible.*

As an accomplished musician, June has been a guest on numerous national television and radio programs, including the NBC *Today* show. She has toured overseas with the USO and been a guest soloist at Billy Graham crusades. Five recordings—*Songs of Surrender, Hymns of Hope, The Whisper of My Heart, The Shelter Under His Wings,* and *The Hope of Christmas*—all reflect her heart of hope.

Learn more about June and Hope for the Heart at...

Hope for the Heart, Inc.
P.O. Box 7
Dallas, TX 75221

1-800-488-HOPE (4673)
www.HopeForTheHeart.org